MAKING INDIGENOUS CITIZENS

Making Indigenous Citizens

IDENTITIES, EDUCATION, AND
MULTICULTURAL DEVELOPMENT IN PERU

María Elena García

STANFORD UNIVERSITY PRESS

STANFORD, CALIFORNIA

2005

Stanford University Press
Stanford, California

Printed in the United States of America on acid-free, archival-quality paper

Library of Congress Cataloging-in-Publication Data

García, María Elena.
Making indigenous citizens : identities, education, and multicultural
development in Peru / María Elena García.
    p. cm.
    Includes bibliographical references and index.
    ISBN 0-8047-5014-9 (cloth : alk. paper) — ISBN 0-8047-5015-7 (pbk. : alk.
paper)
      1. Quechua Indians — Ethnic identity.   2. Quechua Indians — Civil rights.
3. Quechua Indians — Education.   4. Multiculturalism — Peru — Cuzco (Dept.)
5. Citizenship — Peru — Cuzco (Dept.)   6. Cuzco (Peru : Dept.) — Ethnic
relations.   7. Cuzco (Peru : Dept.) — Social policy.   8. Cuzco (Peru : Dept.) —
Politics and government.   I. Title.
    F2230.2.K4G364 2005
    305.8'98323 — dc22   2004008534

Frontispiece photo by the author

Typeset by BookMatters in 10/12.5 Sabon

Original Printing 2005

Last figure below indicates year of this printing:
14   13   12   11   10   09   08   07   06   05

Para tí, abuelita. Por tu cariño, tu corazón, tu cocina, y tu historia.
Y para mi José Antonio. Gracias por regalarme tu vida.

Contents

Photographs appear after page 160.

Acknowledgments

The ideas in this book have made many journeys, and many people helped along the way. First attempts at writing about indigenous mobilization and education in Peru took place at Brown University. At Brown, my dissertation committee — William Beeman, Blenda Femenías, Matthew Gutmann, and David Kertzer — provided invaluable encouragement and support. Their comments on early dissertation drafts gave me a solid base from which to begin rethinking and revising the manuscript that has become this book. Also at Brown, Thomas Skidmore's kind offer of office space in the Center for Latin American Studies (CLAS) gave me a wonderful place to think about, write, and complete my work. At CLAS, Ronald Rathier reminded me every day of the importance of music, food, and happiness, even in the midst of academic craziness. I owe much to him.

In the years since Brown, many colleagues have helped me develop and clarify my thinking through their comments on various drafts and sections of this book. Thanks so much to Patricia Ames, Liza Bakewell, Tony Bebbington, Paul Gelles, Penelope Harvey, Andrea Heckman, José Itzigsohn, José Antonio Mazzotti, Nancy Postero, Deborah Thomas, Donna Lee Van Cott, Patrick Wilson, and León Zamosc for your insightful questions and comments. Juan Carlos Godenzzi, Javier Lajo, Patricia Oliart, and Brígida Peraza, thank you for your sharp critiques and for engaging in critical debates. I am also indebted to Marisol de la Cadena for her helpful comments at the early stages of the manuscript, and to Julia Paley, Joanne Rappaport, Orin Starn, and Mary Weismantel for raising important questions and providing suggestions that helped this book take its current shape.

I want to extend special thanks to Blenda Femenías and Ann Wightman for helping me transform the dissertation into this book. Thank you for sharing with me your wide and deep knowledge of Andean history and ethnography, your experiences with writing, editing, and publishing, and most important, your love of Peru.

I also want to thank my students at Wesleyan University and Sarah Lawrence College for reminding me why I do what I do.

I would not have been able to finish writing this book had it not been for the support and encouragement of many friends and colleagues. I am especially grateful to Carmen Ashhurst, Serafín Coronel-Molina, Brian DeVido, Mary Dillard, Dean Hubbard, Nancye Flinn, Mark Manetti, Greg Medara, Jamee Moudud, Joshua Muldavin, Jorge and Andrea Nállim, Patrick Niehus, Kris Philipps, Karen Rader, Kasturi Ray, Ray Seidelman, Patrick Sweeny, David Valentine, Monica Varsanyi, Allan Walters, Dave Williams, Komozi Woodard, Charles Zerner, Matilde Zimmermann, and Elke Zuern. Jeffrey Lesser has been helpful and inspirational at every stage of this project. Kehaulani Kauanui, David Shorter, and Jonathan Warren have been models of exuberance, passion, and commitment. And Rima, to you I can only say thank you for sharing coffee and martinis, laughter and tears, life and love.

In Peru and Bolivia, many people were critical to the research for this book. The staff at the Instituto de Estudios Andinos Centro Bartolomé de Las Casas in Cuzco, and at the Dirección Nacional de Educación Intercultural Bilingüe in Lima were always helpful. In Bolivia, staff at the Programa de Educación Intercultural Bilingüe para Países Andinos and the Centro de Comunicación y Desarrollo Andino were also wonderful. Also in Cuzco, the staff of CADEP, CEDEP Ayllu, CESU, Fé y Alegría, KALLPA, and Puklasunchis were tremendously helpful. I am especially grateful to Patricia Ames, Martín Castillo, Andrés Chirinos, Rufino Chuquimamani, Alberto Conejo, Gonzalo Espino, Juan Carlos Godenzzi, Luis Enrique López, Patricia Oliart, Pablo Regalsky, and Inge Sichra for all their time and support, and for openly sharing their concerns, critiques, and hopes.

Most important, I am forever indebted to the many *capacitadores,* teachers, community leaders, parents, and students working and living in the highlands of Cuzco who opened their schools, their homes, and their lives to me. I hope that the words on the following pages can at least provide a glimpse of their struggles and in some way join in their own efforts toward social justice.

Mario, Honorata, Alexia, Gaby, y Karen, a ustedes les debo demasiado. Gracias por compartir su vida conmigo, y por ofrecerme el alma y el corazón. María, Ignacio, Eloy, Virginia, y Celia, gracias por enseñarme a hablar nuevamente, y por regalarme un pedacito de su Apu Ausangate.

Many institutions provided support for this project. The Department of Anthropology and the Center for Latin American Studies at Brown University provided institutional support and research grants. I am also indebted to the Center for the Americas at Wesleyan University and to Sarah Lawrence College for supporting and funding my research. Two fellowships from the

Watson Institute for International Studies at Brown University supported both research and writing. A Foreign Language and Area Study Fellowship funded language study in Cuzco, and a Fulbright Dissertation Research Fellowship funded the bulk of ethnographic research in Peru.

A portion of this work (parts of Chapter 3) appeared previously in *Latin American Perspectives* 30(1), Issue 128, January 2003: 71–96, as "The Politics of Community: Education, Indigenous Rights, and Ethnic Mobilization in Peru."

The publication process was made less arduous thanks to the kindness of senior colleagues and friends such as David Kertzer and Jim McGuire, who shared their wisdom. I am also extremely grateful to the thoughtful reviewers of earlier drafts under consideration by Stanford University Press. The good people and fine editors at Stanford University Press, especially Patricia Katayama, Carmen Borbón-Wu, and Anna Eberhard Friedlander, made this process much less painful than I had feared. Their patience and humanity meant a great deal to this first-time author. Finally, I am grateful to my indexer, Bob Schwarz, for his keen eye.

There is nothing I can say here to adequately express my gratitude toward my family, both here in the United States and in Peru. Their unconditional love and support carried me through the cities, valleys, and glaciers of the southern Peruvian Andes and the streets of Cochabamba. Their encouragement has sustained me throughout the writing process. Gracias, abuelita, mamá, papá, Claudia y Fitito. To you, and to the memory of my grandfather, I owe the inspiration for all my work.

I would not have been able to survive graduate school, dissertation writing, life after graduate school, and writing this book were it not for my two beautiful cats, Poet and Micaela. I am extremely grateful to them for always knowing when to lie on my work, nudge me away from my desk, and simply curl up next to me, no matter how long I stayed up working. To them I owe my sanity.

Finally, this book would not exist were it not for my husband, José Antonio Lucero. His gentle but incisive critiques helped me sharpen my thoughts and my words; his tireless readings and rereadings of every single page of this book helped me clarify my arguments; and his always insightful, creative, and bold comments helped me shape this book from beginning to end. No one was more supportive, encouraging, or helpful, and there is simply no possible way that I could have sustained my teaching, my writing, my research, and my life without him. To my *compañero*, José Antonio, I owe everything.

MAKING INDIGENOUS CITIZENS

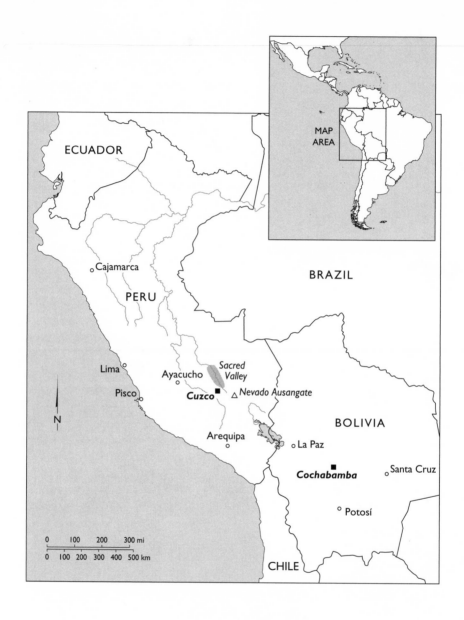

Introduction

> To be Indian . . . we have to speak in our language and
> in Spanish, we have to weave and write, we have to walk
> with our llamas and fly in planes, we have to retain our
> traditions and be modern at the same time.
>
> — Mario, rural schoolteacher in highland Cuzco

Toward the end of my fieldwork in the Peruvian highlands in 1998, my younger brother, Fito, flew to Cuzco for a visit. He had never been to the Andes before, and I was eager to show him all its rugged beauty and, of course, to take him to the communities where I had been conducting research for over a year. He and I had never talked about the specifics of my work. Fito simply knew that I was working with indigenous communities and researching rural education.

Our first outing was a trip to the well-known Sacred Valley of the Incas on a local bus. We walked to the bus stop, bought our tickets, and waited for the bus to fill up and depart. While we waited, a man wearing a poncho and a *ch'ullu* (woven hat) typical of a community located in the highlands above the Sacred Valley rode up to the bus on a bicycle. A young boy, sitting on the handlebars, wore a Ninja Turtles T-shirt, a Chicago Bulls jacket, and Levis jeans, though he was also wearing *ujutas,* the traditional black rubber sandals worn by most indigenous and peasant farmers in the region. My brother was startled when he saw the man and the boy, and watched carefully as the man picked up his bike and handed it to the driver's assistant, who stood on the roof of the bus arranging the passengers' belongings. Fito was even more surprised, it seemed, by the fact that the two men were speaking to each other in Quechua. He observed their interaction for a while, then shifted his gaze to the boy, who had made his way to a woman selling bread, and watched the exchange between them, also in Quechua. At that point he turned to me and said, "I thought only Indians spoke Quechua." I asked him why he did not think the man and the boy were indigenous. He responded: "The man was riding a bike, and his son is wearing a Chicago Bulls jacket. How could they be Indian?"

In retrospect, it seems that in a way, my research in the highlands of Cuzco sought to answer my brother's question. Competing ideas about what it means to be (and to not be) Indian, particularly the troubling distinction — all too commonly made — between modernity (defined as progress and enlightenment) and tradition (read as backwardness and ignorance), have been critical in shaping recent discussions over indigenous rights and mobilization. But more theoretically, this book is about indigenous citizenship and the struggle over representation and voice. In particular, I examine the varying (and competing) representations of indigenous identity, education, and citizenship in local, national, and transnational spaces. These spaces are by no means neatly defined, but rather are themselves zones of engagement in which indigenous community members, state officials, and development practitioners (among others) construct and disrupt, negotiate and contest the means and ends of multicultural policies.

A tremendous diversity of actors have participated in these conversations. The Peruvian state, nongovernmental organizations (NGOs), international development agencies, social scientists, the media, Latin American indigenous leaders and intellectuals, rural indigenous communities in Peru, and indigenous rights advocates (among others) have all deployed their own multiple visions of indigenous representations. This book explores the intersections of recent debates about indigenous rights and empowerment through an analysis of the connections (and gaps) between local, national, and transnational spaces of contention. It does so by looking at the tensions between and within highland Quechua indigenous communities, the state, and indigenous rights activists in Peru and the multiple cultural and political consequences of these tensions.

Specifically, I examine the contradictions of and local challenges to the implementation of development policies, such as intercultural education, that form part of a larger national and international multicultural project. Much is at stake in these debates as they speak to the changing position of indigenous people in the nation-state and in transnational development agendas. As states and NGOs devote increasing attention to what the World Bank calls "ethno-development," it is important to pay close attention to the multiscale and complex construction of indigenous identities and the unequal power relations that complicate even the most well-intentioned efforts at advocacy. For example, as indigenous parents in highland Peru resist state and NGO intercultural education initiatives, they create new local spaces for collective action that have resulted (at least in Cuzco) in one of the very goals of indigenous rights activism, greater local participation in development and politics, albeit through means that activists had not expected. By exploring these and other unexpected turns in Peruvian indigenous politics and grass-roots development, I have tried to emphasize the dynamic and plural nature of identity construction, social movements, and policy initiatives. This is not simply a case of rural communities and their advocates against the neoliberal state, but rather a more complicated story of changing agendas and alliances in which Quechua parents can mobilize against pro-indigenous NGOs, and NGO goals can converge with those of both the state and the international development community. These twists and turns are not unique to Peru but are part of a broad pattern of local and global interactions characterized by contradictory projects of resistance and integration (see, for example, Alvarez, Dagnino, and Escobar, eds., 1998; K. Warren 1998a; and Edelman 1999).

As I try to show throughout the rest of this book, multisited ethnographic analysis is critical for understanding broader (local and global) representations of indigenous organizing, rights activism, and development policies. In the chapters that follow, I explore how debates over education and interculturality (*interculturalidad*) in highland Peru have sparked a "new" round of indigenous activism. The concept of interculturalidad in Peru is similar to the concept of multiculturalism in the United States, though indigenous leaders, state officials, and NGO practitioners stress that the term implies not only the recognition of difference but also "the development of respectful relationships between and among different cultural groups in the country." As one Otavalo friend put it, "multiculturalism is to know that you have neighbors who are different from you, but interculturalidad is when you and your neighbors hold hands to keep each other up [*se agarran de la mano para mantenerse levantados*]." Interculturalidad, like multiculturalism, is a contested term. However, we can try to understand the distinction between them in the following terms: multiculturalism is the recognition of a reality (Peru is a country of a diverse cultural and linguistic makeup); interculturalidad is the *practice* of a multiculturalism in which citizens reach across cultural and linguistic differences to imagine a democratic community. In that vein, bilingual intercultural education is the mechanism par excellence used to foster intercultural unity out of multicultural difference.

In the remainder of this chapter, I look at the particular place that Peru has occupied in discussions about indigenous movements in Latin America, and briefly explore how indigenous citizenship has become a part of new development agendas. Finally, I introduce the people, places, and methods important to this study, and provide a summary of the three sections that make up the rest of this book.

Indigenous Movements and Development Agendas: Repositioning Peru

Indigenous peoples in Peru (and elsewhere) have been and continue to be associated with underdevelopment and poverty (Psacharopoulos and Patrinos 1994) and presented as "archaic obstacles" to the development of "modern" nations (Vargas Llosa 1990). Increasingly, however, tensions between the exclusionary political structure of Latin American governments and the various challenges coming from both local communities in the region and international advocates of indigenous rights have defied this simplistic notion of Indianness (Varese 1996; Díaz Polanco 1997; Stavenhagen 1992, 2002). Indeed, indigenous leaders have been relatively successful in their demands for national and international recognition of indigenous cultural and political rights, and have undeniably challenged ideas about democracy, citizenship, and development.

In fact, the stunning (re)emergence of indigenous peoples as important political actors in Latin America since the 1980s has by now been widely documented (Albó 1991; Stavenhagen 1992, 2002; Van Cott, ed., 1994; Brysk 2000a; Yashar 1998).[1] As many observers have also noted, international institutions have both enabled and reinforced this development through such reforms as Convention 169 of the International Labor Organization, on collective indigenous rights, and the U.N.-declared decade of indigenous people (1995–2004). Also of increasing scholarly interest are the state reforms that have often merged liberal and multicultural projects, what the political scientist Donna Lee Van Cott has called an "emerging regional model of constitutional multiculturalism" (2000: 17; see also Assies et al., eds., 2000, and Sieder, ed., 2002). While some optimistically classify these reforms as ones that inform a "radically new politico-legal order and conception of citizenship" (Sieder, ed., 2002: 5), others point out that the political spaces that have been opened by "neoliberal multiculturalism" are dangerous in that they limit the radical potential of social movements as they "pro-actively shape the terrain on which future negotiations of cultural rights take place" (Hale 2002: 488; see also Gustafson 2002). As scholars have noted about globalizing discourses in general, these converging international and state agendas are double-edged, useful to both movements of resistance and projects of governance (Brysk 2000b, Edelman 1999). Thus we should critically examine new multicultural agendas and discourses that promote the rights of indigenous peoples from both above and below.

The case of contemporary Peru sheds important light on these contradictory processes of incorporation and exclusion when we examine both state multiculturalism and indigenous rights activism. The Peruvian case also contributes greatly to a more plural and multivocal understanding of indigenous politics (Rubin 1997, K. Warren 1998b). Moreover, the exploration of this dynamic field of contention stands in striking contrast to a widely held view of Peru as a curious anomaly.

In a symposium on the Peruvian Truth and Reconciliation Commission (TRC) held at Princeton University in February 2003, several legal and human rights experts commented on the strange turn of events that had taken Peru from the authoritarian rule of Alberto Fujimori to the constitution of the TRC. Most of the speakers were from the United States, though they all had important work and research experience in the country. Each remarked on the "peculiarity" of Peru. One speaker argued, perhaps a bit facetiously, that in Peru, you never know what might happen. "It's a strange country." The one Peruvian member of the roundtable, the well-respected senior anthropologist Luis Millones, then felt compelled to comment: "It is interesting to hear people say that Peru is a strange country. I do not think it is a strange country. I think this [the United States] is a strange country." The panelists and audience laughed in appreciation. Yet through the laughter the question of the peculiarity of Peru still lingered. Indeed, it is a theme that runs through much of the scholarship on Latin America, especially on indigenous politics in the Americas, since the 1990s.

In the context of the region-wide wave of indigenous social movements, dubbed the "return of the Indian" by Xavier Albó (1991), Peru has been the biggest surprise to scholarly observers. In the heart of the Inca empire, a country with a significant indigenous population (estimated to represent around 40 percent of the total), the "indigenous movement" seems to be slumbering, especially in comparison with its neighbors. The anthropologist Paul Gelles writes that "the way that activists have organized along ethnic-based lines in [Ecuador and Bolivia] is virtually inconceivable in Peru" (2002: 246). Similarly, indigenous movements in Peru have been described as "marginal" (Albó 1991), "largely nonexistent" (Yashar 1998), and "a profound failure" (Mayer cited in Yashar 1998). Luis Millones himself has noted how strange this has seemed to some observers:

A year ago, the World Bank decided to make funds available to indigenous populations in Latin America. These were very important funds that would be distributed between Mexico and Tierra del Fuego. To do so, the Bank went in search of the representative indigenous institutions in all of the Latin American countries. And it found itself with the surprising discovery that between Ecuador and Bolivia, there was a country [Peru] without indígenas. (Millones 2000: 79)

Not only is social-movement activity seemingly missing, but according to leading scholars, so are governmental efforts to implement a new kind of multiculturalism. David Maybury-Lewis asserts that while in Ecuador and

Bolivia "channels of participation in national life" have recently opened for native peoples, "this has not happened in Peru" (2002: xix).

Taking the so-called absence of indigenous movements in Peru as a point of departure, most current studies of indigenous mobilization in Latin America either exclude Peru or attempt to explore its "exceptionalism." While it is true that Peru is different from its neighbors, this focus on Peruvian "absence" has obscured the richness of indigenous activism in Peru. As I have discussed elsewhere, indigenous politics in both lowland and highland settings has been vibrant even if it has not always taken the shape of nationwide mobilizations, as in other countries (García and Lucero 2004). If, instead of searching for the sources of Peruvian exceptionalism, we examine closely the interactions between indigenous highlanders, NGO activists, and the state, we confront a different set of questions. Why do people choose or reject Indianness? Who is speaking for indigenous people? Why are local communities mobilizing against NGO and state initiatives ostensibly meant to help indigenous highlanders? How have multicultural education and the politics of culture and language become a terrain of dispute in Latin America? What should indigenous movements look like? In order to move beyond the limits of Peruvian exceptionalism, in this book I try to emphasize the complexity of the cultural processes that provide the elements for constructions of highland indigenous citizenship and intercultural development.[2]

As the anthropologists Kay Warren and Jean Jackson note, "Self–other oppositions, drawn both by activists in their oratory and by anthropologists in their ethnography, turn out to be anything but fixed. Rather, interaction occurs in social fields where alliances shift, definitions are reworked, entities are renamed, and authority is rethought" (2002: 28). In short, we move from taking absence as a point of departure to exploring actually existing multiple and vibrant articulations of indigenous politics. The concept of articulation, especially as formulated by Stuart Hall (1996 [1986]) and used by James Clifford (2001) and Tanya Li (2000), is particularly helpful for understanding how we can move beyond thinking of indigeneity in the all-or-nothing terms of authenticity and invention, cultural survival and extinction.

A theory of articulation is both a way of understanding how ideological elements come, under certain conditions, to cohere together within a discourse, and a way of asking how they do or do not become articulated, at specific conjunctures, to certain political subjects . . . It asks how an ideology discovers its subject rather than how the subject thinks the necessary and inevitable thoughts which belong to it. (Hall 1996 [1986]: 141–142)

The articulations of indigenous politics in Peru reveal important dynamics that cannot be encompassed by views of Peru as simply a case of absence.

As the following chapters show, the conscious manipulation of ethnic labels by Quechua highlanders, the organization of mothers for literacy training, the demand for greater community control of rural schools, and the professionalization of indigenous intellectuals are all examples of indigenous politics at work, albeit in ways that differ in some respects from the *levantamientos* (uprisings) in Ecuador and road blockades in Bolivia.[3] Rather than simply argue for a recoding of Peru as a case of success rather than failure, in these pages I examine the ways in which scholars, activists, and NGOs have participated in the construction of models and expectations that have made such assessments possible in the first place. To that end, the following section explores several scholarly visions of failure or absence and presents a slightly different view of Peruvian indigenous cultural politics, one that challenges representations of an "inadequately" indigenous Peru.

Constructing and Explaining Indigenous Absence

In view of the lamentations over the lack of indigenous political activity in Peru, it is helpful to review three of the most common explanations offered for this absence of ethnic mobilization. Respectively, these approaches emphasize questions of class, politics, and culture. First, some scholars argue that class identities and discourses have historically crowded out ethnic identities and movements. According to this view, the legacies of the populist and corporatist government policies of General Juan Velasco Alvarado (1968–75) continue to classify indigenous populations by class-based labels and social programs. As discussed in Chapter 2, Velasco famously prohibited even the use of the term *Indian*, promoting instead identification as campesinos or peasants. De-Indianization as a strategy of populist reform and of leftist mobilization, then, made ethnic Indian identification unlikely (Gelles 2002).

This argument, however, is unpersuasive, as it simplifies the relationship between class and ethnicity; they are hardly mutually exclusive. Indeed, throughout the 1960s and 1970s, "indigenous utilization of class rhetoric was a political option that did not represent the loss of indigenous culture, but was rather a strategy toward its empowerment" (de la Cadena 2001: 21). Moreover, this view neglects the fact that other Andean states saw comparable efforts to "re-baptize Indians as peasants," as Albó (1994) has put it, yet still boast a resurgence of more explicitly indigenous political identities. This explanation is, at best, insufficient.

A second explanation, drawing on social-movement scholarship, looks to the lack of political opportunity and capability in building supracommunal organizations, due largely to the disastrous effects of civil war (Albó 1991, Yashar 1998). As has been widely discussed (e.g., Poole and Rénique 1992,

Stern 1998, Manrique 2002), the war that raged in the 1980s and early 1990s made Peru an often deadly environment for the kind of explicit organization-building activities of NGOs, missionaries, unions, and indigenous activists that took place in other Andean republics. Political violence, repression, and persecution had a devastating impact on the spaces available for grass-roots organizing. On one side, leftist militants eliminated rival sources of political power; on the other, government forces interpreted any sort of gathering as potentially subversive. This explanation, however, suffers from the fact that organizing did indeed occur during times of terror, and not only despite the violence but at times because of it. Largely in response to political conflict, indigenous communities organized to defend themselves from attack in both highland and lowland contexts. The most notable examples are the Asháninka army in the Central Jungle region and the *rondas campesinas* (peasant patrols) in the Andes (Vásquez, interview, June 2002; Starn 1992, 1999; Sieder 2002). It is also significant that some of the oldest and most active indigenous organizations in Peru are found in zones that continue to be afflicted by political violence.[4]

Moreover, explaining indigenous mobilization through a structural view of political opportunity and capacity, while valuable, tends to assume a rather static notion of indigenous identity politics, one that seems simply to be awaiting the right conditions to emerge through the cracks of uneven states (but see Yashar 1998). A political/structural approach does say much about the conditions for visible protest, but it says very little about the "hidden transcripts" (Scott 1990) and the cultural dynamics of identity formation that are an important part of collective action.

Given the difficulties of class and political accounts, it makes considerable sense to consider more cultural explanations of the nature of Peruvian identities. Among the most influential has been the one advanced by the Peruvian anthropologist Marisol de la Cadena (2000). Closely analyzing the cultural force and particularity of *indigenismo* and *mestizaje* in Cuzco, de la Cadena tries to answer the question of Peruvian exceptionalism. She rejects earlier contentions that Peruvian Indian identity has been erased by national projects of mestizaje. She emphasizes instead the significance of historical conditions that have led Peruvian Andeans (specifically those in Cuzco, or *cuzqueños*) to appropriate and redefine the term *mestizo* as a way "to develop de-Indianization as a decolonizing indigenous strategy" (2000: 325). Examining the discourse and practices of urban cuzqueño intellectual elites, university students, mestiza market women, and others, she argues that they have all expanded their mestizo identity to include indigenous practices. In doing so, these individuals (whom she labels "grass-roots indigenous intellectuals") have redefined dominant notions of mestizo and indigenous identity. Defying perceptions of indigenous identity as "exclusively rural, essentially backward, irrational and illiterate," these intellectuals present indigenous culture as both rural and urban and compatible with literacy and progress. Thus, for cuzqueño grass-roots intellectuals, "indigenous culture exceeds the scope of Indianness and includes subordinate definitions of the mestizo/a" (316). Simultaneously, becoming mestizo does not necessarily mean erasing indigenous cultural identity. In other words, indigenous practices do not disappear when indigenous people learn Spanish and move to the city. Thus one strategy of empowerment employed by indigenous intellectuals in Cuzco is to perform their identity as *indigenous* mestizos. Given this reworking of the terms of Peruvian ethnic and racial discourses, de la Cadena contends that the lack of *recognized* ethnic mobilization in the country is due to the fact that indigenous mestizo activism is not usually considered ethnic activism.

Her contribution is important because it helpfully problematizes the distinction made between the categories of Indian and mestizo, and highlights the complexity of identity formation. Indigenous mestizo activism is an important concept, as it contributes to a more nuanced understanding of Peruvian cultural politics. However, while her contribution is a helpful alternative to the scholarship that emphasizes Peruvian failure, it misses important parts of the story. Specifically, it neglects other forms of activism that cannot be described as indigenous *mestizo* activism. Unlike the urban intellectuals that de la Cadena emphasizes, rural (often monolingual) indigenous parents are also negotiating identity in politically important ways. Additionally, indigenous students and intellectuals in transnational institutes are promoting alternative (local and global) visions of Indianness that challenge dominant categories and structures of representation but reject the label of mestizo.

Accordingly, the research presented in this book continues the critical line of cultural research represented by de la Cadena and others, by suggesting additional ways to move beyond the questions of absence and failure in Peru. Interactions between indigenous parents, activists, and the state suggest the need for a complex view of both social movement and success. Additionally, the transnational nature of contemporary indigenous politics requires viewing Peru as embedded in cultural and political processes that occur at multiple scales. When we readjust our gaze away from national cases and nationwide movements (such as the Confederation of Indigenous Nationalities of Ecuador, or CONAIE), the constellation of Peruvian indigenous politics suddenly appears striking.

Highland communities are the sites of a great deal of conflict, resistance, and organization. The protagonists of much of this activity are Quechua parents who reject programs that, according to NGO activists, are meant to educate their children and in time empower and incorporate their communities in a new multicultural Peru. Activists, state officials, and NGOs are often surprised and disappointed by the rejection of their efforts at advocacy. In their estimation, the obstacles put up by parents might be viewed as an internalized oppression, Quechua subalterns viewing their reality through the eyes of neocolonial elites, victims of false consciousness who are unable to discern their real interests. Given such a diagnosis, the remedy is training, education, and other strategies to raise the consciousness of Quechua community members. However, often these strategies are implemented in ways that seek not to educate but to dictate the new terms of policies that come "from the ministry." Compliance with new reforms is obtained not through new consciousness but often with old-fashioned coercion. Intercultural activists, in and outside government, seem to deliver the same message: The state has given you these programs; participate or lose access to these resources that have generously been offered to your people.

For students of social movements, things seem curiously upside down. The peculiarity of these kinds of interactions is perhaps most clearly illustrated in an encounter described in Chapter 4, in which a state official described her intercultural work and the work of the NGOs (who were often the "executing agents" of state policy) in the communities as nothing less than a social movement on behalf of indigenous people and inspired by indigenous movements throughout the region. If social movements are directed by state policies, one can reasonably ask what the term means and what we should call the resistance to the "movement" from the people on whose behalf it is being constructed.

This contestation over the very idea of "social movement" is significant because it puts into relief the importance of the models of contention analysts use to understand social struggles over meaning and resources. Thinking about both the complex interactions in the Peruvian countryside and the vast literature on social movements,[5] one could ask: What counts as a social movement? One could find plenty of support for a wide range of answers. NGO supporters of indigenous organizing follow many scholars in seeing social movements as the visible protests coordinated by professional activists (Tarrow 1994, Tilly 1993-94). In this view, the training of indigenous youth is a crucial step in the formation of an indigenous social movement. Others, perhaps including the government workers who see intercultural education as a social movement, would adopt the more flexible conception of social movements as "wars of interpretation" that take many forms as they unsettle the dominant meanings and codes of society. In an effort to bring together a fractious field of scholars, Charles Tilly (1993–94) has characterized social movements as "clusters of political performances" involving authorities and challengers. I don't seek to discuss these typological debates here, but taking Tilly's evocative idea, local communities are clearly the sites of political performance by the state, nongovernmental actors, and Quechua families.

This organized and steady resistance of parents to "outside" actors provides many examples of people coming together in the name of their children and mobilizing against the imposition of external policies. Though some may not care to see this resistance in these terms, I cannot think what makes community organizing against intercultural education any less of a movement than indigenous mobilizing against other forms of state intervention. Indeed, as I discuss further in Chapter 1, Quechua communities have organized themselves against a series of external agents, including the deadly forces of both Sendero Luminoso and state military units and the ostensibly more benign forces of international development. The actions and struggles of Quechua parents and intercultural activists are emblematic of the contemporary struggles over the very meaning of citizenship in the Andes.

Intercultural Development: Citizenship and Livelihoods

Throughout Latin America, indigenous peoples are undoubtedly facing new challenges as they are increasingly integrated into national and global contexts (Yashar 1998; Brysk 2000a; Van Cott 2000). One of those challenges is the dilemma faced by indigenous movements when leaders demand the right to participate fully in national society while simultaneously pressing for special and sometimes separate status in that society. Intercultural activists in Peru face this challenge not as indigenous leaders but often as "outsiders," activists not from indigenous communities but working in their name toward what some call a "multicultural citizenship" (Montoya 1998). However, there are some difficulties with the very category of "intercultural activists," as the term can include nongovernmental advocates of bilingual intercultural education, state bureaucrats involved with its implementation, and intellectuals who work both within and outside the state. The trouble in unpacking this label and untangling the actors involved suggests a need not for more specific terms but rather, as shall soon become more apparent, for a more flexible theory of articulation, in the double sense given to the term by Hall, as both a political "cobbling together" and the process of voicing a collective identity.

Activists' efforts to construct indigenous citizenship represent, in their view, a move from the undemocratic subjectivities of prior eras — that is, as members of a separate (and not equal) "Republic of Indians" during colonial times — and as nationalized (and ostensibly de-Indianized) peasants linked to states by populist leaders and policies. Becoming an indigenous citizen in some ways represents a dialectical move to synthesize the (colonial) recognition of ethnic difference and the (populist) policies of national inclusion, but without the hierarchies that both implied. Additionally, indigenous citizenship stands not for what states give to subjects but for the agency and autonomy that indigenous people claim to construct it for themselves. Moreover, it reveals an awareness of the changing historical positioning of "us" (Quechuas) and "them" (state and international agents).

The central arena for the construction of this new kind of citizenship, in the view of activists, is the schoolhouse, the place long recognized as a kind of "citizenship factory" (Luykx 1999). Struggles over citizenship and indigenous politics, of course, go beyond the schoolhouse, as mobilizations around mining, coca, and human rights have demonstrated (Caballo and Boyd 2002, García and Lucero 2004, Youngers and Peacock 2002, SERVINDI 2002b, Rojas 2003). However, intercultural education occupies a special place in the contemporary history of indigenous mobilization. During authoritarian times (1990–2000), bilingual education was one of the few causes that activists could advance without necessarily inviting government repression. In the current moment of democratic transition, bilingual intercultural education remains a central concern of advocates for a truly inclusive, intercultural Peru.

The implementation of intercultural education is important not only for the impact it has had on questions of citizenship, identity, and indigenous self-determination, but also because it forms part of a larger effort aimed at effecting real, palpable material improvement in the lives of Peruvian highland populations. Typically, local and international NGOs are charged with implementing and overseeing these programs at local levels. In recent years, NGOs have played an increasingly prominent role as intermediaries between the state and marginalized groups in Latin America, partly in response to the reduction of social welfare programs administered by the state (Bebbington and Thiele 1993, Fisher 1997, Bebbington 2000). Mounting concern over indigenous rights on the part of international donor agencies has also shifted the balance toward an emphasis on funding NGOs with a focus on indigenous language preservation, cultural revival, indigenous health, and indigenous education. Thus intercultural education programs are an extension of the enterprise of grass-roots development and human rights advocacy that have been the subject of serious scholarly and policy debates (Hornberger, ed., 1997; Healy 2001; Kleymeyer 1994).

The literature on development is vast and it is not necessary to summarize it here. However, for the purposes of this book, it is useful to highlight two distinct analytic approaches to understanding how new development policies, such as educational reforms, work. On one side, such initiatives as bilingual intercultural education are hailed as important examples of the kind of ethno-development policies — advocated now by a striking variety of actors across the globe, including North American and European NGOs and even the World Bank — that no longer see "indigenous culture" as an obstacle to development but rather as an important source of social capital (Kleymeyer 1994, Davis 2001, Healy 2001). From another side, a postmodern scholarly critique has emerged against the discursive power that the development industry has, in Arturo Escobar's (1995) phrase, to make and unmake the Third World (see also Ferguson 1994). Critics such as Escobar argue that development is a dangerous fiction that reinforces unequal power relations by expanding the domain of "states, dominant institutions, and mainstream ways" (Escobar 1991: 667). Marc DuBois levels the charge directly at such local grass-roots efforts as bilingual intercultural education: "small development organizations that operate on a grass-roots level . . . appear to be potentially the most dangerous if a Foucauldian sense of power is used to examine development anew" (1991: 91).

So are the educational changes taking place in Cuzco a part of the new inclusive and culturally sensitive ethno-development or a part of the fictions of progress that constitute new disciplinary strategies targeted at subaltern populations? The position I develop more fully in Chapter 4 is attentive to the questions raised by these perspectives but skeptical of both views. Close ethnographic study of the new opportunities and dangers of changing development agendas and community responses reveals a dynamic field of contestation where possibilities are not defined by the goals of international organizations or the pessimism of Foucauldian views of power. Though it is remarkable that international organizations such as the International Labor Organization, the United Nations, and the World Bank have shifted their energies away from integrationist policies toward multicultural ones, one should still ask how the new multicultural agendas are being forged in Geneva, New York, and Washington, by whom, and on behalf of whom (Fox and Brown 1998). A close look at the cultural understandings of intercultural activists, state officials, international funders, and indigenous peoples is needed to evaluate how inclusive the new policies of intercultural development truly are. Moreover, scholarship on the compatibility of multicultural policies and neoliberal agendas (Wade 1997, Hale 2002, Gustafson 2002) further complicates this story and compels us to look closely at the intersections of global agendas and local practices.

Local ethnographic research can provide valuable insights into the workings of the global discourses and practices of development. Indeed, taking a ground-level view of globalization is perhaps the most powerful and feasible way to capture the imbrications of the local and the global. Local ethnography is also a useful corrective to postmodernist indictments against development writ large that often operate at such a high level of abstraction that the subaltern victims of alleged discursive crimes are ironically far beyond the analytical horizon. The desire for development looks very different after one has spoken with Quechua parents who are concerned about the all-too-real material limitations of rural life, and who fear for the futures of sons and daughters whose best option is often to move to faraway cities and work in conditions of certain exploitation and (often) cruel physical violation.

In order to understand the limits and possibilities of intercultural education as an ethno-development strategy, I have sought to study closely both the formulation and implementation of NGO efforts and the responses of the indigenous community members who are the most affected by those efforts. Throughout this book I suggest that a crucial factor accounting for indigenous rejection (in Cuzco) of NGO educational and cultural reforms is the marked contrast between the ideology behind such programs and their practical implementation. To understand this gulf between NGO goals and community realities, it is necessary to explore the multiple contradictions of development practices. In particular, the tensions between NGO discourses about social equality and the reproduction of ethnic hierarchies, and between their nongovernmental status and simultaneous reliance on governmental authority (especially that of the Ministry of Education and other state agencies), raises questions about their contributions toward grass-roots mobilization and empowerment. While NGOs have often provided alternative spaces for discussion of reform and democracy, we should not assume that there is a clear line separating the budgets, personnel, and agendas of governmental and nongovernmental spheres (Jelin 1998).

In highlighting some of these contradictions, I do not intend to join the chorus of antidevelopment theorists but rather to follow the lead of skeptical yet committed ethnographers of development and culture who are concerned with tracing the unequal material and cultural impacts of specific development policies on rural people (e.g., Starn 1994, Gupta 1995, Gill 1997, Edelman 1999, and Bebbington 2000). I do not seek to defend a separation between the discursive and material stakes of development, for such dichotomies are of little help. Rather, I hope to contribute to the critical but engaged study of the local effects of development policies. Such a grounded view can offer a concrete sense of the social costs of contradictory discursive practices and the human costs of abandoning all hope in development.

In the Field: Places, Methods, and Terminology

In recent years the importance of multisited (and multiscaled) research has become increasingly clear (Marcus 1995). Moving between rural and urban spaces and across local, national, and international scales not only allows multiple ethnographic vantage points but also makes it possible to trace and track the connections and contradictions of cultural politics. It is more apparent now than ever that culture and politics do not stand still for the ethnographer's steady gaze, but rather dare ethnographers to move unsteadily in various contexts (R. Fox 1991, Appadurai 1991). The research for this book was multisited in that I worked in Peruvian rural highland communities, highland towns, highland cities, coastal cities, and among Peruvians in a neighboring Andean country. However, as the field of anthropological research is remapped to include long-distance nationalisms (Glick Schiller et al. 2001), flexible (and diasporic) citizenships (Ong 1999b), and the anthropologist herself (Stephen 2002: 21), we must keep in mind that even multisited analyses inform only part of the story. Additionally, as global technology makes contact and communication easier, and as indigenous and other grass-roots organizations gain access to computers and the Internet, cyberspace has also become an important field research site. While uneven resources still determine access to these tools, the Internet has clearly become a critical site of struggle (Delgado 2002). E-mail and its subscription lists, online newsletters, and Web sites are now legitimate sources of production, negotiation, and reproduction of knowledge.[6] These sites have also facilitated the development of both new and already established collaborative networks of (for example) local organizations and intellectuals, international funders, and social scientists.

Moreover, as those traditionally labeled informants or subjects of research increasingly challenge these and other (unequal) power-laden terms and construct their own representations and interpretations of cultural and political histories, often products of anthropological (mis)understandings (K. Warren 1992, Fabian 2001), they have helped to transform the field of anthropology. In my view, the now common move among (engaged) anthropologists toward "an entirely new set of priorities" (Stephen 2002: 11), including a rethinking of neutrality and observation as political acts (Wright 1988: 365–367, Diskin 1991: 171) and an intimate collaboration from the outset with the community with which one wishes to work, is critical for a more responsible practice of anthropology (García 2000), as well as for the democratization of ethnography and the ethnographic method (Paley 2001: 20).

I should also say a word about my role as a Peruvian-American ethnographer working in the Peruvian Andes. I spent two summers in the city of Cuzco (1996 and 1997) taking courses in language and linguistics at the Colegio de Estudios Andinos and conducting preliminary research before moving to Cuzco for long-term field research in the fall of 1997. By the time I arrived in the city the third time, I had already had many conversations with intercultural activists about the kind of research I was interested in conducting. In fact, my research topic — the connections between bilingual intercultural education and ethnic mobilization in the highlands — was shaped largely by the kinds of analyses that some intercultural activists told me would be helpful to their political and cultural struggles.[7] While my commitment to practice a politically and socially engaged anthropology was an important part of my collaboration with intercultural activists and other advocates of intercultural education in Cuzco, local expectations about me and about my work (not only as an anthropologist but as a Peruvian anthropologist) played a significant role in my initial ethnographic interactions.

Elsewhere (García 2000) I have more fully discussed the connections between identity, ethnography, and advocacy, as well as the responsibilities of anthropologists to the communities with which they work. What is important to note here is that though the term "native anthropologist" (with its essentialist assumptions) is at best a problematic one (Abu-Lughod 1991, Narayan 1993), it captures an idea that indigenous farmers, local intellectuals, NGO practitioners, state bureaucrats, and many others (including colleagues in U.S. academic spaces) used when discussing my work. Acknowledging that Peru is the country of my birth and the Andes the land of my grandfather, many Andeans would use phrases such as "You are like us [*Eres como nosotros*]," "You are authentic [*Eres auténtica*]," and "You have Andean blood, like us [*Tienes sangre andina, como nosotros*]." Significantly, these phrases were usually followed by a statement about how and why this identity tied me to a more socially responsible kind of research. Because I was born in Peru, I was somehow more intimately connected, I understood more completely, and I would contribute (both concretely with material resources and abstractly with academic contributions) more fully to the community.

I could say that being aware of the constructedness of categories and identities made me somewhat skeptical or even dismissive of claims regarding my own "authenticity." Moreover, many of the same people who would validate my Peruvianness on some occasions would also be quick to call me a gringa (or *agringada*) when my views seemed to go against theirs. However, despite the difficulties of the ideas of nativeness and authenticity, in many ways I did feel somehow more responsible to Andean communities. My return to Peru and my work in the Andes were deeply tied to my own family history. Notwithstanding Orin Starn's warnings about Andeanism (1991), I could not avoid a deeply personal and emotional connection with the highlands, not out of a romantic vision of rural Indian life but as a way of looking for my own family's past. In an important way, I was looking for my grandfather, a miner from the highlands of Ayacucho who migrated to the coast and forbade anyone to speak Quechua in his house. His vision of education as a "civilizing" process meant, for him, leaving behind the highlands both physically and culturally. My own parents followed this example even more dramatically by leaving Peru altogether. Ironically, one of the primary reasons my family left when I was only a child was my parents' concern over the progressive education reform policies being passed in the mid-1970s by the government of General Juan Velasco Alvarado (1968–1975). Specifically, the "threat" of the implementation of bilingual education (Spanish-Quechua) at the national level, in both urban and rural contexts, prompted my parents to leave the country in 1976, only one year after Quechua became an official language. Especially for my father, a fierce believer in the power of education (which took him from the economic margins to middle-class comfort), staying in Peru would have only endangered his children's future.

In returning to the Andes I was looking past the complexities of my training as a cultural anthropologist — who should be skeptical of essential and static views of culture — and trying to find what my family had "lost." Although the power of this nostalgia became clear only in retrospect, it is important to acknowledge it here, not only in the spirit of reflexivity but also in recognition of the hold that cultural memory, with all its imaginative force, can have. Twenty years after my parents left the country, and two generations after my grandfather left the highlands, I returned to Andean Peru to support the work of activists promoting bilingual education and working tirelessly to "rescue" language and culture. The irony was not lost on my parents, who still registered their unease about my return to Peru generally and to the Andean highlands specifically. This unease emerged from their concern over the political violence that was still a part of Peruvian life. But as I discuss below, it also reflected ideas about the dominant racialized geographies that divide Peru between a more "advanced" (and whiter) coast where my extended family still lives and the more "backward" (and Indian) highlands that my grandfather tried to leave behind.

Places

My research with highland Peruvians was conducted mainly through work in the department of Cuzco, specifically in the city of Cuzco and in rural communities in both the high puna of the Ausangate region and the warmer climes of the Sacred Valley of the Incas. Following the increasingly transnational trend of indigenous politics, I also conducted fieldwork (for brief periods) among the Peruvian (and Bolivian, Ecuadorian, Chilean, and Colombian) indigenous students at the Bilingual Intercultural Education Program for Andean Countries (PROEIB Andes) in Cochabamba, Bolivia.

My research in Peru occupied nineteen months during the years 1996–99.[8] For most of that time I lived in Cuzco and the surrounding countryside. The first five months of research — including Quechua language study and preliminary fieldwork — took place in the city during the summers of 1996 and

1997. It was during those two summers that I met most of the intercultural activists and intellectuals advocating the implementation of bilingual intercultural education at the Centro de Estudios Andinos "Bartolomé de Las Casas" (CBC), a well-known research institute in Latin America. I spent this time taking classes at the CBC and interacting with intercultural activists from Peru and other Latin American countries and with highland teachers, teacher trainers, and some NGO practitioners who were also taking courses at the CBC. I took courses on Andean linguistics, education reform, and language planning in Latin America. I conducted the bulk of my research, however, between October 1997 and November 1998, though I spent one last month in Cuzco and in Cochabamba in August 1999.

CUZCO: THE CITY

Cradled by the striking Andean mountain range, Cuzco lies at 3,500 meters (about 11,500 feet) above sea level. It was the capital of the Inca empire, and as such, it is considered a city of tremendous historical and cultural importance. Since an upsurge in tourism in the 1960s, foreign visitors have been among Peru's most important sources of revenue, and most tourists visit Cuzco during their stay. The importance of tourism is not solely economic. Representations of Peru and its inhabitants are important elements of transnational tourism that influence the discursive fashioning of "authentic" indigenous identities and the commodification of cultural products.

As one way to maintain foreign interest in the Peruvian Andes, the state became closely involved with the production and promotion of *cuzqueñista* festivals and folklore, cultural representations of Inca history, and local religious rituals and ceremonies (de la Cadena 2000). Cuzco's historical prominence is recognized by most Peruvians, even those in Lima. Yet many *limeños* and others who extol Cuzco as a national cultural treasure also view its inhabitants, and other *serranos* (Andeans), as inferior. Marked geographic distinctions between the coast, the highlands, and the lowlands of the country reflect as well the cultural, ethnic, and class representations that mark people from each region as distinct, a point illustrated by the cuzqueño indigenista intellectual Luis Eduardo Valcárcel in *Tempestad en los Andes* (Tempest in the Andes):

Cuzco and Lima are, by the nature of things, two opposing focal points of nationality. Cuzco represents our mother culture, inherited from the millenarian Inkas. Lima is the desire for adaptation to the European culture. And this is because Cuzco already existed when the Conquistador arrived, and Lima was created by him, ex nihilo. (Valcárcel 1972 [1927]: 110)[9]

Of course, regional boundaries are not rigid and unchanging, as the "Andeanization" of Lima through internal migration illustrates. Nevertheless, despite the demographic complexity of population shifts, as representational spaces the Andean highlands and coastal Lima continue to signify racial and economic contrasts.

While Lima has become the political and economic center of the country, Cuzco continues to be the site of important cultural and political developments. Notably, as I discuss in Chapter 2, many influential indigenista intellectual movements originated in Cuzco.

Because of Cuzco's historical significance as the capital of the Inca empire, several self-labeled indigenous organizations, professing the return of the Tawantinsuyo (the Quechua name for the Inca empire) and proclaiming Quechua (often equated with Inca) identity as part of claims against Hispanic oppression, have surfaced in this city. Despite their claims, however, representatives of some of these groups often treat Quechua Indians and peasants in Cuzco in a derogatory manner. The Academy for the Quechua Language in Cuzco can be seen as one of these organizations. Its leaders, all men in their forties and fifties, proclaim that they are the "new Incas" who must defend the Quechua language against Spanish intrusion, and consider themselves to be professionals and intellectuals of high social status and thus deserving of respect, especially from those of the "lower classes." According to them, they speak the *correct* variation of Quechua (*Capaq Runa Simi,* or High Quechua), whereas highland Indians and peasants speak simply *Runa Simi* (the language of the people). I have also heard some of these representatives refer to the Quechua spoken by indigenous peasants in the highlands as *Allqu Runa Simi,* "the language of dogs."[10] Notwithstanding the problematic elitism of such views, the academy has created several spaces for collaboration with other indigenous groups, activists, and some scholars on the revalorization of Quechua language and culture.

Throughout the twentieth century, Cuzco was also the site of both union activity and intense peasant mobilization, particularly around land recovery (Rénique 1991). The Federación de Trabajadores del Cuzco (Cuzco Workers' Federation), for example, established during the early 1940s, would become the principal leader in demonstrations against landowners during the land invasions of the 1960s (Rénique 1991). Cuzco is also closely associated with intellectual movements linked to education. In 1909 Cuzco was the site of the first university reform movement in Latin America. In 1919 university students chose the city as the headquarters of the National Student Congress. In the 1920s the region was one of the sites where the Comité Pro-Derecho Indígena Tawantinsuyo, an indigenous (and indigenista) political and cultural organization, placed demands on the state for community-controlled schools, and campaigned for indigenous peoples' right to education and citizenship.

THE HIGHLANDS: COMMUNITIES IN THE
AUSANGATE AND THE SACRED VALLEY

My work in highland communities was crucial to understanding the conflict between intercultural activists and the people for whom they claim to speak. Only after traveling to dozens of highland schools and living in several communities for weeks at a time was I able to grasp the depth of the fissures that exist between activists and teachers, between teachers and parents, and between parents and activists. It was also during my time among indigenous parents, children, and community leaders that I developed most of my language skills in Quechua.[11]

I spent several months in communities throughout the Ausangate region, one of the poorest areas of the country. Named after the snow-capped peaks of the Ausangate mountain range (considered a deity by many of those living in the area), this region is one of the most isolated and neglected in Peru. At an elevation of 4,000 meters or over 13,000 feet (its highest peak rises above 6,000 meters or 16,500 feet), only rocks, *ichu* (a strawlike grass), and alpacas (of the same family as the llama) surround the base of the mountain range. The indigenous peasants who live in this cold and arid region are mainly farmers or herders. They harvest potatoes or herd alpacas or sheep. Although they sometimes sell alpaca meat at the village market on Sundays or exchange it for other goods, such as oil, butter, cheese, or eggs, the main source of income for most Quechua highlanders in this region is the sale of textiles. Women weave ponchos, *polleras* (skirts), and other garments for women, and the men work on embroidered *ch'ullus* (hats) and bracelets. Although the men boast that their work is more intricate and delicate, women's weavings are the most expensive. The sale of one poncho at almost U.S.$100 (an extremely lucky and rare occurrence) can provide enough income to support the entire extended family for a month. Most women speak only Quechua, and only some of the men speak both Quechua and Spanish.

The Ausangate region suffers from tremendous government neglect, especially with regard to medical and educational facilities. New school buildings have been erected throughout many highland areas in recent years, but so far none has been built in the Ausangate region. Medical posts are scarce, and their existence does not guarantee equipment or even medical personnel. Teachers in these areas are often expected to care for sick children when parents feel they need help. Yet most of the schools have no first-aid kit, and none of the teachers I met had any kind of medical training.

I lived in Intipacha, a community at the base of the Ausangate, longer than at any other community in Cuzco.[12] I first heard about Intipacha when a North American anthropologist and friend, Andrea, returned from her fieldwork in Peru. Andrea spent several months commuting between Intipacha and Cuzco, learning how to weave, and exploring the patterns in the ponchos and polleras of the area. Our stays in Cuzco coincided once, toward the beginning of my year-long research in the department, as I was struggling to develop conversational skills in Quechua. She told me about her comadre María and her family, and suggested I travel to Intipacha. She said that no one except María's oldest son spoke Spanish. When I decided it was time for me to learn more about the particular concerns of Quechua parents about the implementation of bilingual education in their schools, I thought about María and her family, packed my bags, and set out for Intipacha.

The trip to the Ausangate, especially for an inexperienced woman traveling to the region alone for the first time, feels like an eternity. Before attempting this trip, I had already traveled to the Ausangate with a local NGO, and I felt confident about the route. However, I had traveled in the NGO's four-door pickup, leaving from Cuzco or a nearby town, driving directly to the base of the Ausangate, and stopping only for bathroom breaks. The entire trip took no more than five or six hours. Traveling alone was a little different. On my first solo trip to the communities of the Ausangate, I took a bus from Cuzco to Urcos, a town about one and a half hours from Cuzco. At Urcos I got off the bus and asked when, if ever, a truck or *colectivo* (a minivan used as a kind of taxi) might be leaving in the direction of Ocongate, the town nearest to the Ausangate mountain range. Since colectivos rarely make the seven-hour trek up two mountains to reach Ocongate, on this occasion (and as I would do many other times) I decided to climb onto a cargo truck. I made the trip next to a few other passengers: three teachers and two community members returning home after trying, without luck, to secure a birth certificate for their daughter. The truck made a slow climb up the dirt road that winds around the mountains. I learned on that trip about the importance of handkerchiefs (or any other piece of cloth) to protect your face. Without one it is next to impossible to fend off wind, dirt, and dust from entering your eyes, nose, and mouth. I arrived at Ocongate that evening and found a small room for about U.S. $1.50 to spend the night. I continued my journey to the Ausangate the next morning.

I mention the difficulties involved in getting to Intipacha and other communities in the Ausangate to emphasize the importance of space in the geography of development. The roughly fifteen families that lived in Intipacha were accustomed to traveling great distances for medical care, markets, and legal services as basic as birth certificates and national identification cards. The isolation of Intipacha stands in contrast to the situation of communities in the Sacred Valley.

The Sacred Valley of the Incas is commonly referred to by most cuzqueños as simply *el Valle,* or the Valley. The Valley is one of the most common tourist stops after Machu Picchu. In fact, to travel to Machu Picchu, the best-known Peruvian archaeological site, one must take a train through part of the Sacred Valley and wind down alongside the Urubamba River, considered sacred by most Quechuas in the region. Despite its proximity to Cuzco, the Valley is home to Quechua communities that, like many highland communities, often lack basic social services. As in the Ausangate, children in most Valley communities are often undernourished and sick. Because of the cold and harsh climate, most children live with perpetual nasal congestion and coughs, and most have skin ailments. Regardless of their health, they do their chores, help their parents in the fields, and sometimes attend the community school.

Here, too, most people are farmers, although some men and women work as potters and weavers and participate in the tourist craft fairs that take place on most Thursdays and Sundays in several Valley towns. On these days, men and women from the highlands gather their vegetable produce, their weavings or ceramic pots and plates, and commute to various Valley towns — such as Pisaq and Chincheros — where they join mestizo villagers from nearby areas to sell their goods, primarily to tourists and to some town residents. As in the Ausangate, women still tend to be monolingual Quechua speakers despite some contact with Spanish speakers. However, many of the men from the highlands above the Sacred Valley are bilingual in Quechua and Spanish.[13] One of the most common forms of employment for men in these communities today is working as porters for the thousands of tourists who hike the Inca trail year round. For anywhere from three to five days, these Quechua men carry camping gear, food, clothes, and sometimes chairs and tables strapped to their backs, running ahead of the tour group in order to set up camp for them and have it ready by the time they arrive. Speaking Spanish and a little English has become a necessity for most young men in these communities, who compete for these jobs on a daily basis. Although they make very little money, they still make more than they would by selling their agricultural products, and they also often receive sacks of rice, sugar, or flour from certain tour companies as special gifts.

Because of their proximity to the city of Cuzco, communities in this area receive much more attention from intercultural activists, NGO practitioners, and regional education authorities than do the communities in the Ausangate. I noticed during my first visit to Pacchay, a community above the town of Ollanta (another important archaeological site), that many of the parents seemed more aware of the role and responsibility of state agencies. Unlike many of the Quechua parents I met in the more isolated Ausangate communities, parents in Pacchay and other Valley communities I visited demanded resources with ease, not only from NGOs operating in the region but also from regional state agencies and their representatives. I will discuss the experiences of Quechua parents and community leaders, children, and teachers more fully in Chapters 3 and 4.

PERU IN BOLIVIA: COCHABAMBA AND THE PROEIB ANDES

In addition to my ethnographic research in Cuzco, I traveled to neighboring Bolivia, following a group of Peruvian indigenous students who had been selected to attend a master's program at an institute in Cochabamba. The Bolivian department of Cochabamba shares some important similarities with Cuzco; it is also an important national city and is located in the Quechua valley of the country (in contrast to the high plateau dominated by Aymaras). For my purposes, however, the regional space of Cochabamba was less important than the specific transnational space that the PROEIB itself represented.

As mentioned above, the PROEIB houses indigenous students from five Andean countries. I first heard about the PROEIB in November 1997 during an international conference I attended on intercultural education in the highland department of Puno (bordering Bolivia). As part of a panel on indigenous intellectual traditions, the primary founder and director of the PROEIB, Luis Enrique López, delivered a presentation announcing the inauguration of the PROEIB master's program. López spoke passionately of the importance of training indigenous people to be protagonists in indigenous development and become full participants in the process of implementing the educational, political, and social reforms that were being advocated by a variety of national and international agencies. I was intrigued by this institute, particularly because such a program, although perhaps increasingly common in other Latin American countries, was still unprecedented in Peru. My interest in the program only grew when I learned that Martín, a Quechua-speaking friend who had long identified as mestizo, was selected for this exclusively indigenous program. Soon after he began his training at the PROEIB, I traveled to Cochabamba for the first time, and my friend Martín no longer spoke with me in Spanish but insisted on speaking only in Quechua. This shift in self-(re)presentation was not limited to Martín; it was common to all the Peruvian students at the PROEIB at that time.

After spending a few weeks in Cochabamba, I was surprised to find that students at the PROEIB did not only read about bilingual education methodology and debate language acquisition theories, they also read such theorists as Michel Foucault, Pierre Bourdieu, and Mikhail Bakhtin. Moreover, students were trained in bilingual methodology and theory by European, North American, and Latin American instructors. They discussed theories of power and inequality, and debated anthropological notions of culture, identity, and ethnicity. Moreover, in this cosmopolitan setting, courses stressed the maintenance of authentic indigenous identity, but they also promoted the intellectual development of their indigenous students by providing access to global tools. Students were encouraged to learn several international languages, such as English and French, and they learned how to use computers and navigate the Internet. In other words, being an authentic indigenous intellectual meant being rooted in local histories and identities, and also being well versed in international vocabularies of social theory and technology.

After two visits to the PROEIB, I found that students at this institute were labeled indigenous intellectuals, leaders, and international representatives of indigenous peoples. However, as is often the case, students did not simply assume these designations but continuously debated, challenged, and modified them as they appropriated them. In Chapter 5 I take a closer look at these dynamics.

Methods

Over the course of the nineteen months I spent in Cuzco, I conducted extensive interviews with the many actors directly and indirectly engaged with changes in education policies in the highlands. They included intellectual and academic supporters of bilingual intercultural education, both Peruvian and of other nationalities, public officials, regional education authorities, NGO personnel, *capacitadores* (teacher trainers), directors of schools in the city and in the rural highland regions, highland teachers, highland community leaders, and parents of Quechua children. I also spoke with individuals who did not agree with the concept or the implementation of bilingual intercultural education, such as the directors of three agricultural NGOs and members of the Cuzco Academy for the Quechua Language.

Working with NGOs was both rewarding and challenging. The NGO with which I worked most closely, which I will call YACHANA, had jurisdiction over the Ausangate region. José Muñoz, the NGO's director, was one of the most helpful (and eccentric) individuals I encountered throughout my time in Cuzco. Immediately after our first formal meeting, he introduced me to his entire staff and told them I would be working with them for the following year. The NGO's staff was one of the friendliest and most helpful I met. With them I traveled to and from the Ausangate many times, and I spent days with capacitadores from YACHANA as they prepared for and led teacher-training and *interaprendizaje* (shared learning) workshops.[14] I accompanied local supervisors as they traveled from one school to the next, evaluating teachers, talking with students, and organizing community assemblies and parent gatherings to discuss current educational changes, and I spent many afternoons in Yanamarca, the small town near Cuzco where YACHANA was based, discussing issues such as language policy and the educational needs of highland children with most of the NGO program directors and capacitadores. I participated in similar ways with other NGOs and their personnel, although not to the extent that I gradually became involved with YACHANA's people and programs.

Despite our rapport, however, I noticed after a few trips that both teachers and parents of Quechua children did not always receive YACHANA's personnel with open arms. Though in the past I had traveled to highland communities only with personnel from various NGO projects, once I discovered that teachers and community members did not necessarily think positively of the NGO, its representatives, or the projects they proposed, I changed tactics. First, I attempted to arrive in communities unannounced and walk straight to the school, where I would introduce myself to the teachers, tell them about the research I was conducting, and ask if I could stay in one of the classrooms. I hoped that if I traveled alone, something uncommon in the highlands (particularly for a woman), teachers might not associate me so closely with the NGO assigned to their particular region. Although this tactic seemed to work, better in some schools than in others, it soon became apparent that I would also need to disassociate myself from teachers if I wanted to learn more about the people primarily affected by intercultural education: Quechua children and their parents. After a few months of working mainly with teachers, I refocused once again, and attempted what proved most difficult for me: living with a Quechua family where, except for two family members, all were monolingual Quechua speakers.

The greater part of my time in Cuzco was spent conducting participant-observation research in teacher-training workshops, in interaprendizaje workshops, in *escuelas de padres* (workshops for parents of Quechua children affected by education policy changes), in schools with children, among highlanders in daily life (weaving, cooking, farming), in community assemblies, at ritual events such as weddings, hair-cutting ceremonies, religious fiestas and pilgrimages, and in regional conferences and intellectual gatherings. In the city I conducted extensive bibliographic research at the CBC's library. Also, as part of my work with NGOs I accompanied teachers and capacitadores to communities near the city. As described above, these were usually trips lasting anywhere from one to three days during which NGO personnel participated in community assemblies to discuss community grievances or questions regarding bilingual education policies, the behavior of teachers, and other such issues, or in which they monitored and supervised teachers to ensure that they were teaching with the "appropriate" methodology. Sometimes NGO personnel would hold workshops for parents, in which they tried to convince them of their children's need for education in Quechua and Spanish, and of the difficulties and "cultural aggression" to which highland children were often subjected under traditional education in Spanish.

Between 1996 and 1999 I attended regional, national, and international conferences in Cuzco, Puno, Lima, and Cochabamba. Among these gatherings were meetings about the significance of the Quechua language, about teaching in Quechua, about gender and indigenous education, and about the "cultural recovery of Quechua vis-à-vis the dominant Hispanic society."[15] In addition to participant observation, my field research involved several other methods. Tape recordings of workshops, conferences, teacher-training sessions, community assemblies, school classes, and debates or discussions among intercultural activists and personnel from different NGOs, always with the permission of those being taped, have proved to be crucial supplements to field notes. Both formal and informal interviews were a useful way of noting the kinds of things individuals involved in the implementation of education reform wanted me to know. I conducted thirty-five formal (taped) interviews. These included conversations with directors of NGOs in Cuzco, with the chief of the then UNEBI (National Unit for Bilingual Intercultural Education) in the Ministry of Education in Lima, with leading intellectuals involved in bilingual intercultural education throughout Latin America, with intercultural activists from Peru, with teacher trainers (from both NGOs and the state), and with highland teachers, regional education authorities, and parents. Additionally, I conducted fifty informal interviews, mainly with teachers, capacitadores, and parents who wanted me to record their concerns but felt uncomfortable about tape recorders. Further, surveys conducted in schools (among students, teachers, and parents) and within NGOs (among directors, capacitadores, and some teachers involved with particular NGOs) gave me a sense of the variety of ways in which concepts were understood and interpreted at different levels. Most valuable, however, was simply the experience of living with Quechua children and their parents, sharing experiences with highland teachers, and discussing problems of identity, language, and democracy with activists in Cuzco on a daily basis.

It is important to note that the value of multisited research is not purely methodological. Gaining access to multiple perspectives does of course enable more engaged ethnographic encounters. However, moving among different communities of Quechua highlanders, development practitioners, and state officials involved engaging the political and moral challenges of ethnographic research, that is, justifying one's intervention in and disruption of people's lives. If anthropology is ever to escape its colonialist legacy, it is crucial for ethnographers to recognize, as many have done, the power dynamics involved in this kind of research.

With small gestures of solidarity and support, such as providing basic first aid materials and training to teachers and honest reactions to the work of NGO professionals, I tried to infuse my work with an ethic of ethnographic responsibility. The people who made this book possible were not simply informants but often colleagues, comadres, friends, and individuals who challenged and inspired me. Despite my best efforts, however, I am certain that I gained more from them than they did from me. This book hopefully contributes something to the remaining debt.

A Word on Names and Terminology

In addition to following the standard ethnographic practice of using pseudonyms for specific communities (but not large cities) and "informants" (but not for public officials or leaders), I should make a few additional notes about the names and terms that I use in this book. Throughout this project I have used such terms as *indigenous, Indian, Andean, indígena,* and *mestizo.* Though several scholars have already addressed the ambiguous and problematic nature of these categories, both with respect to Peru (Matos Mar, ed., 1970; van den Berghe 1974a, 1974b; Bourricaud 1975; de la Cadena 2000; Weismantel 2001) and Latin America more generally (Field 1994b, 1996b), these terms continue to be used as ethnic, racial, cultural, and linguistic labels simultaneously. The social, dialogical construction of identities and identity categories means that these words are not stable containers but rather dynamic elements of struggle (Bahktin 1981). In an attempt to avoid some confusion, however, I will briefly discuss these terms and how I use them.

In Peru, the state has often distinguished between highland populations as peasants (campesinos) or Indian peasants, and lowland (rain forest) populations as natives *(nativos),* who are presumed to be more authentically Indian. This distinction was especially marked during the government of Juan Velasco Alvarado (1968–75), particularly in light of his prohibition of the use of the term *indio* for highland peoples. Before the 1960s however, and especially throughout the 1920s and 1930s, at the height of indigenista currents, highland populations were either romanticized (albeit in a paternalistic and condescending manner) as the oppressed descendants of glorified Incas or demonized as enraged Indians intent on "erasing the whites from the nation."[16] While Peruvians today refer to highland peoples mainly as campesinos, the terms *indígenas* and *nativos* are often used in reference to lowland groups. With the ongoing multicultural changes in the country, and particularly with growing national attention to indigenous rights, the term *indígena* is beginning to encompass highland populations as well. The expanding geographic scope of the term *indígena* reflects in part the growing set of international norms that recognize the rights of indigenous peoples throughout the world. "Indigenous education, therefore, is a right of indigenous peoples or first nations [*pueblos indígenas o pueblos originarios*]. This is the meaning that the term *indigenous* has in ILO Convention 169 regarding indigenous and tribal peoples" (Zúñiga et al. 2003: 16). Indigenous people are not only the passive "target populations" of new policies and rights, they are also increasingly recognized for their active participation in the elaboration of new models of development.

The term *indigenous intellectual* is becoming increasingly prominent in the political lexicon of Peruvian indigenous-rights activists. As one consequence of activist efforts to position self-identified Quechua youths as indigenous leaders, this label has evolved into an essential marker for these future leaders. Moreover, the presentation of self of those considered (by themselves and by others) indigenous intellectuals increasingly hinges on individual and group ideas about what being an indigenous intellectual means in practice, as we shall see in Chapter 5.

Though most highland peoples are thought of as belonging to Quechua or Aymara ethnic groups, these classifications were elaborated through colonial processes that attempted to manage the immense cultural and linguistic variation that existed in the Andes. Bruce Mannheim (1984, 1991) eloquently discusses the processes that led to the diffusion of Quechua, as language and ethnic group, throughout what came to be the Peruvian Andes. For the purposes of this study, I use the term *Quechua* to refer to both the language and the indigenous highland population targeted by intercultural activists in Cuzco.

The term *Indian* has two translations in Spanish: *indio* and *indígena*. At present *indio* is most often considered and used as a racial slur. While in some cases this term is appropriated by groups advocating Indian empowerment, it remains mainly a derogatory label. Similarly, terms such as *serrano* (literally "from the sierra" or "from the mountains") and *cholo* (usually referring to a dark-skinned individual with Andean origins — no matter how nebulous those origins may be — in transition to an urban/mestizo lifestyle) are still used as insults by most Peruvians.[17]

Finally, terms such as *Andean* and *mestizo* are broad identity categories that encompass large groups of the Peruvian population. A point crucial to understanding the representation of Andeans was emphasized in 1991, when the anthropologist Orin Starn launched a severe critique against North American anthropologists working in the Andes, accusing many well-known researchers of Andeanism. In his words, Andeanism is "representation that portrays contemporary highland peasants as outside the flow of modern history" (Starn 1991: 64). According to Starn, this view prevented Andeanists from understanding modern questions of identity, ethnicity, and politics in the region. More important, he argues that this viewpoint led them to over-look — particularly during the late 1960s and 1970s — the existing climate of social and political unrest and upheaval throughout the Peruvian Andes, thereby "missing the revolution" that began in 1980. While critiques have also been levied on Starn's representations and misrepresentations of research by North American anthropologists (Mayer 1992: 194–196), his contribution led to much needed debate about previously de-emphasized hetero-geneity and conflict in the Andean region.

The term *mestizo* commonly refers to an individual of mixed ancestry (usually indigenous and European), though it is also used to designate indi-viduals who, regardless of ancestry, speak Spanish and claim Hispanic cul-tural traits, but who are not considered *blancos* (whites). In her book on the politics of race and culture in Cuzco, Marisol de la Cadena (2000) teases out a more complex interpretation of mestizo identity. Drawing on extensive his-torical documentation and on her ethnographic research in contemporary cuzqueño society, de la Cadena explores the evolution of this term and argues that "subaltern cuzqueños have lived, practiced, and created alternative meanings of mestizaje . . . crucially [redefining] the term 'mestizo'" (33). This redefinition of mestizo identity involves the expansion of the term by view-ing it as a "social condition with room *both* for literacy and urban educa-tion *and* for the continuation of regional *costumbres,* the customs that they call authentic" (30). This definition is significant primarily because, unlike most other interpretations of mestizaje, it emphasizes the fact that while becoming a mestizo does change one's social conditions, it does not neces-sarily mean shedding or discarding indigenous customs. I agree with de la Cadena's more complicated view of mestizaje, but I should emphasize that among many people in the region, *mestizo* implies a distance from indige-nous spaces. This distance is seen as positive by those who see Indianness as a sign of backwardness and as negative by those who seek to revalorize indigenous identities and cultures.

As a final note, the terms *blanco* and *criollo* literally designate "white" Peruvians as well as those of European origin, and are usually associated with individuals from the coast. While these labels are often used interchangeably, and those labeled as such are frequently considered members of the upper classes, the term *criollo* has evolved among the popular classes into mean-ing something quite different. In colloquial usage *criollo* designates an indi-vidual from the coast, usually from the lower or working classes, who in a sly, quick-witted, and deceitful manner survives by outsmarting those around him. Notorious for their use of slang and popular jokes, criollos are also described as vulgar and crass. Unless I note otherwise, I use *criollo* to designate the Hispanic elite of Lima, against whom intercultural activists position themselves.

When I use the term *Andean,* I do so as a way to refer to the entire region, or because I am describing someone who identifies as Andean. For example, many of the intercultural activists I worked with identified themselves as Andean (*andinos*), and took pride in claiming an Andean identity. Moreover, most of them were adamantly opposed to being called mestizos. As was made clear to me at both social and professional gatherings, the term was meant to be derogatory. In this way, they linked themselves to traditional indigenista positions about mestizaje. As Mary Weismantel (2001: 260) notes, for José Carlos Mariátegui, one of the most consequential Peruvian indigenista intellectuals, mestizaje produced (in Mariátegui's words) "a sordid and unhealthy stagnation." Most activists identified themselves as *andinos* to signal the importance of their connection to the Andes, rather than accept the assimilationist implication of *mestizo,* as they understood the term.

Of course, as is often the case, it is important to note that there was also tremendous ambiguity and contradiction in both the representation and creation of identities among activists, teachers, intellectuals, parents, and the various other actors involved in the processes I describe. Accordingly, I want to emphasize that the linking of labels to specific groups of people is a political process that involves many actors, including social analysts. Thus my decision to refer, for example, to parents in rural communities as Quechua, Andean, or simply indigenous is not without reservation. My hesitation stems in part from the fact that much of what these parents are fighting against is the imposition of labels from outside their communities. However, these same parents also understand that shifts in labels can have profound consequences. Moreover, during conversations with many of them, the same persons would tell me that they were not indios, that they were campesinos, but that they were also Quechuas (or *runas,* the Quechua term for "people") or indígenas. Close ethnographic study will not reveal that one label is more accurate than any other; my own use of labels recognizes that they are provisional and situational, ready to be rejected and accepted depending on a variety of factors that will be explored in the pages that follow.

Organization of the Book

This book is divided into three parts. Part I, "Politics and Histories," provides a broad historical frame for understanding the contemporary dynamics of Peruvian indigenous cultural politics. For readers already well versed in Peruvian history and politics, this discussion will cover familiar ground. Beginning with the internal war between the Shining Path and the Peruvian government (1980–95), Chapter 1 examines the shifting contexts of state–indigenous relations. I trace changes over time in intercultural activist strategies from relative trepidation in the countryside to a cautious advocacy of language and education rights, and finally to bolder attempts to redefine indigenous identity. Chapter 2 explores the trajectory of Peruvian thought with regard to the place of Indians in the nation. Starting with the indigenista intellectual movement of the early twentieth century, the discussion traces the role of the state, intellectuals, and nongovernmental actors in designing policies aimed at Peru's indigenous population. In a sense, contemporary intercultural activists — while members of a modern NGO development community — are products of this older tradition.

Part II, "Ethnographies," presents three interconnected stories about the construction of indigenous citizenship in Peru. Chapter 3 details the effects of intercultural activism in the highlands by focusing on community politics. Since a crucial aspect of intercultural activism is the promotion of bilingual education — the teaching of Quechua alongside Spanish in rural schools — Quechua parents believe that those most directly affected by these policies are their children. By contrasting the actions and voices of indigenous highlanders with those of intercultural activists, this chapter describes Quechua communities as sites of political struggle in which indigenous people assert their rights in ways unanticipated by their advocates.

Chapter 4 provides an ethnographic exploration of the local effects of international development. Here I examine the gaps and gulfs between the ideals of NGO discourses of interculturality and the everyday inequalities that pervade the work of development workers and education polices. I interrogate the messy boundaries between governmental and nongovernmental actors and spaces that complicate the meaning of both democracy and civil society.

In an effort to examine further the local-global dimensions of ethnicity and development, Chapter 5 explores two important academic centers, spaces that have become critical sites for transnational discussion and contestation over notions of indigenous identity. First, I look at the Centro Bartolomé de Las Casas in Cuzco as a center for intellectual debate and production. As an institution where activists, foreign academics, and local intellectuals can come together to teach and debate matters of "Andean reality," it is a crucial site for examining the dynamics of interculturality. Second, I explore the cultural politics that are simultaneously produced and challenged at the PROEIB Andes in Cochabamba, Bolivia. I discuss the training of students at this institute and examine the complex discourse on indigenous and political identity at this center. I also describe how these transnational networks link professional indígenas to global resources and make them important intermediaries between their communities, the state, and international funders.

Part III presents some conclusions of this book in a final chapter. This

chapter explores the broader implications and contradictions of crafting policies and discourses of cultural inclusion during periods of profound economic
and political dislocation. First, it looks to the surprises and risks of a new
official multiculturalism, which can be considered in some ways an expansion of the aims, means, and contradictions of the intercultural education
policies reviewed in this book. Second, it explores the challenges of forging
indigenous citizenship under the constraints of a new political context but
also through the possibilities offered by transnational memberships that have
reconfigured the foundations of the ideas of political and cultural belonging.
Third, the book concludes by revisiting the all too recurrent specter of terror that has long haunted discussions of social change in Peru. It examines
the implication of both the recent Truth and Reconciliation report of 2003,
which sought to reckon with past horrors, and a reconsitituted Sendero
Luminoso that undermines the notion that violence is a thing of the past. The
question of terror gains yet another dimension of complexity in a post-9/11
world in which the labels *terrorist/terrorism* and *activist/activism* often get
confused. Finally, the chapter examines the lessons that Peru holds for
rethinking the models and metaphors of politics that shape scholarly agendas, development frameworks, and the horizons of political possibilities.

Part 1

POLITICS AND HISTORIES

1 *In the Shadow of Terror*

INDIGENOUS PEOPLES AND THE STATE,
1980–2002

During my seventeen months in Cuzco, I spent many weeks in Intipacha, a monolingual Quechua community at the foot of the snow-capped Ausangate mountains. At the end of one stay in the community, while I packed my few belongings in preparation for my return to the city, Carmen, my *comadre*, called me into her family's eating area.[1] They had prepared *pachamanca*, a special meal (in this case, potatoes, lamb, and alpaca meat) cooked in a makeshift oven underground. There was a large pail of *chicha* (fermented corn beer) on the ground, and I suspected that several bottles of beer, though hidden from me then, would appear later.

Huddling close to each other against the cold night air, we began eating and drinking, and gradually many in the community joined us. One man brought his guitar, another his *charango*,[2] and before I knew it I was asked to change into the traditional polleras (skirts) *allinta tusunaypaq* (for a prettier dance). The dancing began and the drinking continued until Raúl, an unusually tall and serious man whom I had seen little during my time in Intipacha, walked in. I noticed glances toward my compadres Carmen and Ignacio from most people, and an uncomfortable pause in the music confirmed the uneasiness that had suddenly enveloped the room. But, charming and proper as ever, Ignacio recovered the one glass passing around the room, rinsed it out with water, filled it to the brim with chicha, and handed it to Raúl in a welcoming gesture.

Visibly pleased, Raúl took the glass. After slowly and carefully scrutinizing everyone in the room, he offered some drops to the Pachamama (Earth Mother) and gulped down the cold drink. With that the music began again and we continued to dance, though I was now nervous about this man's presence. Everyone in the room seemed to understand something that had escaped me, and although I tried to ignore my nervousness, I was still uncomfortable and my gaze constantly shifted toward Raúl. At the end of a song, as I took the opportunity to rest and have a beer, Raúl approached me. Again there were glances, though this time first toward me and then quickly toward Ignacio. But with a sign from Ignacio, the music continued and people attempted to converse naturally. As Raúl began to speak with me, however, those closest to us stopped talking and listened.

We did not exchange many words, and his comments were short and direct. He said he had come to say goodbye, although he had never said hello. And he said he had come to apologize. I was confused, and when I asked him why, it was he who became confused. He had obviously been certain I would understand. He looked to Ignacio for the answer, and I looked to Carmen. Suddenly Ignacio's cousin Mario, a short, thin, very funny (and by this time very drunk) man, blurted out: "He thought you were a terrorist and that we were all going to be blown up!"

I was in shock. All around me, though, people were laughing. The entire room found this hilarious, but even funnier was the fact that I was entirely unaware that heated debates had gone on during my first week in Intipacha (in June 1998) between Raúl and Ignacio. Some members of the community had been unsure whether I was a threat to the community or simply a well-intentioned anthropologist trying to learn Quechua. While at that time the Peruvian government maintained that the years of political violence were over, for many highland and lowland communities the threat of violence was still real. Raúl and several others in the community were certain that Sendero Luminoso, a Maoist guerrilla movement, had sent me to determine whether any children in the community were strong enough and smart enough to recruit into the organization. As an anthropologist, I was immediately associated with the political left, and because I spent much of my time in the school observing and working with children, my intentions became suspect.[3]

In contemporary Peru, the official years of terror (1980–95) continue to cast a shadow over the country (Basombrío Iglesias 1998). These shadows have come to seem even more menacing as reports appear in the media about the resurgence of Sendero Luminoso. Moreover, the release of the national Truth and Reconciliation Commission's report in August 2003 sparked new debates over indigenous rights, reparations, state accountability, and impunity. Clearly the politics of culture and development in the Peruvian Andes cannot be separated from the lingering effects of more than a decade of violence — much of it aimed at indigenous peoples.

While the present moment is full of uncertainties, I would like to note that the period during which I conducted most of my fieldwork (1996–99) was also characterized by a particular set of ambiguities, hopes, and fears. Intercultural education was being debated and implemented in the context of a tenuous transition away from authoritarianism. Though in a sense activists were continuing work that had been ongoing since the 1960s and

1970s (Burns 1968, 1971), they were also breaking new ground as they sought to broaden their linguistic and cultural work toward more explicitly political activism. Indigenous and peasant political mobilization in Cuzco, in their view, had last erupted over questions of land tenure and agrarian reform (Blanco 1972). While the 1990s bore the marks of these earlier mobilizations, for activists this decade was about a new set of concerns about culture, language, and education (Andrés Chirinos, personal communication).

When I first arrived in Cuzco in 1996, Peruvian indigenous rights activists were hesitant to discuss indigenous rights overtly. Although the war had officially ended in 1995, the political climate was still such that simply discussing politics or raising questions about human rights abuses could be (and had been) labeled subversive by Alberto Fujimori's government forces. In the place of more overtly political work, activists stressed the seemingly less controversial right of indigenous communities to multicultural education and contributed to the promotion of indigenous languages. By the end of my fieldwork in 1999, mounting international pressure for multicultural development and indigenous rights and increasing government acceptance (publicly) for multicultural policies led to more explicit discussions among intercultural activists in Cuzco about indigenous cultural and political autonomy. After the fall of Fujimori in 2000, with the transition government of Valentín Paniagua (2001) and the elected government of Alejandro Toledo, new opportunities for the advancement of the rights of indigenous communities throughout Peru and Latin America drastically reframed state–indigenous interactions. Peru began the twenty-first century with a dramatic explosion of activity in civil society. A striking increase in NGO projects and new social movements, widespread anti-privatization protests, and a proliferation of indigenous organizations characterized what some hopefully considered the post-Sendero, post-Fujimori Peru. It is difficult to write during a time of such rapid change, when news of new organizations and changes in indigenous leadership comes almost daily. Yet it is helpful to think about the cultural politics of the late 1990s in this light, since it seemed to set in motion much of the broader political activity that is evolving today. Consequently, this book focuses on the pivotal years of the late 1990s, during which Peru sought to move from times of terror and war toward reconciliation, peace, and multiculturalism.

Beginning with the internal war between the Shining Path and the Peruvian government, this chapter traces recent political history in the country. It looks closely at the shifting contexts (and their impact) for debates over indigenous rights and state policies, from relative trepidation in the countryside to cautious nongovernmental advocacy of language and education rights, and finally to bolder attempts by NGOs, the state, and indigenous communities to negotiate the terms of indigenous citizenship.

A History of Violence: Terrorism, the State, and Indigenous Resistance

SENDERO LUMINOSO AND "THE INDIAN PROBLEM"

Sendero Luminoso burst onto the scene of Peruvian politics in May 1980 when the group launched its first armed offensive in the department of Ayacucho. Sendero's first attack, burning ballot boxes and voting lists in Chuschi, a small town in Ayacucho, went almost completely unnoticed by government forces. When isolated bombs began to go off in scattered parts of the highlands later that year, no one paid attention. By the end of 1980, however, Sendero Luminoso caught the nation's attention when residents of downtown Lima awoke to the sight of dead dogs hanging from lampposts. Wrapped around the animals' bodies were signs reading "Deng Xiaoping, Son of a Bitch!" According to Abimael Guzmán, leader of the group, the flaws of the post-Mao leadership in China had left Sendero as the new and only leader of world revolution. In Guzmán's words, Sendero was a force that, by encircling Peru's cities from the countryside, would "put the noose around the neck of imperialism and the reactionaries . . . and strangle them" (Guzmán 1988).

Guzmán and his group, likened to Pol Pot's Khmer Rouge in Cambodia because of their ruthlessness, were initially seen as a revolutionary movement that fought in the name of Peru's poor.[4] The movement invoked the ideology of Marx, Lenin, and especially Mao Tse-tung, as the following excerpt from the last public document the group released before the insurrection shows:

> Marxist–Leninist–Mao Tse-tung thought is the ideology of the international proletariat and the general political line of the revolution is its application to our concrete reality, . . . in all its glory the task of the coming revolution is . . . TO BEGIN ARMED STRUGGLE. To begin the hard and prolonged Agrarian War that follows the path of surrounding the cities from the countryside, creating revolutionary bases of support. (Cited in Gorriti Ellenbogen 1999: 56)[5]

What gave this internationalist ideology a more concrete Peruvian connection was the use of the legacy of the Peruvian philosopher José Carlos Mariátegui.

The movement's full name — In The Shining Path of José Carlos Mariátegui — and its highland origins led many to assume, wrongly, that this new organization was a uniquely Peruvian indigenous revolutionary movement. Mariátegui, one of the most respected social theorists of the 1920s, glorified the socialist Inca state, forged important links with indigenista intellectuals, and founded the Peruvian Socialist Party. His ideas about socialism were informed by what he saw as the persistence of "communist" Andean traditions. I will discuss Mariátegui and indigenismo at length in Chapter 2, but what is relevant here is the ideological connection between Mariátegui and Guzmán. For Mariátegui the so-called Indian problem in Peru (how to integrate indigenous populations into the nation) was an economic problem, not a cultural one. It was a problem of land (ownership), labor, and exploitation (Mariátegui 1994 [1928]). Although Mariátegui wrote about "indigenous claims" (*reivindicación indígena*) and "indigenous resurgence" (*resurgimiento indígena*), he was also passionate in his insistence that "indigenous claims lack historical concreteness as long as they remain on a philosophical or cultural level. To acquire [concreteness] . . . they have to be transformed into economic and political demands" (Mariátegui 1972 [1928]: 12). Although Mariátegui became "an ever more silent icon" in Sendero's proclamations (Gorriti Ellenbogen 1999: 56), Guzmán was clearly influenced by his writings about the revolutionary spirit of indigenous populations, and he may have heeded the claim made by Luis Valcárcel (another important indigenista intellectual) that "this indigenous proletariat awaits its Lenin" (Valcárcel 1972 [1927]). It is more likely, however, that Guzmán saw himself as a Peruvian Mao.

Following Maoist revolutionary logic, Sendero originated and developed in the rural countryside. Its birthplace was Ayacucho.[6] In Quechua, Ayacucho means "corner of the dead." It has historically been one of the most neglected regions in the country. Even during the years of agrarian reform in the late 1960s and throughout the 1970s, land redistribution was not successful, and some large landowners and haciendas remained in place. For Guzmán and his followers, Ayacucho was the place from which revolutionary peasants would emerge. Moreover, part of their strategy was to establish themselves in the countryside, consolidate their stronghold by gathering peasant support, and "strangle" the cities that constituted the center of political power.

However, the assumption that Sendero was an ethnic movement, or a movement advocating indigenous rights, was clearly wrong and later dismissed by most observers. Actually, Sendero demonstrated tremendous hostility toward indigenous practices and traditions. Echoing the chilling metaphors of Senderistas, the historian Florencia Mallon states:

The failure politically to engage indigenous traditions and practices, which emerged in the twentieth century among a variety of oppositional political groups in Peru, was reconstructed with the class-based leftist discourses and practices of the 1960s and 1970s, intensified in the Shining Path vision of the 1980s popular war. Indeed, within Senderista strategy, a historically created blindness to Indian-ness, linked to the imperative of total war, transformed communal culture and politics into one more insect to be squashed. (Mallon 1998: 115–116)

During the first few years of organization and struggle, much support for Sendero came from teachers, university professors, and young university students in Huamanga, the departmental capital.[7] Recognizing the significance of the education system for the propagation of their ideology and as an important source of cadres for their movement, leaders of this new organization infiltrated the national teacher's union (SUTEP) as well as various universities throughout the highlands (Hinojosa 1998) and maintained close relationships with highland teachers (Degregori 1998a). Many students at the University of Huamanga came from rural communities in the area, and as the educated children of peasants, they were more easily able to garner support from indigenous peasant communities. Many returned to their homes to promote the Senderista cause. Another important support group were rural youth without a university education, for whom Sendero Luminoso could be a path toward social mobility and away from the "traditional and backward" ways of their parents (Degregori 1998a: 128–131). In a discriminatory system that left many of them with little or no hope for social or economic advancement, Sendero presented concrete steps toward social ascent. Testimony collected by the anthropologist Carlos Iván Degregori (1998a: 130) from a young man in a community in Ayacucho highlights this idea: "[Senderistas] said that Ayacucho was going to be a liberated zone by 1985. A famous illusion that they created among the muchachos was, way back in 1981, that by 1985 there would be an independent republic. Wouldn't you like to be minister? Wouldn't you like to be a military chief? Be something, no?"

During the early years of the "popular war," Sendero accumulated significant support from indigenous peasant communities in Ayacucho. Senderistas reminded community members of the state's neglect, their lack of medical facilities, and the need for better schools for their children. Initially, Senderistas were viewed positively by some as promoters of new forms of community justice and authority. During public trials, for example, they punished cattle rustlers, violent husbands, thieves, and others who were perceived as harming the community. However, by establishing local "people's committees" as replacements of local authority, Sendero also began to alienate elders and others in the community who recognized this as a challenge not only to the authority of the state and individual landowners but also to traditional community customs. Gradually, in an effort to restrict food supplies to the cities, Sendero tried to close weekly markets and control what the community could and could not sell. Eventually militants insisted that farmers produce only enough sustenance for the community and the Party, and forbade them to produce for the market. They banned religious ceremonies, which they considered manifestations of "archaic superstitions," and began to forcibly recruit increasing numbers of children, some as young as seven or eight years old, into their movement.

Sendero quickly became known in highland communities for its ruthlessness toward dissenters. Militants delegated specific responsibilities to individual community members. Those unwilling to perform their duties, communities were told, would die. Moreover, if Senderistas suspected peasants of collaboration with local authorities, the entire village was punished. Lashing and mutilation of suspects was a common strategy, although by 1982 public trials were more often than not becoming public executions. For Sendero, violence and the spilling of blood were necessary parts of their revolution. Guzmán himself referred to the armed struggle as a "bloodbath" (Gorriti Ellenbogen 1999: 98). Every Senderista was expected to die and kill for the Party. Self-sacrifice and self-criticism were critical components of Senderista ideology. As the Peruvian journalist Gustavo Gorriti writes, "Shining Path militants had to be convinced of two things: the need to kill in a systematic and depersonalized way as part of an agreed-upon strategy; and, as a necessary premise, not just the willingness but the expectation of giving up their own lives" (1999: 99).[8] The idea of sacrificing one's life, known as "the quota," and the fanaticism with which militants carried out this sacrifice earned Sendero the reputation of a zealous cult following a fanatical leader. Senderista cruelty quickly became a part of everyday life for indigenous peasants, who began to identify the guerrillas as *ñaqas*, supernatural beings who, in Andean mythology, take human fat and eat flesh. They became "figures of power out of place — not from one's own space and time" (Isbell 1992: 75–76). Increasing resentment from communities, and Sendero's hostile response, generated a rift between the two that would eventually be manifested as overt community resistance against Sendero Luminoso. However, community politics of resistance were complicated by the sudden deployment of military counterinsurgency forces into the area.

THE STATE RESPONDS

The Peruvian government virtually ignored the first two years of Sendero activity. President Fernando Belaúnde was elected in 1980, the year Sendero began its armed struggle. He had been ousted by the military in 1968 because of his failure to deal effectively with guerrilla activity and peasant mobilization in the highlands. For political reasons, upon hearing about Senderista activity in Ayacucho, Belaúnde was hesitant to give too much power to the military, lest he be removed from office once again, and relied instead on local and regional police to maintain social order.[9] However, while politics did play a significant role in his decision, part of the reason for his government's inactivity was also linked to the perceived cultural and racial divide between the Andean highlands and the coast. Most politicians (and many others) in Lima consider the inhabitants of the Andean highlands to be racially and culturally inferior. Despite the fact that peasant mobilizations had rocked the highlands during the 1960s and 1970s, it was deemed unlikely that a movement originating in the highlands could have national repercussions. However, by the end of 1982, Sendero's attacks had become increasingly violent. They had managed to displace police forces from several provinces in the department of Ayacucho, and were preparing to lay siege to Huamanga, the departmental capital. Although several special counterinsurgency units had already been deployed into Ayacucho, it was only after 1982 that the military responded in full force, and they did so with fateful brutality.[10]

The struggle between insurgents and government forces quickly submerged Peru in bloody violence.[11] By 1983, Peru's so-called dirty war had begun (Stern, ed., 1998). While military abuses had already become a part of life in Ayacucho and neighboring departments, political violence and terror intensified between 1983 and 1984. Many of the central and southern highland departments were designated "emergency zones," meaning that the military had complete control over the areas. Antiterrorism laws were passed, constitutional rights were suspended, and movement was restricted. Civilian populations, popular organizations, and university communities were targeted by the military.

The deployment of a specially trained counterinsurgency police, the *sinchis,* escalated violent conflict in the highlands, usually leading to the indiscriminate torture and execution of suspected rebels. With funds and advisers from the U.S. military and CIA, the sinchis were created in response to guerrilla activity in the 1960s as a special antiterrorist unit of the Peruvian Civil Guard. They were already well known for the cruelty they displayed in their repression of demonstrations throughout the 1970s. In Quechua, *sinchi* means "warrior" and "he who can do anything." As an adjective, it means "excessive." Unable to identify militants, the sinchis (and other security forces) equated teachers, community leaders, and all Quechua-speaking peasants with terrorists, and thousands were killed or disappeared as part of government efforts to eliminate the opposition. The presence of a single suspected terrorist in a community sometimes led to the destruction of the entire village. Counterinsurgency forces routinely pulled peasants from their homes and beat, raped, and tortured men, women, and children. It was also common practice for government forces to kill all inhabitants before they left a community to avoid accusations of abuse (Poole and Rénique 1992).

The military's notion of indigenous peasants as terrorists was only a more extreme manifestation of the kind of discrimination that indigenous populations had always faced. The massacre in 1983 of eight journalists in the community of Uchuraccay in Ayacucho and the ensuing investigation by a government-appointed commission headed by the writer Mario Vargas Llosa exemplified traditional stereotypes of indigenous highlanders as violent, ignorant, and primitive.[12] The journalists had been traveling to the community of Huaychao in Ayacucho to verify reports that several Senderistas had been murdered by community members. However, before reaching the community, they were stopped by peasants in Uchuraccay and massacred with stones and axes. The journalists' bodies were mutilated and buried upside down. According to the Vargas Llosa report, the massacre was the result of a cultural misunderstanding. Community members had mistaken the journalists for Senderistas, and had killed them to defend themselves against possible attack, without any participation of police or military forces. For Vargas Llosa and other members of the commission, the massacre was a symptom of "the Peruvian problem":

That there is a real nation completely separate from the official nation is, of course, the great Peruvian problem. That people who participate in the 20th century can simultaneously live in a country with people like the [peasants] of Uchuraccay and [other] communities who live in the 19th — if not to say the 18th — century; this enormous distance which exists between the two Perus is behind [this] tragedy. (Vargas Llosa 1990: 46)[13]

The divide between "deep Peru" (*Perú profundo*) and "official" Peru, often referred to as "the two Perus" (Mayer 1992: 191–194), has permeated debates about nation-building throughout the country's history. The term *Perú profundo* is attributed to the Peruvian historian Jorge Basadre, who first used it in 1943. Basadre distinguished between the juridical invention of the state (*país legal*) and the "deep" nation (*país profundo*) composed of its people. Over time, *Perú profundo* came to mean the "historical roots of Indianness as a component of Peru's sense of nationhood" (Mayer 1992: 192).[14] As part of the background to the official description of events in Uchuraccay, Vargas Llosa questioned whether community members were able to make "moral, constitutional, and juridical distinctions between . . . right and wrong" and described the peasants involved in the massacre as "part of a 'besieged nation' . . . with thousands — perhaps millions — of compatriots who speak another language, have different customs, and who, under such hostile and isolated conditions, have managed to preserve a culture — perhaps archaic, but rich and deep — that links up with the whole of our prehispanic past, which 'official' Peru has disdained" (Vargas Llosa et al. 1983: 32, 36). Vargas Llosa has since expanded on his analysis of "archaic" Peru, and is a vocal proponent of the "sad but necessary" disappearance (via assimilation into the "progressive and modern" national society) of what he calls Peru's "antlike" indigenous populations, particularly if the country is to avoid the kind of "cultural misunderstandings" that occurred in Uchuraccay (Vargas Llosa 1990).

Needless to say, it was extremely dangerous to promote any kind of indigenous mobilization at this time. Indigenous rights advocacy took the form of human rights activism, focusing on denouncing the numerous atrocities committed by both the military and Sendero Luminoso. However, indigenous activism did emerge from within communities, and those communities were increasingly branded not as examples of the failures of nation building but as defenders of the country. Soon organized groups of peasant militias, or rondas campesinas, could count on the state's approval and often its military aid.

INDIGENOUS RESPONSES TO VIOLENCE: RONDAS CAMPESINAS AND INDIGENOUS RIGHTS

In January 1985, Amnesty International reported over a thousand disappearances, and a Peruvian senate commission on human rights found that 2,507 civilians and 4,428 "presumed subversives" had been killed in 1983 and 1984 (Poole and Rénique 1992: 7). Caught between Sendero Luminoso and the Peruvian military's counterinsurgency forces, peasants and indigenous peoples bore the brunt of the violence that enveloped the country. Initially, the brutality of government repression provoked sympathy and support for Sendero among indigenous peasants, even when that support had already begun to erode.[15] However, this quickly changed, and communities began to blame Sendero for the violence and terror that had enveloped their lives. When the army entered a community, Sendero retreated, leaving the men, women, and children whom they had promised to protect at the mercy of government forces.

As indigenous and peasant opposition to Sendero increased, peasants organized into peasant patrol units, modeled after the village patrols in the northern departments of Cajamarca and Piura that proliferated in the 1970s and 1980s in efforts to stop thievery and oversee small public works projects (Starn 1998, 1999). Amazonian indigenous populations in the Central Jungle also formed an organized resistance against insurgents. Specifically, the Asháninka army challenged incursions by both Sendero Luminoso and the Túpac Amaru Revolutionary Movement (MRTA) into their territory (Manrique 1998).

Armed with machetes, knives, and makeshift bombs or guns, peasant men and women organized collectively to safeguard communities against Senderista attacks. Though disenchantment with and fear of Sendero were probably the key reasons for the expansion of rondas throughout the highlands, some argue that another important factor was the improved relations between the military and the peasantry after 1984. After that year, civilian deaths at the hands of the military declined by more than two-thirds, and selective killing, not indiscriminate slaughter, became the norm (Poole and Rénique 1992; Starn 1998). Part of this shift in government policy, however, may have come as a result of peasant initiatives of organized defense. As the Uchuraccay case suggests, by 1983 peasants were already overtly resisting Sendero, and they were "encouraged" to do so by government and military forces.[16]

In 1985, under the new administration of Alan García, the state announced a change in tactics. García stressed the importance of human rights and promised to bring to justice those in the military who had committed atrocities against peasant communities. He also promised an increase in social development programs, which not only would benefit communities in the short run but would have the long-term effect of preventing further violence by making up for past government neglect. Unfortunately, García's promises were not kept. Repression and disappearances increased, and he was unable to implement any of the ambitious social programs he had envisioned. However, the government did shift its antisubversive strategy from indiscriminate targeting of civilians to more selective repression. Moreover, it began to see peasant communities as allies in the war against Sendero.

In national television news reports and pro-government newspapers throughout the late 1980s and early 1990s, cases of collaboration between rondas campesinas and antiterrorist government forces were often cited as evidence of the alliance between Quechua highland peoples and the Peruvian government. For example, the government-controlled media often glossed indigenous and peasant struggles against Sendero as the struggle of "our Peruvian brothers and sisters" against antinationals.[17] In similar fashion, Quechua-speaking officers at this time traveled to the highlands wearing ponchos and ch'ullus and urged their "peasant brothers" to join them in their fight against their common enemy, the enemy of the nation. By 1991, under Alberto Fujimori's regime, the Peruvian army made clear its shift in counterinsurgency techniques when it began a massive distribution of more than 10,000 shotguns to Andean peasants (Starn 1998: 232).

By the early 1990s, more than 3,500 villages in the highlands had organized into rondas to fight against Sendero (Starn 1998: 225). Torture, rape, and murder of suspected Senderistas and sympathizers remained the usual modus operandi of counterinsurgency forces (making Peru the country with the world's highest number of "disappeared" from 1988 to 1991), but communities with organized rondas were less likely to fall victim to such abuses. Although critics sometimes charged that the military coerced peasants into fighting as paramilitary groups that could potentially abuse their own communities, persuasive accounts of the political conflict in Peru suggest that despite these problems, the rondas campesinas played a crucial role in the defeat of Sendero Luminoso (Degregori 1998a; Degregori et al. 1996; Starn 1998, 1999). The rise of the rondas had a clear effect in relocating indigenous people within the national imaginary. No longer "subversive antinationals" or simply "ignorant peasants" belonging to an archaic Peru, indigenous citizens were increasingly represented as important forces on the front lines of defense.

Here it is important to note that there has been some controversy over the depiction of rondas campesinas as indigenous organizations, primarily because of their problematic alliance with the military. However, historically grounded analyses of the rondas in both the north and south (Starn 1999) and examinations of their place in discussions of customary law (Yrigoyen Fajardo 2002) have persuasively argued for a more nuanced understanding of the place of the rondas campesinas in discussions about indigenous rights and politics. Such a nuanced understanding was especially critical when the Truth and Reconciliation (TRC) commissioners debated whether *ronderos* should be considered victims or perpetrators of violence, and whether they and their families would be eligible for economic reparations. [18]

Merging Neoliberalism and Multicultural Policies

MOBILIZING THE POLITICAL OTHER

Belaúnde and García, representatives of the criollo political class, had not been able to stop the terror. Moreover, García's populist policies had immersed the country in economic chaos. In the midst of this political and economic instability, Alberto Fujimori, a virtual unknown, made his entrance onto the political scene. In 1990, in a surprise victory over Mario Vargas Llosa, the son of Japanese immigrants became the new president of Peru. Fujimori presented Peruvians with an alternative to traditional politics. His eclectic movement, Cambio 90 (Change 1990), was composed of a mix of micro-entrepeneurs, teachers, agronomists, engineers, and small-business people. Fujimori, who was himself an agronomist and former rector of the National Agrarian University in Lima, took advantage of the frustration with traditional party politics and presented himself as a political outsider. In addition to the political and professional background of Fujimori and his supporters, their ethnic and class origins played a role in Cambio 90's rising popularity. In stark contrast to the aristocratic and European background of Vargas Llosa and his supporters, most of Fujimori's backers were from provincial backgrounds. Some were from Peru's Japanese community, a group associated with small enterprise, hard work, and honesty. Campaigning primarily in marginalized sectors, such as shantytowns, highland communities, and jungle regions, Fujimori would arrive at pueblos and neighborhoods in his "Fujimobile," a cart pulled by a tractor. Dressed in regional clothes and dancing to local music, Fujimori symbolically closed the traditional distance between political candidates and their constituencies (Oliart 1998).

Organizing around his populist appeal and personality, Cambio 90 won close to 30 percent of the votes in the April 1990 presidential elections. Vargas Llosa, despite predictions of a landslide victory, obtained only 35.1

percent of the votes, not enough to take the presidency in the first round. After a few more weeks of campaigning, Fujimori won the runoff in June 1990. Pitting ethnic outsiders (*"cholitos"*) against the ruling *"blanquitos,"* as he liked to characterize the difference between his movement and Vargas Llosa's party, Fujimori took the presidency with 57 percent of the vote (de la Cadena 2001). After his defeat, Vargas Llosa said simply: "I feel sorry for Peru." He would later claim, after moving to Spain and taking Spanish citizenship, that Peruvians voted not for ideas but "out of some mysterious impulse." Fujimori, in presenting himself as a political "other" or outsider, gained the support of Peruvians who felt excluded by the traditional white ruling elite (Oliart 1998).

NEOLIBERAL POLITICS, AUTHORITARIANISM, AND THE "END" OF CIVIL WAR

Despite his populist promises, Fujimori's regime would combine strict neoliberal economic policies and increasingly authoritarian rule. He began his term by implementing the same economic measures he had denounced when Vargas Llosa proposed them. Known as the Fujishock, the macroeconomic stabilization program was necessary, argued Fujimori, for Peru's reinsertion into the international financial community. The next steps in the state's economic policy would include a structural adjustment through liberalization of the economy, privatization of state-held enterprises, and a reduction of tariff barriers (Poole and Rénique 1992).

The social impact of his economic program was devastating for Peru's poor, and it quickly eroded Fujimori's credibility. By early 1991, after only six months in office, Fujimori was already facing tremendous opposition. Organizing regional strikes and other demonstrations throughout the country, NGOs, teachers, peasant organizations, workers' organizations, and a spectrum of political parties (mostly on the left) led a movement challenging Fujimori's administration and demanding decentralization and autonomous regional development. The strikes were met by violence. Many demonstrators were killed, hundreds were imprisoned, and several opposition leaders were disappeared by the army (Poole and Rénique 1992).

Fujimori's actions in 1991 became increasingly authoritarian. The president had forged strong ties with the military immediately after taking office (Obando 1998). He criticized both the judiciary and the legislature as corrupt institutions standing in the way of what he called "direct democracy," which, he argued, should link the executive and the people. Fujimori also faced what seemed an insurmountable challenge: to stop Sendero Luminoso from destroying Peru. By 1991 more than half the country was declared an emergency zone. This designation meant the eradication of all civil liberties. As the war escalated in Lima, Fujimori announced another sudden change.

On April 5, 1992, the president established an "emergency government of national reconstruction."

In a so-called *autogolpe* (self-coup), Fujimori dissolved Congress and the Supreme Court, and declared that he would reorganize the judicial branch and the general accounting office. Moreover, in what he claimed were efforts to stop drug trafficking and terrorism, Fujimori also disbanded Peru's twelve regional governments and suspended all articles of the constitution that were "not compatible with the government's goals." The president ordered the armed forces and national police to enforce the measures. While Fujimori's actions were severely criticized by the international community and particularly by the U.S. government, most public opinion polls showed that many Peruvians supported Fujimori's extraordinary measures. Since he had taken office in 1990, the Peruvian media, increasingly controlled by the government, had shown a courageous and active head of state traveling throughout Peru and supervising social development projects. At a time when Sendero's message was one of annihilation, Fujimori spoke instead of reconstruction and of generating resources for the country (Oliart 1998: 421).

On September 12, 1992, only five months after declaring martial law, Fujimori and his (now infamous) national intelligence agency (SIN) captured Abimael Guzmán and declared that the war would soon be over. Most Peruvians considered the capture of Sendero's leader miraculous. Psychologically, it was a tremendous boost to the morale of the country. Guzmán had managed to develop a mysterious aura, evident in depictions of him as a mythical or cult leader (Gorriti Ellenbogen 1999). Even before his arrest, Fujimori had consistently tried to "puncture the Guzmán mystique" (Oliart 1998: 421). He was successful after Guzmán's capture. Guzmán was displayed in a cage outdoors, first without a shirt, later in a striped prison outfit. Peruvians saw a fat, defeated lunatic, not the elusive, godlike leader of a movement that had managed to bring civil war to the country. Despite Guzmán's capture, however, Peru was already close to being destroyed.[19] According to the TRC report released in August 2003, 69,280 Peruvians died as a result of this war. Moreover, the country suffered approximately $30 billion in reported damages, and at least 4,000 persons were reportedly disappeared (Youngers and Peacock 2002). Those most severely affected by the violence were indigenous people and their children.

As part of his efforts at state building in the wake of almost two decades of political and economic upheaval, Fujimori embarked on a campaign that proclaimed the prevention of political violence through attention to historically neglected highland and lowland regions and their inhabitants. In his well-publicized efforts at rebuilding the country, Fujimori provided indigenous and peasant populations with roads, schools, medical and agricultural facilities, electricity, and running water, and supported organizations emphasizing community development. Television and magazines constantly featured the president as he traveled around the country, dressing like a "serranito" and dancing *huaynos* in the mountains or floating on a raft down the Amazon in an Asháninka headdress. [20] Emphasizing the importance of a unified nation, particularly in the years immediately after Guzmán's capture, Fujimori continuously pointed to ethnic, cultural, and regional distinctions as parts of one Peru. It was in this context that indigenous rights activists began to advocate more explicitly (although still cautiously) for indigenous peoples through discussions of the preservation of indigenous languages and bilingual education. Although work toward indigenous linguistic and cultural preservation had been ongoing for decades (Pozzi-Escot 1992), since the early 1980s the explicit focus of such work had been on bilingual education methodology, theoretical and social linguistics, and to a lesser extent democratic pedagogies (Hornberger, ed., 1997; Godenzzi, ed., 1992). Throughout my time in Cuzco, particularly toward the beginning, public discussions of indigenous rights, self-determination, and cultural autonomy were minimized. When intercultural activists did speak of indigenous rights and intercultural education, discussions were couched in terms of the prevention of future political violence by addressing the particular neglect of indigenous communities and isolated rural areas.

Fujimori's attempt at unifying the nation was also evident in his public treatment of indigenous and peasant "soldiers" who had fought against insurgents in the highlands and lowlands. Between 1993 and 1999, Fujimori's army trucked thousands of peasant ronderos and representatives of Amazonian militias into Lima every year to participate in the Independence Day parade on July 28. Next to teachers, university students, engineers, nurses, doctors, and squadrons of meticulously dressed policemen, soldiers, and even sinchis, indigenous militiamen and peasant ronderos marched through the streets of Lima (and other provincial capitals) in columns, shotguns and spears over their shoulders, all of them dressed in traditional garb. As Orin Starn observed:

> The extremes of violence and reason, . . . "the Andean" and "the Western," "the primitive" and "the modern" converge in a public spectacle of national unity, staged by the government as part of the cultural politics of state-building in the wake of harsh years of political violence and economic crisis that have torn so deeply at the fiction of the imagined community of a united nation. (1998: 234)

As Starn also noted, however, the poor, dark, and rural combatants with spears and shotguns stand in stark contrast to soldiers with pressed uniforms and high-tech weaponry and government bureaucrats who watch the procession from elevated platforms. Despite the clear persistence of "the desperate inequalities of race and class" (Starn 1998: 235), including indigenous and peasant populations as Peruvians and disassociating them from terrorist groups has been a significant step toward the symbolic incorporation of these populations into the nation. Placing them in opposition to "subversives" has also been particularly important because, especially during the early years of the war, government antiterrorist forces had legitimized the random interrogation (torture) and execution of thousands of indigenous people by labeling them "antinational" simply because they did not speak Spanish (Poole and Rénique 1992: 6). At the same time that the political climate in Peru opened up to more explicit talk about indigenous rights (after 1995), indigenous activism in neighboring countries (especially Bolivia and Ecuador) and the increasing connections between indigenous rights activism and radical politics made indigenous rights activism in Peru a potentially destabilizing form of social protest. Despite the dangers, intercultural activists recognized the changing political climate as an opportunity for advocacy. As we shall see, the changing national political context, as well as the influence of international organizations, opened up new spaces for working toward intercultural programs. Yet these new spaces were also filled by the contradictions inherent in the Peruvian state's attempt to validate cultural difference while also seeking to control the social dangers associated with that difference.

MOVING TOWARD OFFICIAL MULTICULTURALISM

While there are always difficulties in periodizing social and political change, the capture of Sendero Luminoso's leader in 1992 was a clear landmark for war-weary Peruvians. After a bloodstained decade of insurgency and counterinsurgency, the capture and imprisonment of Guzmán heralded the end of terror and the zenith of Alberto Fujimori's heavy-handed presidency. Without its leader and under the pressure of Fujimori's aggressive military campaigns, Sendero's numbers dwindled and its remaining elements sought refuge in the jungles. Peace was seemingly at hand. Moreover, though indigenous people had not been passive in the face of terror, organizing self-defense units in both highlands (e.g., rondas campesinas) and lowlands (e.g., the Asháninka army), scholars often cite the devastation of war as a prime reason for the lack of national mobilizing structures for indigenous people.[21] Thus the end of the violence could represent an opening for more explicitly political organizing.

Organizational environments certainly do not change overnight, but as the nation began to speak of the times of terrorism in the past tense, the political climate was certainly changing in important ways. Notably, Peru enacted a new constitution that, among other things, "recognizes and protects the ethnic and cultural plurality of the nation" by guaranteeing the right of all people to use their own language before the state (Article 2). Additionally, it highlights "the state's obligation to promote intercultural and bilingual education, depending on the characteristics of each region" (Article 17). The constitution also recognizes and "respects the cultural identity of rural and native communities" (Article 89) and protects communal property, though it makes exceptions for land the state deems abandoned.

Characteristic of the contradictions of this period of Peruvian history, however, as Fujimori approved progressive changes to the constitution, he simultaneously dissolved the National Office for Bilingual Education. As the anthropologist Peter Wade has cautioned, "the adoption of official multi-culturality . . . may easily be a tactical manoeuvre for coping with protest" (1997: 107), something that was clearly the case in Peru under Fujimori.[22] While there was much skepticism about the government's commitment to these cultural policies, increasingly the presence and financial support of international actors, such as NGOs and the World Bank, did help institutionalize (albeit slowly) a multicultural development agenda. International (and local) pressure, for example, forced the Fujimori administration to reestablish what is now the Dirección Nacional de Educación Bilingüe Intercultural (DINEBI) within the Ministry of Education.

One crucial source of change at this time was the international environment and the striking advances that indigenous people had made in placing indigenous concerns on the agendas of bodies such as the United Nations and in the programs of national and multilateral development agencies. The year 1989 saw not only the fall of the Berlin Wall and communism but also an increasing concern for other issues and identities around which to conceptualize and foment social change. In 1989 the International Labor Organization revised its convention on indigenous peoples and drafted what would be known as ILO Convention 169. Unlike earlier conventions, which had emphasized assimilationist goals, ILO 169 recognized the existence and legitimacy of the claims of "tribal and indigenous peoples." Moreover, it stressed the obligation of national governments to work with indigenous peoples to "coordinate and systematize" efforts that "protect the rights of these peoples and guarantee respect to their integrity" (Article 2, ILO 169, 1989). Soon ILO 169 was recognized as occupying a privileged place in an emerging international regime of norms that legitimated indigenous demands. "More than any other international document, the International Labor Organization's Convention 169 represents this shift from an assimilation perspective to one that respects and values Indigenous cultures" (*Abya Yala News,* cited in Van Cott 2000: 263).

The United Nations, with a Working Group on Indigenous Populations since 1982, had become increasingly active in this arena, passing declarations upholding indigenous peoples' rights to difference and rejecting all acts of cultural ethnocide or genocide. It also recognized the continuing importance of indigenous issues to international agendas by expanding from the Year of

Indigenous People (1993) to the International Decade of the World's Indigenous People, 1995–2004. Additionally, multilateral institutions, including the Inter-American Development Bank, the World Bank, and the U.N. Development Program, institutionalized special programs for indigenous people (Brysk 2000a: 130–131).[23]

Despite international pressure and the end of extreme political violence in the country, throughout the 1990s Peru witnessed a weakening of democratic institutions, the growing authority and dominion of the armed forces, and an increasingly controlling and authoritarian government (Basombrío Iglesias 1998).[24] Moreover, while the government sanctioned the arbitrary arrest of anyone suspected of subversive activities, it protected its own forces from prosecution for human rights abuses. In June 1995, the government passed a law that provided amnesty for "military, police, and civilian personnel . . . who have been denounced, investigated, prosecuted, tried, or condemned for common or military crimes . . . for all of the events derived or originated upon the occasion of or as a consequence of the struggle against terrorism . . . since May of 1980 until the promulgation of the present law" (quoted in Basombrío Iglesias 1998: 443).

These kinds of challenges notwithstanding, it is undeniable that the changing international environment has put pressure on national governments, a phenomenon Margaret Keck and Kathryn Sikkink (1998) have called the "boomerang effect." While indigenous affairs had long been marginal to the concerns of the national government in Peru, the late 1990s saw even this beginning to change, albeit gradually. "A great part of the indigenous problematic," explained Jaime Urrutia (2001), former head of Peru's Secretariat of Indigenous Affairs (SETAI), "was revived and is debated today due to the pressure and financial funding of international organizations." Even though the boomerang effect in Peru was long constrained by the national context of political violence and repression, international-level politics had a tremendous effect on the local and national development of bilingual and intercultural policies.

The forceful and visible emergence of Latin American indigenous leaders as "new" political actors changed the face of democratic politics in the region. Likewise, the active role of international funding organizations and NGOs in monitoring the effects of state policies on indigenous populations transformed the relationship between ethnic minorities and the state. Finally, the increasing frequency with which indigenous intellectuals travel to and study in European and North American universities, and their expanded participation in international forums for the development of social policy for their communities, also intensified the internationalization of indigenous politics.

In Cuzco, indigenous rights activists began operating more openly immediately after Guzmán's capture, despite the reservations of many involved with education reform policies. Despite Fujimori's increasingly authoritarian actions, in what some cautioned was merely a symbolic nod to international pressure regarding the importance of multiculturalism to democracy, the Peruvian state institutionalized (once again) bilingual education and language preservation programs. While some disagreed, many activists I spoke with felt that, at that time, access to state funds for cultural and educational programs was crucial, not least because it allowed them to work toward their own ideals with backing from the government. Without this backing, many activists told me, they would have been easily targeted as political dissenters, and could have faced incarceration. The activists I spoke with in Cuzco placed their work during the 1990s in the context of these sociopolitical transformations. In 1990 the Peruvian linguist Inés Pozzi-Escot wrote that "indigenous education can only . . . develop within a global politics of language and culture" (415). In 1999, several months after Pozzi-Escot's death, a leading education activist reminded a gathering of academics, activists, and teachers of her words, stating with confidence that "at last, at this point in time, her vision has become reality."

ELECTORAL FRAUD, 'VLADIVIDEOS,' AND FUJIMORI IN JAPAN

The political climate was to change dramatically as a remarkable turn of events led to the rapid unraveling of Fujimori's presidency. In May 2000 his reelection to a third term in office and his blatant persecution of and attacks on the political opposition sparked intense international criticism and brought the legitimacy of his government into further question. Fujimori's repressive tactics reached their apex with the deaths of several Peruvians during protests against his inauguration on July 28, 2000. The protests were led by Alejandro Toledo, an Andean-born, Stanford-educated leader who would later emerge as president. Toledo and his supporters organized a protest march, calling it *"la marcha de los cuatro suyos"* (the march of the four suyos).[25] The name evoked the four corners of the Inca empire, and their gathering in the center of Lima was symbolically a call to unify the nation in opposition to Fujimori. Part of the symbolism of this march was also meant to distinguish between a Peruvian (Inca) leader and an outsider. Toledo managed to use Fujimori's ethnic otherness (the very thing that had helped Fujimori gain the presidency) against him. He also emphasized his own Andean origins as more authentically Peruvian than the Japanese-Peruvian president and more a man of the people than traditional white politicians such as Alan García.[26] Although the march began peacefully, it escalated to violent encounters between government and opposition forces, ending with the burning of the National Bank and the deaths of several people. Fujimori branded the opposition terrorists and pointed to Toledo as their leader, bringing back not so distant images of violence and terror at the hands of Guzmán and Sendero. Soon thereafter, Toledo withdrew from the presidential race, stating that he wanted no part in the corruption and fraud that would once again make a disgrace of the democratic system in Peru.[27]

After ostensibly defeating the electoral challenge of Alejandro Toledo in 2000, the Fujimori administration was rocked by the release of videos that showed Fujimori's spy chief, Vladimiro Montesinos, bribing an astonishing number of politicians. The *vladivideos*, as they were dubbed, unleashed a scandal that eventually forced Montesinos and Fujimori out of the country. Montesinos was apprehended in Venezuela and later jailed in Peru. Fujimori fled to Japan, the homeland of his parents and a state from which he cannot be extradited, where he took up residence as a Japanese citizen.[28] This turn of events sparked tremendous political instability, as almost overnight the country found itself without a president.

Transitions: Indigenous Rights and the Search for Truth

VALENTÍN PANIAGUA, THE TRUTH AND RECONCILIATION COMMISSION, AND INDIGENOUS RIGHTS

The sudden reversal of fortune meant that new elections had to be called, and that Peru was suddenly in the midst of a transition from a decade of war and authoritarianism to, it was hoped, a period of peace and democracy. In the interim, someone had to govern. The task fell to Valentín Paniagua, the president of the Congress, who oversaw the caretaker government that would rule until the 2001 elections. While it lasted only a short time, the Paniagua interim presidency proved to be a crucial period for democracy and indigenous politics.

First, in June 2001, the government appointed a National Truth Commission. Under Toledo, it became the Truth and Reconciliation Commission (TRC). The commission, like many others before it, was formed to investigate the human rights abuses committed during Peru's dirty war and to give a voice to the victims. Although it was originally made up of seven members (including anthropologists, government ministers, and lawyers), it grew to a twelve-person body in September 2001, after Toledo took office and confirmed his support for the TRC.[29] Commissioners traveled throughout the country, held public hearings, and brought the plight of highland and lowland indigenous Peruvians to the national consciousness through televised sessions of hundreds of testimonies.[30] The commissioners interviewed victims, collected testimonies, and prepared a final report, which was delivered on

August 28, 2003. Despite many significant problems, the TRC has been an important (if mainly symbolic) step toward democratic reform. Similarly, the (re)entrance of indigenous leaders into national spaces under Paniagua was a crucial turning point in Peruvian indigenous politics.

In early February 2001, indigenous delegates from the Asháninka, Nomatsigüenga, and Yanesha peoples of the central Amazon region made the long journey to Lima. They requested government attention to various urgent problems, including those created by concessions given to mining and logging companies, indigenous people's lack of land titles, and the ongoing problem of war and violence in their lands. Remarkably, President Paniagua personally received the delegation and promised to form a commission that would, in his words, "study each and every one of the complex problems that you are confronting" (Smith 2001: 84).

True to his word, he convoked the commission on February 28, 2001, with the participation of delegates from ethnic indigenous federations such as the Inter-Ethnic Development Association of the Peruvian Jungle (AIDESEP) and the Confederation of Nationalities of the Peruvian Amazon (CONAP), as well as social scientists and government functionaries. In several productive days it elaborated policy recommendations concerning native communities and natural resources, indigenous territories and violence, and education and health in indigenous communities. Additionally, Paniagua created spaces for continuing negotiations (*mesas de diálogo*) that would discuss, among other things, the reform of the constitution (Smith 2002a). To those who had long worked with indigenous people, the actions of Paniagua represented the opening of a window of opportunity that had been closed for decades. Indeed, the existing government office for indigenous affairs (SETAI) had hardly been a high priority for the government, as suggested by its placement in the Ministry for Women and Human Development, a ministry characterized by such little bureaucratic coherence that the former SETAI director Jaime Urrutia called it a "Frankenstein" ministry (Urrutia 2001: 70).[31]

The actions of Paniagua suggested that indigenous issues would be taken more seriously. Yet, with elections on the horizon, there existed the real possibility that "the window of opportunity would close on July 29, 2001 [the day after the inauguration]," if the next president did not follow through on institutionalizing the recommendations of the commission (Smith 2001: 86).

POLITICIZING RACE AND INDIGENOUS RIGHTS:
THE PRESIDENCY OF ALEJANDRO TOLEDO

Initially it appeared that Alejandro Toledo, who had made much of his Andean ancestry during the presidential campaign and emerged victorious over the former populist president Alan García, would keep that window open. Toledo's highland origins, his self-conscious use of indigenous symbols, and his Quechua-speaking Belgian wife, Eliane Karp, all became important political resources.[32] Toledo also made a powerful symbolic and diplomatic gesture in expanding his inauguration to include a ceremony at the ancient ruins of Machu Picchu. There, at the heart of the Inca empire, Toledo — the Stanford-educated former World Bank employee — seemed to signal his return to a deeper Peru as he addressed the nation in Quechua and Spanish, and, joined by all the presidents of the neighboring Andean states, signed the Declaration of Machu Picchu, a document that pledged the defense of indigenous rights throughout the region.

Moreover, Toledo's party, Perú Posible, brought, for the first time, an Aymara woman to the National Congress. Paulina Arpasi, a former secretary general of the Confederación Campesina del Perú (CCP), has been vocal in emphasizing her role in representing indigenous people in Congress:

I think it's not only necessary for indígenas to know they have a representative in the National Congress, it's also very important for the National Congress to know it has within it a representative of the indígenas. I will change neither my indigenous dress nor my constant defense [*reivindicación*] of the rights of the indigenous peoples of Peru. (Arpasi 2001)[33]

The election of Toledo and Arpasi seemed to challenge the lingering racial hierarchies that permeate Peruvian society.[34] However, since these early moments of promise, Toledo's tenure has increasingly sparked skepticism and critique from indigenous organizations and their advocates.

The organized protest of indigenous people is certainly not new in Peru, but the late 1990s saw a new scale of organizing that has led to the creation of several national indigenous organizations. The dynamic and fluid state of current indigenous politics makes a detailed discussion impossible here. However, during a recent visit to Peru, my husband, José Antonio Lucero, and I met with a number of highland and lowland indigenous leaders who were facing the current transition in Peru with a remarkable combination of newfound organizational energy and long-standing anger (see García and Lucero 2004).

KARP AND CONAPA

In order to understand the dialogue on indigenous rights and movements in Peru, it is important to look at the very visible role played by the president's wife, Eliane Karp. Karp, who speaks Quechua and studied anthropology as an undergraduate, has made indigenous issues part of her official duties as first lady.[35] Paniagua's work was to be taken on by Karp in her self-proclaimed role as president of the new National Commission for Andean, Amazonian, and Afro-Peruvian Peoples (CONAPA). Karp has been recognized for giving indigenous issues great visibility. Indeed, Oxfam's Martin Scurrah notes that Karp has "intervened on numerous occasions in support of or in defense of indigenous initiatives." Scurrah points out that she "promoted the proposal for a chapter on indigenous rights in the new constitution" and has provided certain indigenous leaders with access to the presidential palace (personal communication, 2002). The Aymara indigenous leader Brígida Peraza has also highlighted the new opportunities that have come with an indigenous advocate so close to the president (personal communication, 2003). However, other analysts have articulated less positive evaluations of Karp's role as an advocate for indigenous people. Rather than moving the theme of indigenous politics forward, they say, CONAPA (sometimes called the "Comisión Karp") is a step backward. Karp's decision to head CONAPA seemed to recall the uncomfortable paternalism of older populist politics and invited many charges of conflicts of interest. The controversy around these charges led Karp to resign her leadership of the commission in 2003. It is instructive to describe in more detail some of the critiques that pushed Karp toward this decision.

First, CONAPA was perceived as a step down in stature. As one Peruvian analyst put it, "Rather than being in the charge of a minister, the commission is headed by the first lady [who has no official place in the government hierarchy]. From the negotiation table [under Paniagua], the idea of the commission is downgraded" (Agurto, interview, 2002). Additionally, SETAI, the office of indigenous affairs, was transformed into the technical arm of CONAPA, losing much of the dynamism and autonomy that it briefly enjoyed under Paniagua (Benavides 2001: 104–105). More recently, SETAI was dissolved altogether (SERVINDI 2003).

Second, the political implications of CONAPA are troubling. As Margarita Benavides, an anthropologist who worked actively with the Paniagua-convoked commission, argues, "the most important thing is that the [indigenous] organizations continue to maintain their autonomy vis-à-vis the government" (Benavides 2001: 106). CONAPA, as a governmental but unelected body, puts this autonomy somewhat in doubt, as its members are hand-picked and new international funds are selectively handed out. Moreover, it was difficult to tell where Karp's private NGO, Fundación Pacha, ended and where the public work of CONAPA began, as they all seemed to intersect in the office of the first lady. With new funds coming from the World Bank in 2002 ($5 million for a project on Amazonian, Andean, and Afro-Peruvian peoples), the conditions for co-optation and conflicts of interest were clearly present (Agurto, interview, 2002). Whether one evaluates Karp and her work positively as new advocacy for indigenous people or negatively as state co-optation, it is clear that the political climate has changed for indigenous actors in civil society and enabled a variety of indigenous responses.

MINING, CIVIL SOCIETY, AND PROTEST
IN THE HIGHLANDS: CONACAMI

In 1993, as discussed above, the government of Alberto Fujimori over-saw the drafting of a constitution that finally contained some encouraging language for indigenous people, including articles that spoke of respect for "the cultural identity of rural and native communities" and protection of communal property. However, his rhetoric notwithstanding, Fujimori's reign was in many ways harmful to indigenous people. Not only did his campaign against Sendero turn indigenous communities into battlefields, but his constitutional reforms opened the door for increased activity on the part of extractive industries. For example, in the fine print of the constitution and of later investor-friendly legislation, exceptions were carved out from those protections that facilitated the expansion of mining activities on community lands.

A before-and-after statistical snapshot illustrates the point well. In 1992, before the legal changes, approximately 4 million hectares had been claimed by mining industries. In the years after Fujimori's legal reform, mining claims skyrocketed to cover more than 25 million hectares. "Of the 5,660 [legally recognized] communities in all of Peru, there are mining claims [*denuncios*] on 3,200."[36] Miguel Palacín, the president of an important new indigenous organization, the National Coordinator of Communities Adversely Affected by Mining (CONACAMI), recited these figures with the ease of someone who has told them many times to many audiences as we spoke with him in June 2002 in the Lima office of his organization. Concessions have been granted mostly to transnational mining companies, Palacín noted, most of them Canadian (Palacín, interview, 2001).

This increase in foreign investment may have pleased the economic planners in the government, but for many communities the effects continue to be disastrous. Populations have been displaced, productive agricultural lands have been dramatically reduced in size, and water sources have been taken over by mining interests. In addition, environmental contamination has provoked the outcry of communities such as Choropampa, where a mercury spill resulted in widespread reports of sickness followed by inaction by the company and the state (Caballo and Boyd 2002). To add insult to injury, none of the profits or rents generated from the mining activities benefited the affected communities. Extractive industry, remarks Palacín, is part of the "fic-ticious development" that has trapped Peru. "Before mining, [the northern department of] Cajamarca was the fourth poorest department in Peru; now it's the second poorest."

In the mid-1990s, Palacín and others began to organize protests against this unequal exchange in which state and industry profited while highland communities suffered. Mining companies, however, used the legal system, already tilted in their favor, to denounce Palacín and accuse him of criminal activity. In Latin America, the accused is effectively presumed guilty and often detained indefinitely if he or she lacks adequate legal or financial resources. Palacín was forced to leave the highlands and go into hiding on the coast. Emblematic of the double-edged nature of globalization, however, Palacín received unexpected aid from the north.

News of the trouble Palacín was causing for Canadian companies reached indigenous organizations in Canada through Internet sources. With their own histories of conflicts with extractive industries, Canadian First Nations formally requested that the charges against Palacín be investigated by the state. The state attorney looked into the Palacín case and found that there was no merit to any of the charges, which were subsequently dropped. With this brush with the law, Palacín realized that "the only weapon is organization." Thus in 1998 he led organizing efforts throughout the central and southern sierra to bring communities together. In October 1999 the first congress of a new national organization, CONACAMI, was convened and Palacín was elected president.

Although most of the communities represented by CONACAMI were Quechua communities, CONACAMI did not initially fashion itself as a Quechua organization. Palacín acknowledges some of the difficulties that arose around identity, a theme, he says, "that was not taken up by the organization's leadership, but was present in the base communities, the majority of which are Quechua speakers of the sierra." More recently, the organization has been placing greater emphasis on the question of indigenous culture, locating its struggles within the broader framework of "human rights and the rights of indigenous peoples." Culture, argues Palacín, "cannot be bought. It is the only mechanism of resistance." As Palacin spoke of the national march planned for June 2002, he warned that if President Toledo did not heed their protests, they would soon call for a *levantamiento* (uprising), the word used for the Indian revolts of the colonial period and a term forcefully deployed by CONAIE, the powerful indigenous confederation in Ecuador (see Zamosc 1994).

CONACAMI's increasingly visible role as an indigenous actor, however, is not only about what its leadership says or even what the organization does. As identity formation is always relational and representational, it is important to understand how other actors in the state and civil society shape this new organization's collective identity. While there are certainly different opinions about CONACAMI and its leadership, there seems to be an emerging consensus that it is the most coherent and influential indigenous highland organization to come along in a long while. From the point of view of the state, CONACAMI has attracted significant attention. Eliane Karp, in recognition of the importance of this new organization, named its president, Miguel Palacín, to her commission, CONAPA. Palacín registered discomfort over this selection process and raised serious doubts about Karp's CONAPA, but his presence provided a critical voice and increased the organization's visibility (Palacín, interview, 2002). Although he has since resigned from his post on the commission, Palacín continues to be a visible indigenous leader, as we will see.

From the side of civil society, CONACAMI is gaining important allies. Oxfam America, one of the key international funders of indigenous organizations in the Andean republics, has supported the work of CONACAMI since its formation, and funded exchange programs so that its leaders can share experiences with indigenous organizations in Ecuador (CONAIE) and Bolivia (CONAMAQ) (Naveda, interview, 2002). An evaluation prepared by a lowland organization recognized the need to bring Amazonian and Andean organizations together, making special mention of CONACAMI as "the most representative expression of the highland movement" (CINA 2002: 4). CONACAMI is playing a leading role in the constitution of COP-PIP (the Permanent Coordinator of the Indigenous People of Peru), a new organization that may be the start of what scholars and activists have said was absent in Peru: a national organization that links indigenous peoples from coastal, highland, and lowland regions (see García and Lucero 2004). However, the jump to the national scale of indigenous politics in Peru, as it is everywhere, is complicated.

COORDINATING DIFFERENCE: A TALE OF TWO COPPIPS

Miguel Palacín, along with the leaders of the Amazonian indigenous federation AIDESEP (Asociación Interétnica de la Selva Peruana) and other leaders, has been at the center of efforts to build what has become known as the Permanent Coordinator of the Indigenous People of Peru (COPPIP). It is a pan-ethnic and pan-regional national body. It is not, however, the only pan-ethnic, pan-regional national body that goes by that acronym. There also exists a Conferencia (not Coordinadora) Permanente de los Pueblos Indígenas del Perú that has a different leadership and agenda. Both COPPIPs trace their beginnings to a meeting in Cuzco in 1997 when the Conferencia was founded, but the two camps have different accounts of the division that emerged in the Conferencia in 2002. According to some close to the Coordindadora-COPPIP (headed now by Palacín), the Conferencia-COPPIP (headed now by Eduardo Candiotti Munarriz) entered a leadership crisis in 2002 that cost COPPIP credibility and the financial support of international NGOs (Agurto, interview, 2002). Under the new leadership of Palacín and a new technical team, the Conferencia became a Coordinadora and re-established its ties to the transnational networks that include Oxfam America, among others.

According to sources at the Conferencia-COPPIP, the crisis of 2002 was itself the product of interference by outside actors and the state. The head of the organization's commission on politics and ideology reported:

Coordinadora-COPPIP is a puppet-COPPIP of the North American funders, which in alliance with Karp and her cronies succeeded in dividing the Conferencia Permanente de los Pueblos Indígenas del Peru. Now this corrupt alliance has dissolved, leaving us with the consequences we are now experiencing: two factions disputing control of a World Bank loan for $5 million. (Aranwan, personal communication, April 28, 2004).

These complaints of foreign interference notwithstanding, it is fairly clear that the COPPIP that is gaining important international resources and recognition is the Coordinadora-COPPIP. Why or how the Coordinadora is favored over the Conferencia is beyond the scope of this discussion. However, it is important to note that in understanding questions of indigenous authenticity in politics, researchers should pay attention to the "authenticators" in local, national, and international spaces that privilege some actors over others (Warren and Jackson 2002: 10; see also Lucero 2002).

Despite serious differences, the two COPPIPs do represent an important development for indigenous politics in Peru. While neither faction is an organization in the sense in which the term is usually used to describe the autonomous local, regional, or national federations and confederations of indigenous people that constitute social movement fields, they both represent spaces in which various organizations come together and debate and discuss common issues and strategies, without losing their individual autonomy.[37] Both COPPIPs represent truly unprecedented spaces for the articulation of indigenous political projects and subjects. Their respective contributions and projects are documented online in widely disseminated newsletters. The Coordinadora's newsletter goes by the name *SERVINDI: Servicio de Información Indígena;* the Conferencia's newsletter is called *Indígenas del Peru.*[38]

Interestingly, SERVINDI has published the summary of an evaluation of indigenous-state relations (based on a meeting convoked by Guillermo Ñaco, head of the National Amazonian Indigenous Commission, or CINA) that was critical of Toledo and Karp. The document, however, did not stop short of criticizing the organization, asking, "Is the problem Eliane or the indigenous organization?" In that vein, it called for the strengthening of the Coordinadora-COPPIP so that indigenous peoples would have an independent "space, agenda, and strategy of their own" (CINA 2002: 3).

Clearly, the political context for indigenous movements has changed remarkably in the last few years. On the one hand, this new moment is full of contradictions and may even threaten prospects for indigenous autonomy. On the other, the importance of these new spaces and openings should not be underestimated or dismissed. Despite government intentions, indigenous organizations can use them to demand and obtain attention to specific claims, such as efforts by both Karp and indigenous leaders to amend the constitution to include sections on indigenous rights (e.g., CONAPA 2001). Indigenous organizations and communities are negotiating these new opportunities and challenges on a variety of levels. However, a full understanding of Peruvian ethnic politics and multicultural development requires us to take a step back in time. Accordingly, the next chapter explores the politics of indigenous language and education through an examination of the historical connections between indigenista policies in the 1930s and 1940s, populist reform in the 1960s, and multicultural activism in the 1990s.

2 Race, Education, and Citizenship

FROM 'INDIGENISMO' TO
'INTERCULTURALIDAD,' 1920S–1990S

The cultural politics of contemporary Peru are part of long and fractured histories of the making of race, nation, and state. The "Indian problem"—shorthand for the cultural, economic, and political legacies of conquest and colonialism—occupied a privileged position in debates over the very meaning of Peruvian nationality and the program for Peruvian progress. A remarkable number of solutions have been offered for this "problem," coming from a variety of ideological directions but often grouped under the label *indigenismo*. Remarkably, all these projects evidence an almost constant concern with language and education. In order to understand the current politics of intercultural activism, it is essential to understand how it grows from and in reaction to the patterns of the past. In this chapter I highlight the place of education as one of the principal mechanisms through which "Indians" were to be transformed into citizens. Starting with the indigenista intellectual movement of the early twentieth century, the discussion traces the role of the state, intellectuals, and nongovernmental actors in determining the place of Peru's indigenous population.

The Indian as National Problem

> Colonialism . . . busied itself with the nostalgic idealization
> of the past. Indigenismo, in contrast, has living roots in the
> present. It extracts its inspiration from the protests
> of millions. The Viceroyalty was; the Indian is.
> —José Carlos Mariátegui, 1928

The place of indigenous populations within the social, economic, and political life of Peru was debated by writers, social activists, and politicians even before the country gained independence in 1821. The wars of independence reframed the issue from one of colonial administration to a matter of national liberation and republican governance. This transition from Spanish colonialism to republican independence, as Mark Thurner (1997) and other historians have ably documented, represented a move from "two republics" (Indian and Spanish) to "one divided." The enormity of the challenge presented by Peru's postcolonial situation was something that nineteenth-century liberators preferred not to confront. Benedict Anderson notes:

The independence movements in the Americas became, as soon as they were printed about, 'concepts', 'models' and indeed 'blueprints'. In 'reality', Bolívar's fears of Negro insurrections and San Martín's summoning of his indigenes to Peruvianness jostled one another chaotically. But printed words washed away the former almost at once, so that, if recalled at all, it appeared an inconsequential anomaly. Out of the American welter came these imagined realities: nation-states; republican institutions, common citizenship, popular sovereignty, national flags, and anthems, etc. (1991 [1983]: 81)

These "imagined realities" could not erase colonial continuities as the class and racial stratification that represented "deep Peru" constituted an obstacle for the modernizing vision of national elites. The weight of the past, the "backwardness" of the Andes, weighed on the minds of liberal nation-builders like a nightmare. Indians represented a problem that was to be solved. It was not only the ruling Peruvian elite that saw the indigenous populations as the cause of Peruvian underdevelopment. In the early-twentieth-century thought of José Carlos Mariátegui, the currents of international socialism converged with new ideas about how indigenous people themselves would be the solution to Peru's problems (Becker 2002).[1]

As we saw in Chapter 1, Mariátegui extolled socialism as the solution to Indian oppression. For him the Indian problem was a problem not of race but of class. Mariátegui often stated that debating the "Indian problem" as a problem of race was in effect racist because it implied that its solution would include the racial improvement of indigenous populations. He saw mestizaje as an example of how other nations (such as Mexico) claimed to address this problem but in reality only reframed it, leaving intact notions of racial inferiority.

Instead, Mariátegui argued that the oppression of indigenous populations derived from the system of land tenure. Thus, an end to feudalism was an end to Indian oppression and the first step toward restructuring society along socialist lines. These views are eloquently expressed in his most famous collection of writings: *Siete ensayos de interpretación de la realidad peruana*

(Seven interpretive essays on Peruvian reality, 1994 [1928]). However, although Mariátegui discussed the possibility of indigenous revolution, the underlying assumption was that Indians were not ready or able to liberate themselves. Therefore, it was important for others, as Peruvians, to identify with and advocate for their indigenous brothers and sisters. This solidarity could be expressed through literature. In one of his writings, Mariátegui discussed the importance of literature, and specifically of indigenista literature, to Peruvian political thought (Mariátegui 1994 [1928]: 229–348).[2] He distinguished between three distinct types of literary genres about the Indian — *indianista,* indigenista, and indígena — and examined their political significance (Kristal 1991: 17–18).

According to Mariátegui, indianista literature portrayed an exotic and idealized image of the Indian. In their nostalgic representations of Andean life and their refusal to take on the more politically significant topics of abuse and marginalization, Mariátegui saw indianista writers as furthering the exploitation of indigenous populations. Moreover, he described indianista ideology as racist: "To subscribe to [*indianismo*] is to fall into the most naive and absurd mysticism. . . . It would be senseless and dangerous to oppose [the racism of those who demean the Indian with] the racism of those who glorify the Indian with messianic faith" (Mariátegui quoted in Becker 2002: 204). In contrast to indianismo, he defined indigenista literature as one that reflected the commitment of nonindigenous writers to the protection and defense of the Indian (Kristal 1991: 17), and extolled indigenistas as indigenous advocates: "The authentic indigenistas — who should not be confused with those who exploit indigenous issues . . . — collaborate, consciously or not, with a political and economic project of reclaiming [indigenous rights]" (Mariátegui 1994 [1928]: 332). At the same time, this Peruvian intellectual was clear in his distinction between indigenistas and indígenas. Indigenistas, he claimed, would never be able to portray the "real essence" of indigenous life. After all, indigenista literature was still "a literature of mestizos" (332). Moving away from traditional Marxist views on the peasantry, Mariátegui believed that only indigenous peoples could represent themselves "objectively," and that it was only "when they were capable of producing [indigenous literature]" (332) that society would obtain true accounts of indigenous history and cultural politics. Mariátegui thus modified and almost inverted Marx's Brumairean formulation by insisting that indigenous people, for a while, might have to be represented, but in the end they must represent themselves culturally and politically.[3] According to him, until indigenous peoples reclaimed their rights and emerged from their places of marginalization, they should be protected and represented by indigenistas.

*Indigenismo: From Liberation to Assimilation
(1840s–1930s)*

> As we continue to study it, [it is clear that] the indigenista
> current [is less about] simple literary factors [than about]
> complex social and economic factors.
> — José Carlos Mariátegui, 1928

Indigenismo first emerged in the mid-1800s as an urban-based literary movement that highlighted the exploitation and marginalization of the Indian in Peruvian society (Kristal 1991). Indigenistas wrote novels, poetry, and short stories about rural (glossed as Indian) lifeways as a way both to inform urban society about the plight of indigenous peoples and to glorify the indigenous past. Although it began primarily as a cultural movement, indigenista ideology during this time was influenced by political conversations about "the Indian problem" (Mariátegui 1994 [1928]: 328). At the same time, it deeply penetrated political discourse. While mestizaje became the preferred nation-building project of politicians and intellectuals throughout most of Latin America (Stepan 1991, Larson 1995), in Peru it never became an official nation-building racial project (de la Cadena 2000).

However, there were clearly different moments and manifestations of indigenismo. For instance, many Andean indigenistas, such as Luis Valcárcel, forcefully rejected cultural and racial mixing and claimed that mestizaje produced "nothing but deformities" (Valcárcel, cited in Marzal 1995). For others, such as Manuel González Prada, highland Indians had to be "nationalized" through benevolent programs of community education and economic integration (Kristal 1991, Marzal 1981).[4] Each of the indigenista currents was tied to distinct ideas about economic and cultural progress, and about the place of Indians in the nation.[5]

Indigenistas started from the assumption that the solution to the principal social problems in Peruvian society could be found by exploring "the Indian problem." As Mariátegui so eloquently discussed, for indigenistas the Indian problem was tied to the feudal system and the landowning elite who perpetuated it. Throughout the mid-1800s, as the Peruvian nation was being shaped, liberal indigenistas spoke out against the feudal system of landownership and advocated freeing the land and liberating the Indian in order to move the nation toward modernization and progress. Liberal politicians and intellectuals, concerned with building the infrastructure necessary for an export-oriented Peru, demanded indigenous labor for work on the railroads and ports and in cotton and sugar plantations on the coast (Kristal 1991). Thus the liberation of indigenous hacienda laborers was connected to the opening of the market and to the repositioning of indigenous work as part of that opening. In various forums, such as the journal *La Revista de Lima,* these intellectuals accused the landowning elite of responsibility for the "degradation of the Indian," and put forth instead their views about the connections between race and work: "The Indian's freedom . . . is just as sacred as that of any white. . . . Work must be free to be productive" (J. Ulloa, quoted in Kristal 1991: 30).

After Peru's defeat in the War of the Pacific with Chile (1879–83), new nationalist currents arose. Many Peruvians, among them well-known indigenistas, blamed the country's defeat on its regional and ethnic diversity, specifically on the lack of indigenous nationalist sentiment (Bonilla 1987).[6] For instance, Manuel González Prada, poet and social analyst of the late 1800s, argued that Peru had lost the war because it was not a unified nation. The lack of national unity, he claimed, was linked to the lack of a national consciousness among the indigenous population because of its historical marginalization and oppression. Once again, González Prada's ideas connected the "national problem" (lack of political, cultural, and economic integration) to the "Indian problem." However, the problem was no longer only about the emancipation of indigenous peoples, but also about their so-called rehabilitation through education in Spanish (Deustua and Rénique 1984, Kristal 1991). One of the best-known indigenista writers of this time was Clorinda Matto de Turner. Her most famous work, *Aves sin nido* (Birds without a nest, 1995 [1889]), paints a brutally frank picture of the oppression of highland Indians. It goes one step further, however, blaming priests, judges, governors, and the Peruvian nation generally for "abandoning and destroying indigenous culture" (Kristal 1991: 145) and, by extension, preventing the young nation's economic and political progress.

Despite their progressive intentions, racist discourse was a significant part of the arguments advanced by some indigenistas. After lamenting the abuses committed against indigenous people and pressing for indigenous education as a form of acculturation, these social thinkers stated clearly that part of the solution to Peru's problems of economic and national integration was to "improve the race" through immigration. A review of Matto de Turner's work sums up the sentiments among those sympathetic to both indigenous integration and eugenic immigration policies:

One of the principal errors committed [by Peruvians] is the impolitic abandonment of the indigenous race. The Indian, more Peruvian than we, roams through the jungles and mountains, or vegetates in the highlands, or is stupefied among the European races of the coast. . . . I applaud immigration because I recognize the urgent need for a blood superior to ours to reestablish honorable sentiments, inculcating again the notion of duty. (Emilio Gutiérrez de Quintanilla, quoted in Kristal 1991: 146)

Throughout the first decade of the twentieth century, indigenistas continued to proclaim conflicting ideologies about the Indian as national problem. Whether indigenistas proposed an economic opening through the freedom of indigenous labor or national integration through indigenous education, the landowning elite was staunchly opposed to the emancipation of the Indian. Thus, increasing conflict between landowners and indigenistas inevitably centered on the place of indigenous peoples in the nation's economic progress. By the 1910s, debates over the Indian problem had moved beyond intellectual and elite circles. In such cities as Cuzco and Puno, the plight of indigenous communities and indigenous struggles became topics of daily discussion in newspapers and journals (Deustua and Rénique 1984: 69–75). The editorial staffs of many newspapers were made up of indigenistas, some of them recognized intellectuals. In Cuzco, for instance, Luis E. Valcárcel, a prominent indigenista intellectual, was both on the editorial staff of Cuzco's major newspaper and an important presence at the university and in intellectual circles. He wrote academic analyses of Inca history and culture, and promoted a more radical view of indigenous liberation in the Andes, forcefully expressed in his book *Tempestad en los Andes*.

This radical view did not fare well toward the end of the decade. Between 1918 and 1923, indigenous peasant rebellions rocked the department of Cuzco (Deustua and Rénique 1984: 69–96). Valcárcel and other indigenistas who advocated an indigenous uprising defended these land invasions, connecting them to broader social and cultural liberation. However, others, indigenistas among them, saw these rebellions as a threat. Moreover, influenced by daily newspaper articles emphasizing the abuse suffered by Indians and the glorification of the Incas, landowners and other cuzqueños had visions of an indigenous Saint-Domingue and heard echoes of the armies of Túpac Amaru and Túpac Katari:[7]

This ill-directed native agitation is not only of interest to rural landowners, but is one that must awaken in all of society a solidarity movement, indispensable given the somber threat of the Indian multitudes, which, if left without control to finish their work of destruction in the countryside, will then attack [urban] settlements and exterminate their inhabitants. . . . [The] Indian not only intends to reclaim the land that he says landlords have taken from him but wants to restore the Tawantinsuyo empire and the cult of the Sun and to cleanse the national territory of whites. (*El Comercio*, September 15, 1922, quoted in Deustua and Rénique 1984: 78)[8]

In the midst of the escalating political upheaval, Augusto Leguía became president of Peru (1919–30). His government, which he called Patria Nueva (New Fatherland), was initially imbued with a strong populist sentiment. As part of his political discourse, Leguía expanded on González Prada's concern over the national integration of the Indian, while simultaneously highlighting the importance of the modernization and industrialization of Lima through foreign (primarily North American) investment. Moreover, with Leguía, indigenismo also became official state policy (Deustua and Rénique 1984). Leguía's official indigenismo, like all politics, was messy and contradictory, and it shifted along with his political allegiances. For instance, despite his claims to "protect the Indian race," Leguía's encouragement of foreign investment alienated those liberal indigenistas who had earlier pressed for the freedom of Indian labor as a way to promote export-based economic growth, creating yet another rift among those concerned with indigenous populations.[9] Nonetheless, official indigenismo would have significant consequences for indigenous–state relations during this time. Not unlike attempts by contemporary states to manage difference and dissent, Leguía's efforts to institutionalize an indigenous rights agenda was, at least in part, a response to the political upheaval caused by the rebellions. Leguía's promotion of the indigenous cause was also motivated by his search for political support.

The constitution of 1921, a document that gave legal recognition to indigenous communities for the first time since independence, was drafted under Leguía. Also during the 1920s, a series of laws and new institutions and organizations, such as the Bureau of Indian Affairs, opened up channels for indigenous demands for education, land, and suffrage. Additionally, in an effort to garner support for his administration, Leguía endorsed several indigenista projects, such as the radical Comité Pro-Derecho Indígena Tawantinsuyo. This committee was particularly important, and it has become symbolic of both grass-roots and state initiatives. A "radical indigenista national project" (de la Cadena 2000: 89), the committee brought together indigenistas based in Lima and in various coastal and Andean provinces, as well as self-identified indigenous and peasant leaders. As the first national indigenista organization, it had its headquarters in Lima but formed subcommittees in "the most diverse departments, provinces, and districts" (Deustua and Rénique 1984: 74). Founded by members of the Asociación Pro-Indígena (Pévez 1983), the committee demanded indigenous literacy and citizenship rights (Deustua and Rénique 1984, Mallon 1998, de la Cadena 2000: 89–97).[10] As Marisol de la Cadena has noted (2000), their demands for indigenous citizenship were a significant challenge to dominant definitions of Indians as illiterate, traditionalist, and backward. Instead, committee members pushed for the (re)presentation of Indians as literate, modern citizens who were proud to be indigenous, and who would work toward a progressive Peru through indigenous emancipation.

In June 1921, with strong support from the Leguía administration, the committee held its First Indigenous Congress, the first of several to come.[11] These were public spaces where intellectuals and indigenous peasant leaders could come together to discuss indigenous empowerment. However, despite the president's endorsement of the organization, members of the National Congress in Lima condemned the committee, primarily because the Congress was composed largely of landowners and the committee supported and even encouraged rebellions and land takeovers (de la Cadena 2000, Deustua and Rénique 1984). Increasing tensions in the administration, among indigenistas, and even within the committee exacerbated the already tense political climate. Some indigenistas saw Leguía as a supporter of Indians, while others accused him of political opportunism and of not going far enough toward indigenous emancipation. Moreover, conflicting ideas about the rights of landowners and indigenous workers further developed the tensions between intellectuals and indigenous leaders. In his book *Cuestiones indígenas* (Indigenous issues), Luis Felipe Aguilar, an indigenista lawyer from Cuzco and representative of the Bureau of Indian Affairs, wrote that indigenous peasant leaders of land recovery movements (e.g., the Comité Tawantinsuyo) were "false indigenistas," "worse than landlords because they led [indigenous peoples] to believe in the restoration of the Inca empire and the quick return of their lands" (quoted in Deustua and Rénique 1984: 90).[12] In addition, concerns over antinationalist movements did not help the committee's image. Its gatherings were perceived as subversive by some, while others described its members as instigators of racial wars, particularly when national conferences brought hundreds of indigenous participants, dressed in traditional clothing and speaking Quechua, to the Peruvian capital to demand citizenship rights (de la Cadena 2000: 93–94).

As a result of these and other tensions, the committee's leadership split (Kapsoli 1984). Those who espoused more radical paths to empowerment and conservative supporters of state indigenista policies finally split in 1923 with the debate over the passage of the Ley de Conscripción Vial, a law that once again put in place a system of forced labor for Indians (de la Cadena 2000: 96). As a result, the more radical leaders resigned; the new leadership named Leguía as honorary president of the committee and the minister of government, a landowner, as vice president (Kapsoli and Reátegui 1972, de la Cadena 2000). These events coincided with a shift in the administration toward a more authoritarian and repressive form of government. By 1927, Leguía outlawed the committee and imprisoned many of its leaders. In the same year he announced that any claims made by indigenous peoples had to be made directly to the government or to the Bureau of Indian Affairs, recognized at this point as the official government institution for indigenous affairs (Kapsoli and Reátegui 1972). The institutionalization of indigenismo meant, among other things, that once again social movements outside the scope of specific designated (indigenous) spaces were to be repressed and their leaders persecuted.

The indigenista project in the late 1800s and early 1900s was a varied one. The distinct political and ideological positions of elites shaped the forms that indigenous protection would take and the place Indians would occupy in the nation. For the socialist Mariátegui, Indians were at the center of a revolutionary project that would redefine the Peruvian nation; for the conservative González Prada, they were an obstacle to national progress that could be overcome only through education (in Spanish) and immigration. Moreover, tensions between indigenous peasant leaders and indigenistas, particularly during Leguía's term, were complicating the debate over the place of Indians in the nation. In particular, the Comité Pro-Derecho Indígena Tawantinsuyo, despite its internal contradictions and despite racist indigenista attacks against them, promoted an alternative national project that placed indigenous (literate and modern) Peruvians at its center. To understand the contemporary challenges posed by these debates (more fully explored in later chapters), it is helpful to understand the political and intellectual indigenista project that came together in the 1940s. This decade is especially important for understanding indigenistas' ideas about modernity and the ways in which bilingual education could enable Indians to become actors in the making of modern Peru.

"No Soy un Aculturado": Indigenista Languages of Tradition and Modernity

> I am not an acculturated [Indian]; I am a Peruvian who
> proudly, like a happy demon, speaks in Christian and
> Indian tongues, in Spanish and in Quechua.
> — José María Arguedas, 1968

From the heavy paternalism and even racism of some earlier indigenista projects, indigenismo in the 1940s sought to return to the Mariateguian vision in which indigenista advocacy would pave the way for indígena agency. Less concerned with the language of integration and assimilation, prominent intellectuals began to see bilingual education as a way to enhance the capacity of indigenous people to be autonomous actors in constructing a modern and plural Peru. Moreover, the education of indigenous people would not be, as the Comité Tawantinsuyo had demanded, conducted in Spanish, but would be a bilingual program that valorized indigenous languages within a nation-building framework. Thus indigenous liberation and the construction of a plural Peruvian nation came together in the same nationalist project. This thinking is most clearly expressed by José María Arguedas.

Arguedas, a novelist and anthropologist from the department of Andahuaylas, was perhaps the most impassioned advocate of the cultural prominence of indigenous highland peoples. His defense of the Quechua language specifically was reflected in his literary work, and he became known for his extensive use of Quechua along with Spanish in his writing, including poetry, short stories, and novels (Escobar 1984). Like some indigenistas, Arguedas highlighted the oppression of indigenous peoples. Unlike many of them, however, he also wrote about the challenges of migration and modernity, and labeled himself a "modern Quechua."

In 1935 Arguedas published his first collection of stories, marking a radical shift in indigenista literature and politics. In these stories Arguedas moved away from the "purity" of indigenistas' portrayal of indigenous culture and toward a more fluid definition of identity and cultural modernity. As an anthropologist, he registered strong resistance to the overly romanticized notions of earlier writers and a strong concern for the actual situation of indigenous peoples. Recognizing his own "happy demons" of hybridity, Arguedas anticipated the contemporary anthropological appreciation of the cultural multiplicity of individuals and society. Moreover, he was an early advocate of what we would now call engaged anthropology, as his scholarship and writing grew from his political and personal commitments. He was imprisoned in 1937, accused of communism. While in prison, his conversations with communist activists highlighted for him the tensions between his admiration of socialist thought and his concern for Andean culture (Flores Galindo 1992). However, in Arguedas these concerns complemented rather than conflicted with each other. His guiding orientations and inspirations, he explained, were the socialism of Mariátegui, which gave his energy direction, and the dynamic plurality of Peru, which had given it an unparalleled cultural richness. "There is no country," he declared, "that is more diverse" (Arguedas 1993 [1968]: 99).

During the 1940s, indigenistas began working closely with Peruvian and foreign ethnologists conducting research of contemporary life in indigenous communities. Indigenismo then became infused with a social-scientific air, and gradually the implementation of any state program targeting indigenous populations required consultation with and the agreement of ethnologists working in the designated areas (Valcárcel 1981: 368–369). In 1946 the Peruvian Indigenista Institute was founded, and the Ministries of Education and Public Works also began to promote programs highlighting the "cultural recovery" of indigenous language, art, culture, and religion.

At this time Arguedas worked as curator of folklore in the Ministry of Education. Working under the cuzqueño indigenista Luis Valcárcel, who had been Arguedas's history professor and by this time was minister of education, Arguedas stressed the importance of teaching indigenous highland peoples in Quechua. As a result of Arguedas's work, and under the influence of Valcárcel, the Ministry of Education began to implement bilingual education in indigenous schools in 1945 (Contreras 1996). His experience as a primary-school teacher in one of the most desolate regions of Cuzco provided him with a clear understanding of the adverse conditions and difficulties faced by teachers working in indigenous areas. Through the ministry, Arguedas also advocated teacher training in bilingual pedagogy. For indigenistas there existed a crucial ideological difference between bilingual education and education in Spanish. National integration and diversity, in their view, were not clashing themes, but rather two grand melodies that could be harmonized.

Because of his radical promotion of the Quechua language both within highland communities and among intellectuals and bureaucrats in Lima, contemporary intercultural activists often describe Arguedas as a mediator between indigenous and European populations, an indigenista intellectual able to reconcile notions of modernity with those of tradition. Juan Carlos Godenzzi, a leading advocate of indigenous rights and bilingual education, writes: "For Arguedas, access to modernity [did not] imply the destruction of what is Quechua; one can be Quechua and modern at the same time" (Godenzzi 1997: 243). Intercultural activists today, like Arguedas, are concerned with the cultural politics of both modernity and tradition. Much of their work is an attempt to return to an indigenous/traditional identity, although they are still clearly influenced by Arguedas's attempts to perpetuate a modern idea of the Indian against the notion of cultural purity. As it was for Arguedas, for intercultural activists the emphasis still lies on national belonging as indigenous peoples, proud to be different.

From Indians to Peasants: Reforming
Education and Language

> Pedagogy [exists] so that the oppressed may obtain the
> conditions necessary to discover and conquer himself . . .
> as subject of his own destiny. . . . He is not something
> to salvage, but rather an agent who must shape himself
> responsibly. Education must be the practice of freedom.
> — Paulo Freire, 1969

The class-conscious discourse of the 1960s marked a departure from Indianness. The concern became less about indigenous culture and more about a new kind of revolutionary nationalism, in which categories of class and nation (peasant and Peruvian) would bury the "old" ideas of culture and race.[13]

General Juan Velasco's Revolutionary Government of the Armed Forces

(1968–75) emerged in reaction to social unrest and the rise of peasant and guerrilla movements in the highlands in the 1950s and 1960s.[14] Declaring the necessity of transforming Peru's basic economic and social structures as the only way to counter instability and a future insurgency, Velasco announced that his government would seek a third path to development that was "neither capitalist nor communist" (Cotler 1983). Accordingly, Velasco nationalized foreign-held companies, promoted worker-managed enterprises, and attempted to raise popular consciousness and mobilize previously nonparticipatory sectors of the population (Cotler 1983, McClintock and Lowenthal 1983).[15]

In an attack against class and ethnic divisions, Velasco also launched a series of social reforms aimed at improving the conditions of peasants and indigenous peoples. These reforms fundamentally challenged the existing power dynamics throughout the country (Cotler 1983, Turino 1991). Velasco's radical agrarian reform — often cited as a turning point in Peruvian history — was officially initiated throughout the highlands on June 24, 1969, the national Day of the Indian. On this day Velasco announced the massive and forceful handover of large estates by landowners to their former serfs and employees. Moreover, he prohibited the use of the term *indio,* replacing it with *campesino* (peasant). In a televised speech he stated:

Today, for the Day of the Indian, the Day of the Peasant, the Revolutionary Government honors them with the best of tributes by giving to the nation a law that will end forever the unjust social order that impoverished and oppressed the millions of landless peasants who have always been forced to work the land of others. . . . The Agrarian Reform Law gives its support to the great multitude of peasants who today belong to indigenous communities and from this day forward — abandoning unacceptable racist habits and prejudices — will be called Peasant Communities. . . . To the men of the land, we can now say in the immortal and liberating voice of Túpac Amaru: Peasant: the Master will no longer feed off your poverty! (Velasco Alvarado 1995 [1969]: 265)

While this move created the category of highland "peasant communities," it was not until 1974 that Velasco legally recognized and organized Amazonian peoples as "native communities," further reinscribing the distinction between highland and lowland peoples.[16] In an effort to integrate highland peasants into the national economy, Velasco's plan included the redistribution of all haciendas by 1975.[17] Although the idea was simple — distribute land among those who work it — the reform's implementation was largely unsuccessful and fell short of the goals set by Velasco and his government.[18] In the Andes, less than half of landless peasants actually received land, and in the coastal and jungle regions, cooperatives established from expropriated plantations were plagued by mismanagement. While the reform effectively ended landowners' control over peasant workers, it also greatly exacerbated tensions between ethnic groups, particularly between highland peasants and lowland "natives" on the one hand and the criollo middle and upper classes on the other.

Another critical step in government efforts at incorporating highland peoples into national spaces came with the development of educational reform and state-controlled media. Explicitly challenging the national educational system formerly in place, Velasco stated in 1971:

The educational reform of the revolution aspires to create an educational system that satisfies the necessities of the entire nation; that will reach the great masses of [indigenous] peasants, always exploited and always deliberately kept in ignorance; that will create a new consciousness among all Peruvians of the basic problems of our country; and that will contribute to forging a new type of man within a new social morality. (Velasco Alvarado 1972: 63)

However, it is important to note that for Velasco, what was valuable about Inca imagery and the Quechua language was not that they were "Indian" (a term he effectively exiled) but that they were Peruvian. Though refracted through leftist nationalism, Velasco's project was still a part of the contradictions of the long century of indigenismo that had sought both to evoke and to erase the Indian problem. His educational reforms, for example, tapped into indigenista discourse by stating that education should be modified to fit Peruvian social reality. Tellingly, these reforms were part of what was called the Inca Plan (Zimmerman Zavala 1974).

Velasco launched three major initiatives with respect to education. First, the Education Reform of 1972 sought to extend increasing control over the education of all Peruvians, though it targeted primarily indigenous communities. Education would be decentralized and gradually placed under local control through the establishment of community educational nuclei (NECs). These NECs were institutions organized and run by indigenous communities with support from regional government agencies; through them teachers, parents, and community leaders alike were responsible for the implementation and development of education in particular communities. Essentially, this was one of Velasco's attempts to promote self-sufficiency and confidence among indigenous and peasant groups.

Second, the National Policy of Bilingual Education, also of 1972, advocated the implementation of bilingual education in all highland, lowland, and coastal areas where languages other than Spanish were spoken. Finally, a law making Quechua a national language co-equal with Spanish was passed in 1975. The law stated that after April 1976 the teaching of Quechua would be obligatory at all educational levels. Further, all legal proceedings involving monolingual Quechua speakers would have to be conducted in Quechua (Escobar et al. 1975: 61–63). This law, more than all others, emphasized the cultural and ethnic diversity of Peruvian society. Significantly, it highlighted the two areas where language had been previously used as a mechanism of domination over indigenous speakers: the courts and the schools (Escobar et al. 1975, Turino 1991: 274). According to many of the intercultural activists I interviewed, this law was also the one that evoked the strongest reaction by middle- and upper-class society in Lima against Velasco and his government. Placing the Quechua language on an equal footing with Spanish was understood by these groups as symbolically placing Quechua and other indigenous people next to those of European background, and as representative of the limits the Velasco regime posed to development and "progress."[19] By legislating Quechua as a national language next to Spanish, Peru became the first Latin American country to officialize an indigenous language. However, by placing Quechua next to the dominant language, Velasco also brought racial prejudices to the surface. His use of indigenous language and symbols tainted his initiatives with images of indigenous revolutions, one of the factors that led to his replacement with Francisco Morales Bermúdez, another military leader, in 1975.

With the change in presidents (1975) and in constitutions (1979), the law making Quechua an official language was changed to include Quechua not as an official national language but rather as "a language of official use in the areas and in the way that the Law mandates." However, the law that would mandate where and how Quechua could be considered an official language was never developed (Pozzi-Escot 1981, Rojas 1982). Known as "Phase 2" of the Revolutionary Government, this and other changes were a systematic dismantling of many Velasco-era reforms, including the emphasis that had been placed on rural and indigenous rights, including education.

One of the changes that came about during the second military government was an escalation of the tensions (already heightened under Velasco's government) between the military and the national teachers' union (Sindicato Unico de Trabajadores de la Educación Pública, or SUTEP). Uneasy relations between members of SUTEP and agents of Velasco's government due to disagreements over education reform policies led to the persecution and eventual deportation of several highland teachers and activists (van den Berghe 1978, Hinojosa 1998: 70–71). Gradually the educational system came to be seen as a vital terrain that the state had to control and protect from the forces of subversion. In the 1980s this concern was only exacerbated by the political fact that the leadership of Sendero Luminoso and many of its supporters had emerged from Peru's universities and public schools. The schools, once places where indigenous people could be brought into the nation, were becoming a minefield between the forces of order and those of insurrection.

As we saw in Chapter 1, the 1980s were a difficult time with regard to indigenous development policies. Trapped between two armies, indigenous peoples and anyone who spoke up for their rights bore the brunt of political violence.[20] Despite the political climate, there were some developments in language and education policies aimed at indigenous peoples. In 1985, for example, Quechua and Aymara alphabets were given official sanction, and in 1987, after approximately ten years of inactivity, President Alan García (1985–90) reinstated the Department (Dirección General) of Bilingual Education. The next few years signaled the beginning of a new opening for proponents of what for the first time the government would call bilingual intercultural education (EIB). In 1989, the García government approved the Bilingual Intercultural Education Policy, with its goal of promoting a "national identity characterized by an awareness of being united in diversity" (Zúñiga et al. 2003: 25). It also characterized EIB as democratic and participatory. The incoming government of Alberto Fujimori promoted its own National Policy of Intercultural Education and Bilingual Intercultural Education in 1991, seeking to expand the scope of interculturality from the old confines of the "Indian problem" to embrace all members of the ethnically, culturally, and linguistically diverse national community. In at least the rhetoric of the new proclamations (if not the underfunded budgets of new programs), one could make out echoes of Arguedas's "happy demons" that celebrated diversity.

With the increasing attention to these matters, advocates for indigenous rights were able to speak more loudly about cultural rights through the publication of books and articles about language, and they participated in conferences and debates about the standardization of indigenous languages, cultural identity, and education reform. Additionally, the capture of the Senderista leader Abimael Guzmán in 1992 inspired hopes for the end of more than a decade of war and opened a window of opportunity for a new attempt to return to an Indian problem that in the eyes of a new generation of intellectuals and development professionals had only gotten worse.

Contemporary Education Reform and Indigenous Development

> To support [our indigenous peoples] involves not only
> providing them with benefits in the present but also
> securing their future. There is no better way to do this
> than through education, so that the natives will be agents
> of their own progress.
> — Alberto Fujimori, 1999

Intercultural activists are struggling with the legacy of indigenismo in Peru. On one level, the contemporary project is a resurrection of the indigenista project (as practiced by Valcárcel) of providing indigenous people with the tools necessary to become agents of their own history. In the terms of Mariátegui's typology, Valcárcel promoted the move from indigenista representation to indígena self-determination. For him indigenous peoples were at the center of a revolutionary project, one that saw indigenous actors creating a new society. While for some, national integration would happen through education in Spanish, for Valcárcel and Arguedas, education was critical for developing indigenous autonomy, but it had to take identity and culture into account, which is why they worked toward bilingual education and training. However, this new society existed within the parameters of the Peruvian nation. Theirs was a national project. It was about being proudly Peruvian, but a Peruvian who embraced national diversity. It was also about redefining indigenous peoples as a critical part of a modern nation.

The contemporary project is also about positioning indigenous peoples as actors in the making of their own history. It is about preparing them, through education that emphasizes their culture, history, and identity (or activist interpretations of them) as positive and crucial components of Peru as a multicultural nation. Work in the Ministry of Education, changes to the national curriculum, and an emphasis on intercultural education at all levels of society (even if implemented only in indigenous rural areas), make this, in some ways, still a national project. However, it is also a project that challenges the imagined community that is Peru.

Intercultural Education: Shaping Diversity,
Imagining Unity

According to Juan Carlos Godenzzi, former head of the National Directorate of Bilingual Intercultural Education (DINEBI), bilingual intercultural education in Peru was initially promoted (as intercultural — not only bilingual — education) in the 1980s (Godenzzi 2001).[21] Strongly supported by multilateral organizations (e.g., the World Bank, the Inter-American Development Bank, the Fondo Indígena) and international funding organizations (e.g., the German Technological Institute [GTZ], Oxfam America), Peruvian intellectuals, among them linguists, anthropologists, and progressive educators, worked toward what they called a "liberating education." Proponents of intercultural education distinguish clearly between their "progressive and culturally sensitive project" and previous assimilationist policies. Rather than utilizing indigenous languages only as a way to ease the transition to Spanish, intercultural methodology promotes the maintenance of indigenous languages and the teaching of a second language (most commonly Spanish), as well as the acceptance of and respect for cultural difference.

Looking to the many cultural and political gains made by their Ecuadorian and Bolivian indigenous neighbors, Peruvian supporters of intercultural education pushed for indigenous rights by focusing on language and cultural rights. As I discuss in Chapter 1, the tremendous political violence of the 1980s in Peru created a climate of terror that left little room for overt political challenges against the state. Thus, intercultural activists reframed debates over indigenous politics, turning them into "safe" discussions about language and culture.[22]

Clearly, the political context in which intercultural activists worked had a tremendous impact on their activism, and to a certain extent shaped the limits of what many activists called "intercultural mobilization." In contrast to other cases throughout the region, where mobilization came *before* policy changes, intercultural activists in the 1990s argued that in Peru changes to national policy (such as constitutional and education reform highlighting the significance of cultural and ethnic diversity) were important preconditions to the development of significant mobilization. Despite difficult times, however, local NGOs (with international funding) were already working toward the implementation of intercultural education in highland and lowland areas in the early 1990s.

According to intercultural activists, the implementation of EIB was a significant grass-roots challenge to national education policies mandating that all public education take place in Spanish, and an important gain for intellectuals and activists in the country working toward indigenous cultural rights. However, EIB also grew out of international trends in indigenous education that formed part of broader multicultural development projects, and from its initial stages it was quickly subsumed into state education reform projects promoting national diversity.

As mentioned above, the state gave renewed attention to intercultural education in the late 1980s and early 1990s with the resurrection of the Department of Bilingual Education (in 1987) and the adoption of two national EIB policies (1989 and 1991). These national policies, however, were never adequately funded. To make matters worse for EIB proponents, Fujimori disbanded the Department of Bilingual Education in 1993.

Largely in response to pressure from intercultural activists, local NGOs, and various international organizations, the department was reestablished in 1996, though most of its funding was cut off during the last months of 1996 and the first months of 1997. With the reinstatement of the (renamed) National Unit for Bilingual Intercultural Education (UNEBI) in the Ministry of Education in May 1997, the minister of education invited Juan Carlos Godenzzi, an Andean linguist and one of the leading intellectual advocates for intercultural education, to act as its chief.[23]

Godenzzi moved from Cuzco to Lima to head the UNEBI in May 1997, and remained in that position until September 2002. According to Godenzzi, between 1997 and 2001 the UNEBI (with only five staff members) produced ninety-four bilingual teaching manuals, in Aymara, five regional Quechua variations, and various Amazonian languages (Godenzzi 2001). UNEBI staff also facilitated — with some help from NGOs, universities, and research institutes — bilingual training for over 10,000 teachers working in rural bilingual areas, and provided enough materials so that "each and every classroom in the area where bilingual intercultural education is implemented has its own bilingual library" (Godenzzi 2001: 6).[24] In the years between 1996 and 2000, when I conducted the bulk of my field research, there was a sense that new resources could inject new life into previously anemic efforts. Despite these hopes, there continued to be gaps between the official rhetoric of intercultural education and the pedagogical realities in local schools. Some critics saw this period as one devoted more to the bureaucratic empowerment of the UNEBI, which pursued its agenda with little input from communities, than to responding to the specific needs of educators, parents, and children (Zúñiga et al. 2003). This top-down approach to interculturality stood in sharp contrast to the democratic and participatory promises of the new government agency. Since the fall of Alberto Fujimori in November 2000, there has been an increased emphasis on issues pertaining to indigenous rights. Reflective of this trend, the UNEBI expanded to sixteen staff members and was renamed the National Directorate of Bilingual Intercultural Education (DINEBI) on April 5, 2001, by Valentín Paniagua's transitional administration. According to intercultural activists, the change in name from Unit to Directorate reflected the state's continued and increasing support of EIB as part of national education policy (Godenzzi, personal communication; Zúñiga et al. 2003).

No longer only a unit within a division of the ministry, the DINEBI now has more control over policy decisions, and accordingly may have a more profound impact on legislation affecting bilingual education and language policy (Zúñiga et al. 2003). One of the DINEBI's first actions was to establish a fifteen-member National Consulting Committee of Bilingual Intercultural Education. Of the committee's fifteen members, nine are described as "indigenous professionals" (Godenzzi 2001: 4). The committee held several national-level gatherings to consult with intellectuals, NGO workers, teacher trainers, and bilingual teachers, and then drafted a report on the national politics of languages and cultures in education. Based on this report, the DINEBI prepared a "Strategic Plan" (*Plan Estratégico, 2001–6*) for the future development of bilingual intercultural education in the country. These steps are part of the effort to institutionalize bilingual intercultural education as part of state — and not only government — policy. The distinction between state policy (*política de estado*) and government policy (*política de*

gobierno) is important, as (according to intercultural advocates) state policies remain fixed regardless of future changes in government personnel and
ideology, whereas governmental policies come and go with specific political
parties and their representatives. This new state policy is directed, it should
be stressed, to a national society, not just an indigenous minority. In one of
the first information pamphlets distributed by the UNEBI, its authors state
that Peru's "multicultural condition . . . challenges [Peruvian] education to
promote interculturality as the fundamental principle leading to national
unity" (UNEBI 1998). According to documents like this one and representatives from the Ministry of Education, intercultural education is a national —
and not an indigenous — project.[25] Intercultural education, then, is considered an educational process that, taking the country's cultural diversity as
backdrop, teaches "intercultural dialogue" and promotes respectful interaction among individuals and groups of different cultural backgrounds in
order to achieve national unity. Accordingly, a crucial part of the practical
implementation of this definition is that intercultural education reflects only
a "diversification" of the existing national curriculum, and not a separate
project. There are no special EIB curricula. Instead, the national primary
school curriculum has been modified ("diversified") to include methodologies for acquisition of a second language (to be implemented only in areas
with indigenous populations) and culturally sensitive wording and illustra-
tions. In other words, intercultural education is intended for every Peruvian
citizen. *Bilingual* intercultural education, however, is implemented only in
rural and "marginal" urban settings.

Many of the activists I spoke with disagreed with this distinction, saying
that an important part of their intercultural project was to insert indigenous
languages in nonindigenous spaces, since (according to them) much of the
problem of indigenous marginalization lay in the cultural and linguistic discrimination they and their languages face. Others, however, agreed with the
UNEBI's distinction between "intercultural" and "bilingual-intercultural"
spaces of action, claiming instead that this was the only way to advance
indigenous rights "in a realistic way" that would not, as one linguist put it,
"divide the fatherland."

Intercultural activists in Peru are clearly struggling with the various historical legacies of Peruvian indigenismo. A 2003 report on EIB, for example, worries about the danger of collapsing the difference between an "education for Indians" (with all the racist and paternalist baggage the phrase
carries) and an "indigenous education" (with the stress on indigenous
agency and rights) (Zúñiga et al. 2003). Even in the seemingly more enlightened efforts of the new DINEBI, neoindigenista technocratic policy-making
styles clash with hopes for greater indígena empowerment.

DINEBI officials and EIB activists, however, are not only part of historical patterns. They are also members of broader transnational networks that take part in contemporary debates over indigenous development and new social movements. Their work has been influenced by two recent developments in the region and the world. First, indigenous movements throughout the 1990s in Latin America have been pushing for self-determination, challenging the very definition of the nation-state (Stavenhagen 1992). In this way, activist projects to help give indigenous people social and political capacities are also about challenging the nation.

Second, a surprising new development agenda that blends neoliberal and multicultural issues has provided local activists with a transnational source of legitimacy and financial resources (Brysk 2000a; Gustafson 2002; Van Cott 2000; Hale 2002; Lucero 2002). Both new constitutional reforms and economic development strategies now explicitly embrace multicultural realities and leave behind older notions of assimilation. Though this official multiculturalism is in many respects new, it is not that far removed from previous efforts to make indigenous people relevant actors in a multicultural modernity. And like those previous moments, unequal power relations among indigenous people and their advocates continue to present new challenges.

Indigenous people are well aware of the indigenista project, past and present. For indigenous people and activists alike, the term *indigenismo* is tainted. It is seen as a paternalist, unequal relationship. In Peru, I witnessed many heated debates among activists about the label. They rejected the term *indigenista* or *neoindigenista* (which observers sometimes use to describe their work and writing). Instead, they presented themselves as working within the broader, international context of indigenous activism, and as advocates for indigenous people at a time when indigenous people did not have organizations or leaders of their own.

Often pointing to powerful ethnic federations in Ecuador and Bolivia, activists in the 1990s argued that Peru still lacked autonomous political actors and thus that there was a need for them to work in preparing indigenous people to take on this role. Programs in education are not about controlling indigenous people, activists argued; rather they are meant, in the spirit of Mariátegui and Arguedas (and against the paternalism of González Prada), to empower them. Yet, while contemporary activists seek to claim selected parts of the legacy of these towering indigenistas, they prefer the language of interculturalidad.

Since 2001, an increasing number of indigenous organizations in Peru have embraced bilingual intercultural education as an integral part of the struggle for both cultural and political rights. In fact, "bilingual intercultural education" has become a phrase pointing to broader concerns over democracy, self-determination, citizenship, and social justice. However, there are some important tensions in the structure and function of the project of intercultural education, as EIB is often portrayed as an initiative that comes from civil society and forms part of indigenous rights discourses, and at the same time as a project designed by the state. Moreover, intercultural discourse about democracy, respect for diversity, and indigenous rights notwithstanding, there is still a wide gap between intercultural rhetoric and its implementation in indigenous communities. The dynamic relationships between intercultural activism and indigenous agency are the topic of the second part of this book. Together, the three chapters that follow are ethnographic explorations across various scales — local, national, and international — of the negotiation and contestation of indigenous politics.

Part 11

ETHNOGRAPHIES

3 *Community Politics and Resistance*

CHALLENGING REPRESENTATION

> If [intercultural activists] want to keep our children from
> learning Spanish, then they do not want to make things
> better, they want to keep us at the lower levels of society.
> They say they want to help us, but then why do they want
> our children to believe they are Indians, if Indians in our
> country are always at the bottom?
>
> — Quechua father in Intipacha

In multilingual, multicultural nations such as Peru, education becomes inextricable from questions of minority rights and relations of power. Consider the testimony of a Quechua farmer in the mid-1970s:

Because we are Quechua, because we speak our language and live according to our customs, and because we don't know how to read and write, we live in the world of the night. We have no eyes, and we are invalids like the blind. In contrast, those who know how to read and write live in daylight. They have eyes. It is senseless to stay in the world of darkness because we must progress to be like those who go to school and have eyes. Going to school, we open our eyes, we awake. (Quechua testimony in Montoya 1990: 94)

This testimony is a version of what is commonly referred to in the Andes as the "school myth." Collections of indigenous conceptions of school, reading, and writing (Ortiz 1970; Montoya 1990, 1998) and analyses of the unequal social relations reproduced in rural schools abound (Molina et al. 1972; Portocarrero and Oliart 1989; Howard-Malverde and Canessa 1995). Always present in the many versions of this myth is the idea that the process of learning how to read and write is painful, but that learning these skills will allow one to "see," and thus to change and progress.[1] Furthermore, according to these testimonies and to the many highland people with whom I spoke, it is not only writing, but writing in Spanish, that empowers one in Peru.

According to many language professionals, this myth has harmful cultural consequences. The acquisition of Spanish among indigenous highlanders is often interpreted (by state bureaucrats, NGO practitioners, intercultural

87

activists, and others) as a loss of indigenous language and culture. Moreover, many Peruvian activists and intellectuals attribute this to the paradoxical role that education has played in the Andes. As Rodrigo Montoya states, "On the one hand, [schools] contribute to the liberation of feudal oppression, and on the other, they liquidate indigenous culture" (Montoya 1986: 251). Clearly, the concept of cultural loss is problematic. Analytically, culture is more dynamic than this. Academic discussions have moved away from essentialist notions of "cultural survival" and present instead culture as "continually reworked understandings of the world" and as something that "is not 'lost', but transformed" (K. Warren 1992: 205; cf. Clifford 1988; Gould 1998; and Hale 1994b). However, given the dominant (and racist) representations of Indian backwardness that make Quechua identity and language seem like obstacles to progress, it is not surprising that many activists use the language of loss to describe the experiences of indigenous students in classrooms. Indeed, in their view, each day of school reenacts the act of conquest, in which European forces vanquished indigenous ones.

Since the encounter between Andeans and Europeans, education in the Andean region, especially the learning of reading and writing, has been linked to struggles of class and identity. Throughout colonial times in Peru, education among Andeans was a privilege limited to the Indian elite, and it was directly tied to Spanish strategies of colonization (Lockhart 1968; Stern 1982; Montoya 1990; Mannheim 1991: 65). By the 1900s, Quechua highland peoples continuously expressed their need for Spanish as a step toward social mobility, and demanded the right to education, especially to read and write in Spanish, and to build schools for their children in their communities (Montoya 1986, 1990). Current indigenous and peasant struggles in highland Cuzco also highlight the inadequacies of schools and education, whether teaching is conducted in Spanish or in Quechua. Often, as parents voiced the significance of education for their children, they also recognized and complained about the shortcomings of the educational system, both before and after the insertion of intercultural education. One common complaint had to do with the schools themselves. I heard many descriptions (by teachers, indigenous parents, and activists) of highland schools as "decrepit." In fact, high on the list of indigenous demands placed on the Fujimori administration by the mid-1990s were new schools. Relegated to remote areas, highland schools usually lack the most basic material resources. Students are lucky if they have chairs to sit on and tables or desks to write on. In some cases, they are lucky if they have paper and pencils. Of the dozens of schools I visited, only two had anything that could be called toilets: holes in the ground around which the community had erected walls. But more than the buildings themselves, parental concern was mainly with the teaching imparted in schools, and particularly with the teachers responsible for their children's education.

During four trips to Cuzco between 1996 and 1999, I tried to understand the goals and ideals of bilingual intercultural education in the country by exploring the diverse dimensions of its implementation. I spoke with NGO program directors, national and regional state representatives, teacher trainers, highland teachers, indigenous parents, aunts, and uncles, and indigenous children throughout the department of Cuzco. What I found, as is often the case with bilingual education, was a powerful rejection, by indigenous parents and many highland teachers, of intercultural education in practice. The association of indigenous language, indigenous identity, and low socioeconomic status seemed absolute to parents, who preferred concrete results (seeing their children speaking and reading in Spanish) to abstract talk of social and economic rights. Although many indigenous parents with whom I spoke were sympathetic to the ideals behind intercultural education, and had in some cases been open to trying out "the new education," after a few years and myriad problems with lack of resources and confusion over teaching methods (among other issues), they grew tired of waiting for results.

This rejection of bilingual education stands in contrast to the findings of linguists and activists who point to growing grass-roots demand for intercultural education. Zúñiga and her colleagues (2000: 40–43) offer the results of survey research that reveal that there is "clear and overwhelming" demand on the part of teachers and indigenous parents for bilingual education. Seventy-five percent of parents surveyed believed that education of their children was better when it was in both their native language (Quechua or Aymara) and Spanish; over 90 percent of teachers expressed support for the superiority of bilingual education over education in either the native language or Spanish alone. These responses, however, need to be placed in context before they can be accepted as compelling evidence of popular demand. There is a difference between opinion over a proposed curriculum and the reactions to an implemented one. While parents may express support for bilingual education, this initial support does not preclude serious concerns about the ways in which schools are run, lessons are taught, and community voices are heard.

Some of their concerns revolved around the contradictions parents saw in activists and teachers who promoted indigenous language learning while sending their own children to foreign-language institutes or to nonbilingual schools in the nearest city. Moreover, group discussions about interculturality, the respect of cultural difference, and "horizontal" (democratic) behavior rarely translated into changes to educational spaces and interactions. As I discuss more fully in Chapter 4, teachers complained that teacher training sessions were not long enough for them to grasp the nuances of the new teaching methods, and that while they were expected to implement these novel ideas in creative ways, they were not provided with the resources necessary to put them into practice.

An additional complaint of parents against intercultural education was that it was just another way to keep them from learning Spanish, and thus from being able to make their way (*insertarnos*) — on their own terms — into Peruvian society. As in previous periods of indigenista reforms in which the "Indian problem" was to be solved by non-Indians, indigenous people were understandably concerned about the distance that separated them from their advocates. A critical source of tension between proponents of intercultural education and indigenous parents is the difference in ideas about language maintenance.

While a strong motivation for intercultural activists is indigenous language revival and maintenance, most of the indigenous parents and community leaders I spoke with did not believe that learning Spanish would in any way detract from their ability — or their children's — to speak, understand, and (if literate) read in their native language. Moreover, drawing from a reality that usually allows indigenous children only an elementary education (and only four or five years at that), indigenous parents often stated that spending two years learning in the child's native tongue — as bilingual intercultural education methodology dictates — before tackling Spanish is just too much time. Clearly, for indigenous Peruvians, becoming literate is not equated only with learning how to read; it is equated with learning how to read in Spanish, and disassociated almost entirely from indigenous languages. While the historical and social conditions that have merged to establish Spanish as the dominant language in Peru remain in place, intercultural activists are actively trying to change this by arguing that the development of indigenous languages — alongside the acquisition of Spanish — does not have to detract from the socioeconomic advancement and empowerment of indigenous peoples. In fact, not only does learning and developing indigenous languages not detract from the advancement of indigenous peoples in Peruvian society, activists argue, but it can actually foster their democratic inclusion in the nation.

This chapter details the effects of intercultural activism in the highlands by focusing on community politics.[2] In particular, I examine the concerns of Quechua parents and highland community leaders about family and community, and their explicit attempts at determining their place in the nation. By contrasting the actions and voices of indigenous highlanders with those of intercultural activists, this chapter shows how some Quechua communities in Cuzco have become sites of political struggle in which indigenous people assert their rights and transform local politics in ways unanticipated by their advocates.

Power and Representation: Searching for Indigenous Autonomy

Wrapping an alpaca blanket around my body, already layered in thermal underwear, two long-sleeved shirts, a sweater, and a fleece jacket, I sat huddled close to Juana, a good friend and the director of a small school in Ccara, a community in a harshly cold and desolate region of Cuzco. We were listening to a small group of authorities on education policy, including a representative of the Peruvian government's regional education center, a teacher trainer from a local NGO involved in education programs in the area, a health specialist from the nearest medical post (about a five-hour walk), and a teacher from a community near Cuzco. Packed into one of the school's three classrooms, women and men from Ccara listened patiently to the reasons the visitors presented for the forthcoming change in their children's education. By way of introduction, the NGO representative proudly informed them that Ccara had been chosen as one of ten communities that the Ministry of Education in Lima had recently added to its jurisdiction. This meant, among other things, that teaching at their school would no longer be conducted in Spanish only.

At this point, the highland teacher who had come with the authorities launched into a discussion in Quechua about the importance of using a child's native language prior to a second language — in this case Spanish — in teaching reading and writing. "If your children learn how to read and write in Quechua," he said, "they will then be able to learn Spanish much better and faster than if we try to develop reading and writing skills in a language with which they are not familiar." At this, some of the parents began talking among themselves and demanded the right to speak. Realizing that the community members' concerns might not be heard, Luis, the president, stood up and challenged the proposal. In eloquent Spanish, he claimed to speak for all the parents of children in his community and stated that teaching the children of Ccara in Quechua would only limit their future possibilities. "They learn Quechua from us, their parents, in their homes with their families. In school they need to learn the skills that will help them become something more than just campesinos. Look at you," he said, pointing to the teacher. "You are dressed in *misti* [mestizo] clothes, you speak Spanish and probably English, and you are in a position of power. Did you learn how to read and write in Quechua or in Spanish?" Luis was not only underlining the importance of Spanish. He was also challenging the pedagogical optimism of activists who saw Quechua instruction as a way to improve education generally and Spanish language acquisition specifically. Highland communities have had too much familiarity with disappointing state reforms to accept these new promises uncritically.

The struggle for language rights and higher-quality education in Peru has often been at the heart of debates in the highlands about the rights of indigenous Peruvians as full citizens of the nation-state. In the 1990s, initiatives by advocates of bilingual intercultural education — such as teacher-training workshops, parent schools, and the implementation of intercultural programs in highland classrooms — developed into new spaces for sociopolitical debate and action. Parents of Quechua children in Cuzco's highland schools told me they rejected bilingual education and generally saw proponents of intercultural education as outsiders trying to impose disadvantageous educational changes. The teachers with whom I spoke in both the Ausangate and the Sacred Valley either rejected the program or found it worthy in theory but impossible to implement, even after intensive training workshops and sessions geared toward inculcating in them an intercultural mentality. These teachers continue to face tremendous obstacles in their routine attempts at teaching indigenous children, although they now criticize intercultural activists specifically for presenting pedagogic guidelines that, according to many of them, have proved useless for the improvement of education in the highlands. These are not minor disagreements. At stake are both urgent material concerns over livelihood (struggling against poverty) and the cultural unease of conflicting notions of belonging (being Quechua *and* Peruvian).

William Roseberry provides a useful framework for thinking about these conflicting visions of language and culture. He argues (1996: 83–84) that we should understand ethnicity and nationalism as "languages of community and contention":

Languages of ethnicity [and] nationalism . . . draw upon images of primordial associations and identifications but take their specific and practical forms as languages of contention and opposition [in the present]. They typically involve movements for "our" people, "our" culture . . . against . . . minority rule. The images, and the movements they inspire, are products of and responses to particular forces, structures, and events . . . and they derive their community-forming power from their apparent relationship to those forces and events.

Much of the conflict over representation comes from the strikingly different languages used by intercultural activists and community leaders to describe and imagine indigenous Peruvians. The confusion over who "our people" are and who should speak for them is central to questions of indigenous self-determination and autonomy. The ambiguities and tensions involved in the development of "languages of community" are certainly not new. Chapter 2 described how indigenismo, as an intellectual, cultural, and political project, was itself characterized by similar contradictions.

It is useful, however, to take a closer ethnographic look at how these tensions are influencing the contemporary lives of some indigenous Peruvians. By exploring the criticism of bilingual intercultural education and the conflict caused in highland communities by its implementation, my research in Cuzco reveals the interaction of "languages of contention and community." These languages point to both the efforts to reimagine a more inclusive inter-cultural Peru and local struggles to set the precise terms of that interculturality. Thus the following pages explore the particular ways in which ethnicity in the Peruvian highlands is being played out as teachers, parents, and activists attempt to renegotiate in different ways the relation of indigenous people to the Peruvian nation-state.

Commonly considered an "oppressed language" (Albó 1977), Quechua is intimately linked to the struggle of its speakers against imposed linguistic, cultural, religious, and political structures.[3] Whereas in many parts of the Peruvian Andes such imposition has usually involved mandatory schooling of indigenous Quechuas in Spanish, in highland Cuzco indigenous peoples now struggle against what they perceive as the imposition of education in Quechua.[4] Remarkably, not one parent I spoke with ever expressed an unqualified positive opinion about the implementation of the "new education." Although many of the parents with whom I spoke did recognize the goals of the program, for instance, they also stressed that the pursuit of those goals did not take into account their reality. Parents were certainly not against preserving Quechua. However, they either saw Quechua preservation as a process their families practiced outside of school or saw Spanish acquisition as more vital for their children's future.

I should stress, however, that concerns over bilingual intercultural education were complicated. For some, this kind of education had to be openly rejected because in their view it could only hurt their children's chances for social mobility. Others disagreed with some aspects of the new education policies, but were reluctant to reject all the policies and goals out of hand. Moreover, there were also differences in how community members, teachers, NGO workers, and state officials spoke about community responses to bilingual intercultural education. Not surprisingly, these representations also varied across contexts and audiences. In schools, ministries, and NGOs, EIB discourses could take different shapes, as we will see. Indeed, bilingual education itself was a very contested term, as it meant one thing for communities (i.e., we want Spanish) and another for intercultural activists (i.e., indigenous language instruction is as important as Spanish). While there were various ways in which communities reacted to these new policies, I never encountered any community that embraced the reforms enthusiastically. Though parents certainly reject mistreatment of their children and recognize the discrimination against them in highland schools, they also express their belief in education in Spanish as one way to mitigate these prejudices.

It is also worth mentioning that during all of my trips to Cuzco, the parents, teachers, and community leaders with whom I spoke often expressed their confidence in Quechua as a language that will never disappear. In her examination of bilingual education in Puno, Peru, in the 1970s and 1980s, Nancy Hornberger alludes to this faith in the lasting capacity of the Quechua language, which she terms a "linguistic ideology of loyalty" (1988). Activists, however, fear that teaching Spanish at the expense of Quechua will inevitably lead to the extinction of the Quechua language and, by extension, to the loss of Quechua cultural practices and identity.

On a bright winter day in June 1998, I met a man from Urubamba (in the Sacred Valley) while I was waiting for a friend at the regional office of the Educational Services Unit. He was there to ask about "the new education," as he called intercultural education. We talked a little (in Spanish) while we both waited, and one of his remarks stayed with me: "If my son loses his culture, it is because he wants to. And he will never lose it, even though he may choose to hide it. But that is just survival. It is our right as Peruvians."

I asked many parents from communities in both the Ausangate and the Sacred Valley if they worried that by going to school to learn to read and write in Spanish, their sons and daughters would forget Quechua, lose their identity, or become mestizos (a transformation often discussed by activists as a consequence of monolingual education). These are some of the responses I received:

Choque: You [anthropologists] care about our culture. We, too, care. We will never be able to be mestizos, really. We are campesinos, but by learning how to read and write, our children can defend themselves in the mestizo's world.

Ignacio: It is not that education erases our identity. What it erases, in part, is the identity assigned to us by those who are not like us.

These voices reveal important insights about the structure of the debate over education ("you anthropologists" and "those not like us" vs. "we campesinos"). They also suggest that their own identity (Quechua/indigenous/campesino) is more complicated and perhaps less fragile than activists suggest. Aware of the power of imposed labels, Choque and Ignacio view Spanish-language education as providing tools to improve indigenous lives and to fend off the cultural and physical threats of the outside world. As in many postcolonial settings, learning the language of the oppressor is an important way to resist that oppression.

Indeed, some prominent indigenous intellectuals have gone so far as to appropriate Spanish as an "indigenous language." The distinguished Aymara leader and former vice president of Bolivia Victor Hugo Cárdenas remarked at a 2001 conference on indigenous movements:

I know that Spanish arrived with the Conquest. But today Spanish is not the language of the conquistador. Today, it is an indigenous language. Native indigenous languages along with Spanish are our languages [idiomas propios]. Moreover, an indigenous person has to know an additional foreign language, otherwise indigenous peoples will be the objects of study of yesterday's anthropologists, museum objects, not the subjects of development. (Cárdenas 2001)

While some might say this is simply the old message of assimilationists, Cárdenas is making a more radical Bakhtinian move, recognizing that language is not the unproblematic property of any one individual or group, but the very terrain of contestation on which people make lives and communities (Bakhtin 1981 [1934]: 294). Although defending, maintaining, and preventing the so-called deterioration of Quechua is of vital importance to intercultural activists, many highland teachers and NGO practitioners as well as indigenous people themselves perceive the acquisition of Spanish as essential for social advancement.

Nevertheless, many activists working in Cuzco as professional linguists are concerned with the "loss" not only of indigenous culture/identity but of indigenous languages. Linguistic studies about interference or borrowing, for instance, focus primarily on the influence of Spanish on Quechua (Godenzzi, ed., 1992). Highlighting the negative consequences of such influence, these writers emphasize the diglossic condition of Quechua in Peru (Cerrón-Palomino 1982, 1989) and note the diminishing numbers of monolingual Quechua-speakers as primary justification for efforts to rescue, revitalize, and spread Quechua throughout the highlands (Gleich 1994). However, the question of language rights is often complicated when the speakers of "endangered languages" struggle not for the defense of their own language but for the acquisition of a second language, usually the dominant language, as a strategy for pursuing economic betterment. While the social and political conditions that create such a need should continue to be challenged, linguistic studies focusing on the revival or rescue of indigenous languages should also consider the often conflicting demands made by the speakers of those languages.

Intercultural activists are working toward the elevation of Quechua to equal status with Spanish by promoting Quechua literature, writing scientific articles in Quechua, and working toward developing computer keyboards compatible with indigenous languages. As we will see in Chapter 5, they also focus on Spanish, English, and "global tools" as part of the training offered to select indigenous intellectuals. However, Quechua parents and community leaders in Cuzco told me that proponents of EIB do not address the linguistic hierarchies in place in the country today. Though intercultural activists recognize these hierarchies and acknowledge that they will take a long time to change, their work with teachers, parents, and children does not seem to take them into account. Discussions about this with highland teachers and indigenous parents evoked comments that painted images of idealistic activists who "have no idea about the real world we live in." Teachers often stated that activists "assume that we are already in an intercultural environment." But, as one indigenous parent said, "even if they think they live in an intercultural country, we know we live in a racist one. Our point of departure in battling racism is to educate our children. And educating them means that they will learn Spanish."

Politicizing Community: The Struggles of Quechua Parents

As a way to promote their ideals among parents who tend to reject bilingual education, intercultural activists began establishing parents' schools (*escuelas de padres*) in early 1998. These "schools" are gatherings of intercultural education advocates, NGO workers, teachers, and parents in which all are expected to interact and discuss the educational changes taking place in highland schools, and the problems that, according to intercultural activists, hinder children's learning. Organizers of these schools tell teachers that their principal purpose is to educate parents about their children's health, to convince them of the positive effects of intercultural and bilingual education, and to provide an intercultural forum in which they can raise questions and exchange ideas. The activists and teachers who lead these schools address issues such as malnutrition, first aid, family abandonment, school dropout rates, child abuse (physical, emotional, and sexual), and illiteracy.

I attended ten escuela de padres gatherings. Two took place in the same community; the others were dispersed in communities throughout the Ausangate. Many attempts to inaugurate these schools in various other regions of the Cuzco highlands failed for lack of parental interest or attendance. However, intercultural activists working in the Ausangate had been more successful.[5] Gatherings were usually announced two weeks in advance at community assemblies, they were always held in community school classrooms, and they had to be scheduled around the agricultural calendar.

The first time I attended an escuela, I arrived in the highland community of Yanacocha with Silvia, a friend from the nearby medical post. Taking advantage of the advertisement of these schools as forums for "discussions about community development, such as bilingual education," Silvia was planning to integrate a discussion about highland children's health into broader discussions about education. The meeting was scheduled to begin at 9:00 in the morning. We arrived at 8:45, and the room was already full. Approximately twenty men and women were in a small classroom. Most of the men were seated on chairs, desks, or benches that had been made available for the meeting. Except for a select few, the women were all seated on the dirt floor of the classroom. As they waited for the organizers to arrive, the men sat quietly and the women tended to the infants that most had brought with them. Once the session leaders entered the room, the parents rustled around a bit, but no one spoke until the director welcomed them, in Quechua, and announced the inauguration of Yanacocha's first escuela de padres. Immediately after the welcome speech, the director turned to Silvia, introduced her, and informed the parents that she was there to talk to them about the "proper" way to care for their children, especially about hygiene.

The entire session was about child health care, and took place in both Quechua and Spanish. The session leader, Silvia, and the teachers present addressed the parents in Spanish first, later translating what they had said into Quechua. Both mothers and fathers were visibly uncomfortable as topics ranged from the eating patterns of children to menstruation and birth control. For most of the session, there was almost no discussion and the voices that filled the room were those of Silvia and the teachers. When two hours had passed, the director declared the end of the session, and stated that the next meeting was scheduled for two weeks from that date. As the session leaders and teachers applauded, parents seemed a bit confused. Turpo, the community president, stood up and asked, in Quechua, why there had been no discussion about education. When the director replied that that was the topic for the next gathering, Turpo argued that parents had come to the escuela because they had been told that they would be able to discuss their children's education. As Turpo's impatience became increasingly apparent, the director reminded him that two weeks from that date they would gather to discuss education. Turpo, however, declared that parents did not want to wait another two weeks to discuss what was happening in their schools. Finally the community president and the school director reached an agreement, and the next meeting of the escuela was rescheduled for the following week.

More parents than had attended the first gathering attended the second meeting of the escuela in Yanacocha. This time, the session was led by one of the two teachers stationed in Yanacocha. The teacher began the discussion by asking parents, in both Quechua and Spanish, to evaluate Peruvian education, placing emphasis on the differences between education before (the most recent) bilingual education reform and after. One after another, men stood up and talked, in Spanish, about respect. The first man introduced himself and gave his testimony:

Before, we were hit if we spoke Quechua; we were not allowed to speak the language anywhere, not even outside of school. If a teacher saw us talking in Quechua, he would yell at us and we would get it in school the next day. Now, we are told these things will change. Our children will not be hit anymore and they will learn in Quechua and schools will teach Quechua and Spanish.

When he sat down, a second man gave his statement:

Once I was in the market with my friend, and we were talking to each other in Quechua, and we ran into our teacher from school. He heard us and said, "You dumb Indians. You will never be anything but dumb Indians because you will never learn." My friend and I didn't go to school again for a week because we were scared of the teacher. But the next time we went to school, he had not forgotten, and he gave it to us with the stick. But the worst part was not the pain of the stick. It was the shame of what he said about us being dumb and being Indians. Now, they tell us, our children will not be ashamed, and I think that is good.

Four more men stood up after the first two, all speaking about similar experiences and ending with short acknowledgments of the potential benefits of bilingual education for their children. Encouraged by the apparent support of the community for bilingual-education policies, the leader thanked the fathers who spoke for sharing their stories and used them to justify what he called "the new education." Launching into a discussion about the importance of developing self-esteem among children and using their "previous knowledge" to build new concepts, he then shifted to statements about increased parental involvement with their children's education: "You are now responsible for your child's education. It will no longer be the sole responsibility of the teacher, because you need to work with your children so that they will be better citizens."

At this last statement, one of the mothers present gathered her skirts, picked herself up from the ground, and began to speak in Quechua:

Our husbands have not made themselves clear. We do not think this change is good for our children. They speak Quechua with us, and they should speak Spanish in school. That is what school is for. If it is for teaching Quechua, why should we waste our time sending our children to school, when they can speak at home? And being a citizen means speaking Spanish.

Finished, she sat back down abruptly and nudged her husband. Acknowledging his wife's request, the father stood up to speak:

As my wife has said, we are not in favor of this change. We think that now teachers are not expected to do any work, and that you want our children to stay poor and be like us. What I want most for my son is that he is not a campesino, like me. And being an Indian is worse! So you shouldn't tell [our children] to be Indian!

This statement seemed to loosen up many of the school's participants. One by one, fathers stated their objections to what they described as the imposition of policies that would only further their children's marginalization in society.

The leader seemed somewhat taken aback by the suddenness of these attacks, but he regained his composure quickly and countered with a set of questions: "How much did school help you? Do you think you speak Spanish well? Did going to school and being spoken to only in Spanish help *you* become wealthier? Don't you understand that this change is not an option? It comes from the Ministry [of Education] and is mandatory."

Education reform initiatives came as much from intellectuals and development professionals as they did from the state. Moreover (as Chapter 4 illustrates), many bilingual programs were funded and run by NGOs or co-managed by NGOs and the state. However, due in large part to statements like those made by this session leader, parents increasingly assumed that education reform was a state initiative, and they began to act out against bilingual education policies by demanding changes from the state's regional education offices and their representatives. Significantly, during municipal and other local government elections in October 1998, a group of fathers from several highland communities organized to vote against the candidate who supported bilingual education, and made the two-day trip to the city of Cuzco to participate in the elections. When I spoke to them about their decision, all of the men made clear that this was their only reason for voting. This example is particularly striking in view of the fact that indigenous campesinos in the highlands were ambivalent at best about the election process, recognizing the corruption characteristic of formal politics in Peru.

The efforts to legitimize educational changes by using the state backfired. After the session of the parents' school, activists were unable to schedule another meeting. Parents were angry with both the state and the NGO. After the meeting, a father named Tomás confronted the session leader with an interesting question: "You want us to say it's good that you teach our children in Quechua," he began. "But if that's so good for our children, why don't you teach your own children in Quechua too? Why do you send them to French or English institutes?" Pointing to the fact that many activists send their children to the Alliance Française or to the North American Institute in Cuzco and not to regional Quechua-language institutes, this father was making a statement about the socioeconomic and ethnic identities associated with language. In Peru, as in most Latin American countries, not everyone can afford to send their children to private language institutes. By emphasizing the real connection in Peru between language, class, and prestige, Tomás was making a simple but powerful point: Teach our children Quechua and they will remain poor. Teach them Spanish, English, or French and they will get ahead. When I spoke with Tomás later that evening, he reiterated these concerns: "If Quechua were privileged, the situation might be different, and we might even want our children to read and write in our language. But until that happens, our tactics for the improvement of our children's education are still determined by our reality."

Intercultural activists often express frustration about parents' "lack of understanding" and lack of support: "I wish they would see that we're work-ing for them and that what we want is for them to realize that they have rights. That they have the right to use their language and to education, for example, because they are citizens." The activist who said this, an education specialist and NGO worker from Cuzco, insisted that the parents' rejection was due to a lack of understanding, a lack of internalization of their rights as citizens of Peru. She failed to see that parents rejected bilingual education for the same reasons she thought they should support it. Trying to exercise their rights to language and education, parents demanded the right to access to the dominant language and to education that would provide that access.

I attended another parents' school gathering during a trip to Uppis, another community in the Ausangate region of Cuzco, later that year. Like the others I had been to, this meeting ended in tense confrontations between indigenous parents and the teacher leading the discussion. An aspect of the meeting that had also been a part of previous meetings was the escalation of tension after a few women spoke, sometimes directly contradicting their husbands' statements. During this meeting, however, one of the couples in the room had been unified in their critiques of bilingual education, and they had been equally vocal in expressing their discomfort with education reform. When I asked them why they had attended the meeting and how they felt about their children's education, the husband answered:

We came because they said benefits would come to those who were here. But we also came because we wanted to have our voices heard, and we didn't want our children to go to school to learn Quechua. We will continue to fight because if we allow this to happen, our children will continue to exist in this country without being part of it.

The notion of children existing in the country "without being a part of it" was something I heard many times in Cuzco and throughout other high-land regions, both from indigenous parents and from teachers, NGO work-ers, and intercultural activists. This seemed to be a preoccupation that both sides had in common, although once again the difference lay in the solution to that problem. While parents stressed Spanish instruction for their already Quechua-fluent children, activists sought to "elevate" Quechua as a written language first, then move to Spanish. Given these contrasting visions, con-flicts between parents and activists were hardly surprising.

With the spaces opened by intercultural activists to include indigenous par-ents, new and unexpected possibilities began to emerge. Rather than being a stage on which parents were expected to follow activist scripts, these gath-erings allowed indigenous parents in general, and mothers in particular, a space in which to construct alternative readings of the needs of their children and their communities. Unlike activists who feared for the extinction of Quechua in a Spanish-dominant world, parents described another reality in which Quechua was already a language of community and Spanish-language acquisition was more important to their children's ability to master what Roseberry calls a language of contention. Teach children only in Quechua, parents seem to say, and they remain in the same marginalized space and place they are now; teach them Spanish and they acquire the means to contest this marginalization. Some might argue that indigenous parents' desire for Spanish was a symptom of their colonial position. They were seeing themselves, as Frantz Fanon might say, through the eyes of their oppressors (Fanon 1963). In other words, they were the familiar victims of false consciousness, unable to see clearly the source of their misery or the way to escape from it. While not diminishing the ideological force of racism in Peru, I think it is a mistake to dismiss their concerns. Rather than see their consciousness as "objective" or "false," it makes more sense to follow Antonio Gramsci (1971) in seeing that like the "consciousness" of all groups, theirs is composed of contradictory elements. These elements can shift as parts of dynamic processes of resistance and adaptation. As other scholars have noted, to understand these processes anthropologists must engage in close ethnographic examinations of the interactions between state and community, dominant and subaltern groups, and men and women (Hale 1994a; Roseberry 1996; Hall 1996 [1986]).

"Our Husbands Have Not Made Themselves Clear": Indigenous Women, Education, and Power

By late 1998, indigenous parents in various communities throughout the Ausangate region had grown impatient and decided that they would no longer await a solution from outsiders but would rather work among themselves to develop an alternative to the educational changes being imposed in their communities. At many of the gatherings I attended, I was struck by the important role that women played in setting the tone of the exchanges between parents and activists. While in some ways they would conform to the expectations of what some might consider broader Andean and Peruvian patterns — they sat on the ground while their husbands sat above them, they spoke in Quechua while their husbands spoke in Spanish, they allowed their husbands to speak while they listened — it did not take long for indigenous mothers to move out of these assigned roles and take the lead in bringing up questions their husbands seemed reluctant to ask. Though de la Cadena (1995) is right in saying that women are "more Indian" in that they often lack the access to specific urban labor markets and to Spanish-language acquisition that allows their husbands to pass as mestizo, it is worth emphasizing that the ties that indigenous women have to family and home also represent resources with which they can defend their children's interests. Negotiating the terms of their own "contradictory consciousness," indigenous women are clearly aware of the gendered nature of economic opportunities as they protect the interests of their children, their daughters in particular.

Gloria, a mother I met at one of the escuela gatherings told me about her daughter, Laura, who had recently moved to Cuzco to work as a maid. With difficulty she recounted the painful story: "The man from that house abused her. . . . He knew he could do it because no one would care about her; because she had no one in Cuzco. Now she has returned and . . . she will stay with us. She can't speak Spanish, and that's why she was abused." Gloria also told me that her own parents had sent her to school, where her male teacher raped her. Ashamed, she had never told her parents about his abuse, but she had refused to return to school, and because of this she had been severely punished by her father. "My brothers also took advantage of the fact that my father hit me, so they would beat me up too and call me stupid because I didn't like school. But I knew it would be worse if they knew why I didn't want to go. I was afraid they would hit me harder for that." Inhabiting the intersecting spheres of racial and gender inequalities, Gloria and other Quechua women faced especially difficult choices. Gloria feared what would happen to her daughter if she sent her to school, and this is why she had sent only her sons there.

In the Andes, it is common for girls to stay home and boys to go to school (Harvey 1989; Ames 1999; Oliart 2000). This practice is not always or only the result of the kind of violence Gloria described (see also Harvey 1994); it can also be attributed to the gendered ideas about progress, social mobility, and work that define and devalue women, especially indigenous women (Bourque and Warren 1981; de la Cadena 1995). However, since 1998, working to increase girls' attendance at school has become an important part of the struggle for intercultural activism. It is remarkable, though, that old gendered ideas are at work even when girls go to new intercultural schools, where they are often expected to help with lunch, and can begin to eat only after the boys have been served. While they remain a challenge for the "new education," these gender inequalities have been a subject of discussion among activists and teachers.

Intercultural activists are increasingly sensitive to the importance of addressing both gender and ethnic inequalities. By 1998, most conference meetings and workshops incorporated gender into discussions about health, reproductive rights, domestic abuse, and economic opportunities. These discussions were also clearly about gender and not just women, as they explored the ways in which both men and women were part of the problems of and solutions to gendered inequalities. Reflecting the spirit of intercul-turality that opposed separatist agendas around ethnicity or gender, activists sought to weave these discussions of gender within broader conversations of community and development. This strategy may have also reflected the importance of gender in the agendas of international funders. The idea of lit-eracy workshops for mothers fitted nicely within these growing concerns about gender and development. But the push for these workshops, at least in the Ausangate, seemed to have come not only from the NGOs but also (and in many cases primarily) from indigenous women.

In late 1998, Gloria told me about new ideas for literacy workshops. Gloria had heard that mothers had begun to organize in nearby communi-ties: "I heard some mothers talking the other day about learning how to read and write so they can teach their children at home. This would be good for me, so I can teach my daughter, and she doesn't have to go anywhere. Do you know anything about this?" she asked. Gloria's comments were the first I had heard about this idea. I soon became aware, however, that women in various communities throughout the Ausangate region were demanding lit-eracy training for mothers from the NGOs working in their community schools. The women's strategy was to propose to teachers and NGO repre-sentatives that if they taught mothers Spanish by teaching them to read in Quechua ("the way they say they teach our children"), then the mothers would support the activists' efforts to modify their children's education. "If we learn Spanish," Rosario, a mother from another community, told me, "then we can help our own children, especially if the schools are teaching in Quechua only." These mothers were proposing to take control of what their children learned by consciously developing a way to use NGOs and intercultural education for their own purposes.

During a trip to another community in the Ausangate, I discussed these experiences with Ignacio, the community president. After some general con-versation about education I asked him if he had heard about any women in the community who had been organizing literacy workshops. He had. "[A group of mothers] just asked Madre Leticia [one of the regional bilingual-education supervisors] about this a few days ago. She thought it was a great idea, . . . and asked the NGO director. But she says the NGO can't get some-one up to the community to teach them until next month." Unfortunately, by the time mothers were beginning to organize into literacy groups (in late 1998), I was preparing to leave the country, so I was unable to attend or fol-low the development of one of these groups. However, when I returned to Peru in 1999 I found out that two of the NGOs with which I had worked in Cuzco were becoming more and more involved with adult literacy. The director of one of them was working on a request for funding for such a proj-ect. The NGO personnel with whom I discussed these initiatives all stated that it was a sign of the patience and tolerance of mothers and the intransigence of fathers who continued to challenge their programs. "I love watching these women try to learn how to read. You should see their faces," Ilda, a program coordinator, told me. "They are so happy, and for us this is a great sign of their acceptance of Quechua and of our goals."

I left Peru as these workshops were beginning, and it is important for future research to document how these workshops are working and what changes, if any, have come about in indigenous women's ideas about language and intercultural education. The women with whom I spoke before the establishment of these workshops were set on one goal only: learning Spanish. I wondered what would happen if they began to read in Quechua. Could they then read literary works by Arguedas, for example? And if they were then able to learn Spanish, would they organize schools for their daughters? Could this lead to different ideas about women's rights? Indigenous feminisms? Further investigation would do well to focus on these questions and the state of current NGO literacy programs.

In August 1999 I talked with Andrés, a linguist and strong advocate for intercultural education, about the challenges intercultural activists faced in the coming years. When I asked him specifically if the parents' schools had helped in their endeavor, he replied unenthusiastically: "Some. I've heard about literacy programs that some NGOs are conducting with mothers. That seems to be a positive result." For Andrés, it seemed, the fact that mothers were learning how to read and write in Quechua and Spanish was a "positive result" that was not worthy of much of his attention. Meanwhile, Quechua mothers were looking to their children's future by learning skills that would help remove them from the margins of Peruvian society. In doing so, women were actively redefining the scope and content of the program.

Crafting Spaces for Indigenous Empowerment: Community-Controlled Schools

Even if including the concerns of Quechua parents is part of activists' theoretical goals, by the end of 1999 they had failed to do so in practice. Although many acknowledged the importance of Spanish, for example, the implementation of the program in highland schools still focused on Quechua. The parents with whom I spoke in the late 1990s told me that this made them feel that activists like Andrés disregard their opinions. While many activists clearly state that they recognize the importance of indigenous participation in the development of education and language policies that affect them, they also question indigenous parents' capacity to choose what is best for their children and underestimate their understanding of bilingual education "as a project and as a pedagogical innovation." Consider the words of Andrés, one of the most vocal proponents in Cuzco of bilingual intercultural education. Though he considers himself Andean and a speaker of Quechua, his own language suggests the need to explore the outsider/insider divide that often separates activists from communities:

What we want is the affirmation of all our indigenous people in the face of social discrimination. But to do that we need to rediscover our own culture, and Quechua highlanders need to discover new possibilities of reading their own reality. I think parents of Quechua children are only very much aware of their reality today. Unfortunately, unless they can look ahead — and I know it's hard to do when you have to look at your present, not your future, to survive — parents will remain opposed, in general, to bilingual intercultural education and to us. This also means that because of their attitude, parents will keep their children in their existing conditions of marginalization.

Andrés's comments and those of many other activists projected images of parents discriminating against their own children. As Miriam, an NGO program leader, put it, "They don't even realize they're hurting their children's self-esteem and development because of their own narrow views." This attitude was not lost on parents or on community leaders, and many talked openly with me about their concerns regarding the intentions of intercultural education advocates. "We understand what they want to do," Roberto, father of two and president of a community in the Ausangate, told me:

They think we're stupid. They talk to us as if we were dumb. Why would they think we want to hurt our children? If this education they proposed proved better, then we'd accept it. But we have no results. They've given us no results. And *we* live this reality. They are outsiders. We know what our children need, so they don't have to experience the kind of marginalization that we have. . . . What we need is our own school, run by our own community, with our own wise men [*yachaqkuna*] to teach.

The reference to Quechua wise men or elders as teachers surprised me, because these men are respected for their extensive cultural and religious knowledge and tend to speak only Quechua. The reference to a community-controlled school intrigued me, especially when I thought back to the demands for literacy, education, and citizenship of the Comité Tawantinsuyo in the 1920s. As we saw in Chapter 2, the Comité Pro-Derecho Indígena Tawantinsuyo was one of the organizations most active in demands for literacy and citizenship rights at the turn of the century. In a declaration made at the end of their First Indigenous Congress in 1921, the committee extolled literacy and schooling as paths to the acquisition of full citizenship for indigenous peoples. Part of the statement reads as follows:

Gamonales know that their rule will end the day the Indian learns how to read and write, and that is why they prevent the functioning of schools. But now the Indians are ready to do by themselves what the Supreme Government would not be able to. . . . The organized community should support the school they already have or build another one, at their own expense. . . . If ten years from now each community has its own school, the fate of the Indian will change. . . . Respected for his knowledge, the Indian will have strong fists to defend his rights. (*El Tawantinsuyo*, cited in de la Cadena 2000: 90)

It is important to note that, historically, community schools have been tied to indigenous movements and rights. Many indigenous peoples knew of this history, talked about it, and recognized that education was a form of national integration.

Something else struck me about the initiative to organize community schools. Before this conversation with Roberto I had traveled to Bolivia, where a friend and director of an NGO based in Cochabamba had been involved for many years with the creation and development of a Quechua community-run school. In Raqaypampa, community leaders had hand-picked several yachaqkuna to be trained in bilingual literacy and pedagogy by the NGO. Having first established their own school parallel to the local state school, parents in the community gradually began to withdraw their children from the state school and enroll them instead in their own. Eventually, after years of conflict with the state, residents of Raqaypampa won, and the state school was shut down (CENDA 1988).

Returning to Roberto's comments, I asked him to expand on his reference to the Quechua yachaqkuna. He smiled, understanding my confusion, and said, "A new kind of yachaq. Not elders, but young ones, who are from our community, but who speak Spanish and can help us." He said that this was something that he and the other community leaders had discussed several times and that they were just trying to figure out how to carry out their plan. Mainly, they were concerned about training the yachaq, whom they had already selected, so that they would be capable of teaching their children in Spanish.

Raqaypampa in Bolivia was an exceptional case. The community's school had held on for more than thirty years, evidence of the tremendous commitment on the part of community members to maintain their autonomy in the face of constant challenges by government authorities. It was also a reflection of the NGO personnel's commitment to assist Raqaypampa with its leaders' demands, even after significant disagreement with them (CENDA 1988; Pablo Regalsky, personal communication). The case in Cuzco in the 1990s was different because all of the NGOs in the area working with education were linked to official state policy, which did not provide room for separate or parallel educational structures. As of 1999, communities in Cuzco had been unable to set up independent schools. Nevertheless, this initiative on the part of Roberto and the community's leaders was an extraordinary demonstration of the kind of local activism that has developed in the highlands as a response to dissatisfaction with bilingual education. Even as intercultural activists lament the absence of grass-roots mobilization (or at least the kind of mobilization they would like to see), Quechua parents in the 1990s were increasingly not only discussing their dissatisfaction with the educational program and with the state but acting upon their feelings.

Intercultural Policies: Challenges and Possibilities

In August 2002, during the Fifth Latin American Conference of Bilingual Intercultural Education in Lima, the participants, who included indigenous leaders, intercultural activists, and social scientists, drafted a document titled "Multilingual Reality and Intercultural Challenge: Citizenship, Politics, and Education." The first part of the document is worth citing at length:

Democracy and citizenship in Latin America are aspirations for us all; however, they are still more of a promise than a reality, especially for indigenous peoples. Our societies have not stopped discriminating against certain categories of individuals and peoples [personas y pueblos]; and they continue to allow intolerance, inequality, and authoritarianism. Broad sectors of the population have no rights; other sectors do not respect the rights of others. Our societies are fragmented and still suffer modes of domination and exclusion. It is for this reason that indigenous peoples are more vulnerable to injustice, corruption, confrontation, and poverty. . . . Despite educational reform . . . there still have been no adequate responses . . . that might allow for a more visible role for indigenous leaders in their own development. The education offered to most [indigenous peoples], particularly that offered to indigenous women and girls, is devoid of quality and of linguistic, cultural, and pedagogical relevance. (Declaración de Lima 2002: 1.1, 1.5)

For indigenous rights activists, education, particularly bilingual intercultural education, holds the promise of a more equitable, diverse, and respectful society (Godenzzi 1996, López 1996). Its proper implementation is a pledge to eradicate poverty in indigenous communities while simultaneously promoting indigenous autonomy and cultural pride and demanding social, cultural, economic, and political rights. However, as the critical tone of the declaration indicates, there is still much work to be done.

In one of her earlier examinations of a bilingual education project in the southern Andes, Nancy Hornberger explored what she called "bilingual education success, but policy failure" (Hornberger 1987: 205). Looking at teacher-pupil interactions and developments in language ideology within Quechua communities and among children and their parents in schools, she concludes that the failure of this particular project was due especially to the problems of implementation, to a rift between national language policy and the project's goals, and to the low status of Quechua in Peruvian society. "In every case, what is needed for successful language maintenance is . . . autonomy of the speech community in deciding about use of languages in their schools and a societal context in which . . . incentives exist for [their] use" (1987: 224). Hornberger's conclusions in the 1980s are still relevant today. For example, the implementation of bilingual intercultural education appears to have received a much more positive response from indigenous communities in the Amazonian region. Leaders of Amazonian indigenous organizations, activists, and both Peruvian and foreign anthropologists have painted a more positive picture of indigenous-activist interactions and community education (Pérez 2002; Ames 2002; Dean 2002). For example, teachers in those community schools are also members of the community, often young people. Moreover, all community members, especially indigenous parents, participate in intercultural workshops, and in some cases work closely with intercultural education activists in determining the best way to implement education reform in community schools (Dean 2002). Indigenous parents in the Amazon, it seems, have more of a say in what is taught and how it is taught.

A thorough examination of the differences between highland and lowland experiences with bilingual intercultural education would be an important way for future research to begin to document, analyze, and confront both the setbacks and advances in intercultural education and indigenous cultural rights. It seems to me that the principal challenge to bilingual intercultural education is the fact that indigenous parents in the highlands of Cuzco (and possibly elsewhere) have an entirely different understanding of language rights, indigenous rights, and the right to education than intercultural activists do. "Even if in theory bilingual education is better for our children," commented a Quechua indigenous community leader in the Ausangate, "in our everyday reality, and for our future, it's disastrous." Concern for the future affects activists and parents equally but for very different reasons. If intercultural activists and policy makers are serious in their defense of intercultural education as a means to alleviate social injustice for indigenous peoples and create a nation more respectful of difference, indigenous concerns about education should not be dismissed, but rather incorporated into new agendas, both in theory and in practice.

In this chapter I have examined some of the contradictions and unintended consequences of intercultural discourse by focusing on the strategies used by indigenous parents and leaders to bypass the limitations that they claim activists are placing on their children's education. Paradoxically, the efforts both of activists to revalorize Quechua and of parents to secure access to Spanish-language instruction are important parts of indigenous social move-

ment politics in Peru. Along with the striking advances of indigenous movements in many Latin American countries, proponents of intercultural education can claim many victories. Constitutional reforms that recognize and
legitimize linguistic, cultural, and ethnic diversity, the creation and maintenance of institutes and programs for indigenous students, and the development of education materials in dozens of indigenous languages are only a few
examples of the kind of progress made by advocates of cultural rights. Yet
the inconsistencies between rhetoric and implementation still need to be
addressed. For instance, the DINEBI boasts that every classroom in indigenous schools where bilingual intercultural education is implemented has its
own library (Godenzzi 2001). But during my visits to dozens of bilingual state
schools in the highlands, I only saw one that had a library; teachers were still
waiting for the library materials they had been promised. Similarly, though,
according to state documents, more than 10,000 teachers have been trained
in bilingual education methodology, there is little emphasis on evaluation of
the training (or the trainers), on follow-up with individual teachers, or on
feedback from teachers about the positive and negative aspects of training
sessions. In other words, there seems to be a more immediate concern with
quantity than with the quality of education and training.

Bilingual intercultural education is a bold initiative, but as currently implemented it leaves many gaps. There is first the disconnect between the rhetoric of inclusion and the underfunded and paternalistic practices that still
tend toward exclusion. Second, there is the gulf between the ideological
authors of new policies and the teachers and trainers charged with the more
difficult task of implementing those ideas. Finally, there is the lamentable distance between those who make policies and those who must live with the
effects of those reforms. Similar gaps can surely be found in most democ-
racies, but the true test of democracy lies in closing them. If governments,
activists, teachers, and students succeed in bridging the distance between the
promise of intercultural education and its current state, Peruvian democracy
will be greatly in their debt. However, we should not forget that the quality
of democracy is not solely a product of local actors but increasingly is shaped
by the interaction of local, national, and global forces. The following chapter looks at how those forces are at work in the interactions of NGOs and
the state.

4 Conflicted Multiculturalisms

NGOS, THE STATE, AND THE
CONTRADICTIONS OF RIGHTS ACTIVISM

In February 1998 I was looking at the records of an NGO in a town near Cuzco. I ran across a survey conducted ten years earlier (1988) that had been designed by a sociologist based at the Instituto de Estudios Peruanos in Lima. The survey was intended to get a sense of the importance that parents in highland communities and small villages placed on their children's education. Most of the questions were the stuff of statistics: "How much money do you spend on your child's uniform?"; "How far does your child travel to get to school?"; "How many grades, if any, has your child repeated?" Some of the questions were a bit more involved, but the one that caught my attention the most asked, "Who do you think should manage your community's school?" Below the question were several choices: (1) Nongovernmental organization (NGO), (2) Ministry of Education, (3) Teachers, (4) Religious leaders, (5) Community president, (6) The community, (7) Other. The vast majority of parents chose the Ministry of Education; the second most popular choice was an NGO.

Undoubtedly, such studies lent credibility and respect to the subsequent collaboration between the ministry and NGOs in implementing intercultural educational policies over the next several years. However, by the time I conducted my research in various highland communities of Cuzco in 1998, I found almost no sign of the popular support that the decade-old survey described. Far from being seen as the source of solutions, both the state and NGO actors were now described as part of the problem. Indeed, in many communities one could hear increasing talk about local control over schools precisely because the ministry and the NGOs "don't understand our reality." In order to understand the sources of this dissatisfaction and its implication for the cultural politics of contemporary education policies, this chapter explores the many tensions with the project of multiculturalism, and the landscape of uneven power relations on which teachers, parents, development professionals, and state officials contest the substance and form of intercultural education. Through an ethnographic exploration of the local effects of international development, this chapter also addresses the role of international organizations in shaping state policy and local identities. However, this is hardly a case of outsiders simply imposing agendas and beliefs. Rural teachers and local activists continuously reinterpret and transform projects even as they claim to be carrying out internationally funded mandates. In the following pages I focus on the local dynamics of implementing bilingual intercultural education, cultural revival, and language revitalization programs among indigenous communities.

I should add that my research cautions against common assumptions made about NGOs as unfailingly progressive spaces in civil society. While well-intentioned activists may indeed challenge institutional forms of discrimination, they often leave other troubling racial and class hierarchies firmly in place. Moreover, we should be careful not to confuse activist voices with the voices of those they claim to represent. However, although the ethnographic materials presented here paint a critical picture of current efforts, I would like to stress from the outset that my critique is a plea not against NGOs or activism but rather for more nuanced analyses that emphasize the contradictions of development and the tensions between rhetoric and practice.

Promoting Interculturalidad? The Contradictions of Indigenous Rights Discourse

In May 1998 I traveled to a highland community in Cuzco with personnel from TADEP, a well-respected NGO with a long history in the region. This was my first trip to the countryside with this NGO. I was traveling in a pickup truck with two teachers, a project coordinator, the director of the NGO's bilingual education project, and a state representative. As the truck made its way around highland peaks, NGO personnel talked with Mercedes, director of the regional office of the national Education Services Unit (USE) about tensions between parents and teachers in the community of Paccha Pata over educational changes.

Mercedes had recently received a letter from a group of parents complaining about the work conducted by the NGO in their community and demanding that the teachers be replaced. The letter had been written by the community president on behalf of the parents, none of whom could read or write, after a community meeting where all but a few women had vowed to drive the teachers away.

When we arrived at the end of the dirt road, we began the hour-long hike to reach Paccha Pata. I was impressed by the USE director's energy and good humor throughout the trip, especially because, according to her, she had actually arranged for a community assembly in order to "engage in dialogue over the community's concerns about bilingual education and the methodology being used by the teachers." We reached the community school by noon and sat in the courtyard to await Mercedes's instructions. After inspecting the three classrooms and confirming that the community had been informed about the assembly, she led us to one of the classrooms. Once we were all seated, she began to speak, her tone of voice rising gradually:

As most of you know, I received a letter from the members of this community stating that they reject the proposal for bilingual intercultural education and that they want the teachers to stop teaching in Quechua or to be replaced. In my opinion, this letter is a reflection of three things: (a) parents in this community still don't understand what bilingual intercultural education means; (b) you teachers have not done your jobs; and (c) the NGO has not been successful in training teachers.

Mercedes continued, emphasizing her support for bilingual intercultural education as well as her links to the Ministry of Education. She stated that teachers should present the educational changes as a proposal coming from the government, not from the NGO. According to Mercedes, the NGO should be represented as an "executing agent" (*ente ejecutor*) that simply carried out government policy. As she neared the end of her lecture, she highlighted the importance of achieving an "education that liberates, not one that binds individuals to the existing power structures." It didn't seem to matter that she was a representative of the Ministry of Education, the most significant power structure with regard to education in Peru. She finished her speech with the following words:

You must be aware of the importance of forging an alliance between peasants — whom we now call indígenas — and teachers in order to advance a liberating education. This liberation will be possible only if the vertical structure that exists today is broken. Indigenous education is a social movement, not a pedagogical innovation. But the pedagogical advances we work with provide us with tools to meet the challenges we face. Without a social movement, it won't be possible to achieve our goals.

It was striking to hear her blend forcefully two seemingly contradictory messages: this must be done because the state has decreed it; this must be done because the social movement demands it. Yet far from being exceptional, these kinds of tensions seemed to be woven into the very fabric of bilingual intercultural education policies.

Often, NGO personnel were expected to reach several communities in a region that had recently been designated an intercultural education zone. The standard procedure seemed to be the following: NGO program directors and teacher trainers would reach a school, interrupt class, ask for the school's director and teachers, and announce the educational change. Despite constant dialogue among NGO activists about democratic and horizontal relationships, any resistance to bilingual education was almost always met with the same response: Educational reform was not an option. It was official policy.

In Cuzco in the 1990s, at least six NGOs worked on education reform. Activists from these NGOs emphasized indigenous self-determination both in their conversations with me and in their organizations' mission statements. They also promoted bilingual intercultural education as crucial to the cultural and ethnic autonomy of indigenous peoples. One NGO program coordinator told me about what she saw as the importance of bilingual education:

By teaching children in and about their native language and by providing them with the opportunity to learn the dominant language as a second language — second to their own — children will learn to value their culture and language, and thus be able to raise their self-esteem, defend themselves from discrimination and abuse, and chart their own course through history within the dominant society.

Yet these efforts to help indigenous people "chart their own course" often mean in practice that indigenous people must follow the course set by the state. A large part of the international movement for indigenous rights has involved incorporating the state and highlighting its responsibility as an active agent in the implementation of social programs benefiting indigenous groups. The leaner and meaner neoliberal Latin American state, in turn, has looked to nongovernmental actors to implement these new governmental goals. In the process, neoliberal multiculturalism has had the surprising effect of remapping Peruvian civil society in such a way that it seems to include the NGO and state officials (the active agents) but exclude the local communities (the passive beneficiaries). In an inversion of much of the optimistic expectations about civil society, in this case social movements were the products of state policies, not local community activism. Describing a conflict between communal forms of justice and NGO discourse on the rule of law and human rights in Ecuador, John Beverly describes a dynamic similar to the one I observed in Cuzco: "In a certain sense, this conflict could be seen as one between the logic of *community* (indigenous, Quichua-speaking, peasant, rural, poor) on one side and *civil society* (urban, white or mestizo, Spanish-speaking, literate, Eurocentric) on the other, with the state, curiously, in the position of intermediator" (1998: 278). In the case of education reform in Peru, the state was less of a mediator as it sought to act on community through civil society.[1]

Returning to Paccha Pata, I spoke with all three teachers after the meeting, while Mercedes and the NGO director left to bring the community together for the assembly. They were angry, and felt that Mercedes had been offensive to them. "It's easy for her to say we haven't done our job," said one teacher. "She doesn't even know the kinds of problems we have to deal with, especially because of these dumb campesinos." When I was unable to hide my reaction to her last two words, the teacher apologized. "Excuse me for saying so. It's not that I think all campesinos are dumb, but they never told us anything. We didn't know they were so angry with us. Besides, it never matters to the NGO if parents say they don't like Quechua or bilingual education. They just tell us to go on with our job."

As the assembly of community members came together in an open field next to the school, I sat down on the grass and waited for the discussion to begin. It was noon and the sun was strong. Men who had been working in their fields walked up to the gathering, some holding sickles and other tools, and stayed standing. Women began to sit down on the ground in a circle, surrounding the men, nursing their children or talking to one another. When everyone had gathered, there were approximately fifty people present. To begin the assembly, the president introduced both the state USE official and the NGO program directors, but before he had finished his introductions, Mercedes abruptly interrupted him and addressed the community. Speaking in broken Quechua but in an extremely authoritative tone, she made her point in less than five minutes.

All of you know why I'm here. I wanted to come so I could address the entire community directly. I want you to know that if I ever receive another letter like the one I was sent, I will take away your teachers, but I will not replace them. If you want your children to be without teachers, then keep mistreating the teachers you have now. Bilingual intercultural education is not an option. It's government policy, and it's in your schools and communities now because it's better. It's not just about Quechua, it's about your children having the right to speak both Quechua and Spanish.

After a few more comments, Mercedes introduced the project coordinator who had accompanied the teachers and the program director in the truck, saying she would take the next hour to explain in detail what intercultural education meant for their community and for their children. Mercedes stepped aside to let Ilda begin her work. When she tried to do so, however, the men cut her off. One by one they angrily refuted Mercedes' comments. "What right do you have to tell us about our children's rights?" shouted one man. Another followed suit: "My little brother is in the second grade. He's not learning Spanish, and people like you who can't even speak Quechua are teaching him in his own language. He won't even be able to speak well in Quechua if we let you stay here." This brother's comments were especially significant. Proponents of bilingual intercultural education have frequently claimed that one of the consequences of traditional teaching in Spanish is that indigenous children are "left ignorant of essential cultural [and linguistic] knowledge of both Quechua and Hispanic culture" (Montoya 1990: 275). Apparently some community members believed that instruction only in Quechua by persons alien to their culture would also lead to the deterioration of their language. Thus the community member described a double failure of intercultural education: it failed to provide both what the community wanted (Spanish instruction) and what the state and NGOs declared as its goal (revalorization of indigenous language and culture).

During the years I spent in Cuzco, this was only one of many times I heard intercultural activists invoke the state — identified as the government, the president, or the Ministry of Education — as a way to legitimize their authority. In fact, it was a common strategy used by teachers, trainers, and other regional education authorities when parents steadfastly refused to accept bilingual education policies in their schools. According to many activists I asked about this, "it helps them listen if they think it's mandatory." And once parents are "listening," activists can talk about the importance of cultural respect and present the pedagogical justification for bilingual intercultural education. After this trip, I asked one of the program coordinators why they linked themselves to the state. He replied forcefully: "We're not linking ourselves to the state, but for now, we do depend on [the ministry], for example, for materials, like bilingual teaching guidelines." Another activist replied to similar questions that invoking the ministry was unfortunate but necessary, although only at the beginning. "Things will change when Quechuas look beyond simple language issues, and to more political ones," he said. This activist ignored the fact that these "simple language issues" not only had been politically important for decades but had become important topics of debate among parents precisely because activists infused them with political import by imposing language policies that Quechuas found unacceptable.

(Re)making Identity: Training Intercultural Teachers

> Bilingual intercultural education gives us the tools to explain critically and scientifically [to highland teachers and parents] the meaning of that Andean cosmology they have; that magical world they have. Then, when we've managed to make them understand, we've achieved self-esteem and security. We are thus reclaiming what belongs to them. We are creating identity.
> — Lucho, teacher trainer

Highland teachers are considered by activists to be the agents primarily responsible for promoting the valorization of culture and language among highland children and their parents. Accordingly, two of the principal mechanisms through which activists envision the execution of social reform are teacher-training workshops (*talleres de capacitación docente*) and shared learning workshops (*talleres de interaprendizaje*). In an attempt to mold teachers' thoughts about indigenous culture, language, and education, these gatherings, led by capacitadores, emphasize intercultural ideology, "constructivist" pedagogy, and techniques for the practice of interculturalidad. During these workshops, activists mark a clear separation between new teaching methodology and the training received by highland teachers at teacher-training colleges, called *normales*.

Teachers working in the highlands, usually called "rural teachers," come from highland towns and villages, although some are from hamlets and some from the city of Cuzco. Often the only choice available for peasant and working-class youths aspiring to education beyond high school is the regional normal. Because middle- and upper-class youths attend universities, students who attend a normal school are stigmatized as lacking the intellectual capacity for a better education ("She didn't pass the university entrance exam, so she had to settle for being a teacher") or the money to pay for it. Distinctions are also made between normales for rural areas and those for urban areas. Like the rural teachers who are commonly perceived as less prepared or less competent than those working in urban areas, normales catering to rural students are considered less rigorous than urban teacher-training schools. The system itself is subject to the same prejudice. Entrance standards for rural normal schools are more lenient than those for urban ones, for example. Partly because of these factors, highland teachers are commonly scorned not only by their urban colleagues but also by their pupils' parents, who criticize their teaching (especially if the teacher speaks with an indigenous accent), their lack of commitment to students, and their (openly expressed) desire to leave the community. Since most highland teachers are not from the communities where they work, these men and women live in small rooms attached to the schools. Few schools, whether they have four, five, or six grades, house more than two or three teachers. Thus, living alone far from their families and usually having few contacts outside the school, teachers in the highlands are notorious for taking long weekends. It is normal for a teacher to teach on Tuesday, Wednesday, and Thursday, catch a bus to the nearest town or to Cuzco that afternoon, and not return until the following Tuesday morning. These extended weekends are cited by parents, supervisors, and many others as examples of highland teachers' irresponsibility and lack of commitment.

While it is true that many teachers do take advantage of the isolation of their schools and the lack of supervision in not attending school much of the time, they are also subject to tremendous abuse by education authorities, among others. For example, teachers working in rural areas, especially in more isolated highland regions, are supposed to be paid a bonus, called a "rural percentage." This percentage is frequently missing from their paychecks, however. If teachers demand this pay, to which they are entitled, they are often threatened with being fired. One teacher with whom I spoke described what happened when he traveled to Cuzco to demand the missing portions of several checks. "After almost five hours of waiting," he told me, "this woman behind a big desk said: 'If you're not happy, we'll just give your job to someone else.' And I looked and there was a long line of people waiting to take any job, anywhere." Another teacher's comments about teaching in the highlands were, sadly, representative of many of the complaints I listened to:

It is very rare for a teacher to teach in the countryside by her own choice. Almost always she is angry . . . because she didn't manage a position in an urban school; even in a village or town. . . . And usually the reasons why [a teacher] gets sent to the countryside are because he didn't have someone vouching for him, because he didn't have enough money to bribe the educational authorities, because he's not a member of the government's party, or, if the teacher is a woman, because she didn't sleep with the man in charge of placements.

For these and other reasons, not least of which are teachers' own racial and cultural prejudices against their indigenous students, highland teachers are often eager to exchange their jobs for urban teaching positions. All but a handful of the teachers I met asked me if I could do something about their placement. "This isn't teaching," complained one. "These children just can't learn anything. And I shouldn't have to live among such filth. This is punishment. . . . Can you help me transfer to a civilized school?" This teacher's request for a transfer of schools was also a plea for help with the following year's placement process, whereby only certain teachers are selected for rotation to another school.

This placement process also depends on whether a teacher is *nombrada* (appointed) or *contratada* (contracted). One way to achieve a *nombramiento* (appointment) is to know someone with influence who will vouch for you (most teachers hoped I might be that person); the other way is to take a yearly test and get a high score. An appointed teacher has the option of staying in a school for as long as he or she wants to, and receives better pay. A contracted teacher is rotated from year to year, from school to school, and is often assigned to schools where appointed teachers don't want to work. Usually highland teachers in isolated regions are contracted, while those in urban areas are appointed. I witnessed an example of the kind of distinction made between contracted and appointed teachers when I visited Mallma, a community near Mallqucha at the base of the Ausangate. A few months earlier, the regional USE (educational services unit), based in Urcos, a town near the city of Cuzco, needed to replace their director. Because the teacher in Mallma knew the USE's former director and had recently acquired an appointment, the teacher was chosen to replace him as the USE's new director. Meanwhile, the USE filled the teacher's place in Mallma with another contracted teacher. The new teacher noticed that his rural bonus was missing from his paycheck. When he went to Urcos to rectify the situation, he was informed that the teacher he had replaced had done them a favor by taking the position as director of the USE at such short notice. To make up for such an inconvenience (and despite the fact that as director he earned much more than even urban teachers), the rural percentage of the new teacher's check was automatically sent to the new director.

Conflict between teachers aside, even if teachers were from highland towns, their profession placed them in a higher social stratum than the Quechua farmers and herders whose children they would teach. Teachers clearly reinforced these class distinctions, linked to ethnic and cultural differences, thus exacerbating the already strained relations between them and highland parents. As we have seen, one way teachers marked these perceived differences was by pointing to community members as "less civilized," "dirty," or "ignorant" and bemoaning the need to live among such people. Another was by frequently highlighting the fact that they were in the highlands only because the job market wasn't good that year, and that next year they would certainly be teaching in the city of Cuzco.

Despite these problems, intercultural activists insist that the decisive factor in obtaining educational results remains the teacher. Aware of the problems teachers face and of the prejudices they hold against indigenous children, activists say that teacher training is of primary importance to the effective implementation of bilingual education in the highlands. However, their efforts in this area may not be providing the kinds of results they had in mind.

According to activists, the training received by teachers at the normales aims toward homogenization and assimilation to the dominant language and culture. "This kind of racist and culturally insensitive teaching methodology has been the norm in our country during this whole century," one NGO program director told me. "This is the principal problem we encounter," he continued, "when we try to teach them about interculturalidad, for example." As Lucho, a teacher trainer, explained to me, because of the "racist training" imparted at the normales, "teachers' pedagogy and mentality have to be substantially transformed before indigenous education in Peru can become truly liberating." According to intercultural activists, teacher training sessions are the first step toward such an ideological and pedagogical transformation. In these sessions, activists argue, teachers become aware of the importance of indigenous language and culture almost immediately. Although activists also acknowledge that "in many cases, the radical ideas of bilingual [intercultural] education do not outweigh tradition" (López 1995: 27), they usually claim that teachers are easily "awakened" from their ethnopolitical slumber: "It's important that we rescue, revalue, resuscitate even, an entire culture that's asleep in [teachers]," one activist told me. "We need to wake them up."

For intercultural activists, teacher training questions not only teaching practice but also highland teachers' visions and individual behavior in the face of diversity. According to Luis Enrique López, "teachers must be convinced of their pupils' real potential for learning and intellectual development, and of the potential of the given indigenous people, of their skills, knowledge, languages, values, beliefs — in sum, of their culture" (1995: 30). Activists are convinced that after appropriate training, teachers will come to share in their ideals. "I've already seen it happen!" Lucho told me, elated. "They come to the sessions, very hesitant at first, and strongly opposed to bilingual education. But by the time they leave, they've realized its potential and the significance of their own culture, which they've suppressed for so long."

After attending many of these training sessions, I understood what Lucho meant. Teachers' *public* attitudes toward interculturalidad and bilingual education were noticeably different toward the end of the sessions than when they had first arrived. I wondered, however, if teachers' ideas would change again once they returned to teach in the highlands. This didn't seem to concern Lucho, whose only reply when I posed the question was "Well, we have to start somewhere, and we're beginning forcefully!"

I attended a dozen teacher training workshops in Cuzco. Although workshops vary from NGO to NGO, the workshops I observed usually lasted for either two weeks or ten days, with activities lasting approximately six hours each day. The workshops emphasized similar goals and were similarly structured, and all seminars touched on the following subjects: (1) the importance of writing in Quechua, (2) how to teach reading and writing in both Quechua and Spanish, (3) the concept of interculturalidad and its implications and applications in everyday life, and (4) the importance of language and culture as vehicles for social change. Teacher training was originally supported by resources from regional NGOs and by international funds. Since 1996, however, funding has also come from the Peruvian government.

For intercultural activists, the National Teacher Training Program (PLAN-CAD), the program through which they obtain state funds for training highland teachers, has been a symbol simultaneously of state support for intercultural education and of state control. On the one hand, using resources allocated for PLANCAD-related activities, activists are able to channel funds for the production of materials used in training workshops. Further, because the Ministry of Education expects an increasing number of teachers to be trained in current pedagogical theory, activists have been able to argue for additional resources geared toward training capacitadores. Yet government support, however minimal, forces activists to limit the kinds of questions and debates that emerge in training sessions. Moreover, the ministry occasionally sends supervisors to monitor sessions over one or two days, evaluate their effectiveness, and report back on their content. These men usually know nothing about Quechua or about the philosophy behind cultural and language preservation movements or behind bilingual intercultural education. Without a thorough evaluation of the application of this training by highland teachers in rural indigenous school settings, it would be difficult to gauge the effectiveness of these sessions, yet the supervisors who monitor workshops in Cuzco rarely set foot beyond the city limits. Another issue fueling some activist worries about the PLANCAD program was the claim by some NGO project coordinators that teachers selected for training under PLANCAD were government "spies." NGO concerns about government supervision and control serve to remind us that the lines between civil society and state are not always as blurry as they might seem. At least in the minds of activists and government officials, it was clear that power and resources emanated from the still-authoritarian state of Fujimori. Although uncomfortable with the state presence, activists — as we have seen — also invoked state power to establish their authority in the communities. The shifting boundaries of state and society were part of the complex cultural politics of reform and the administration of difference.

Despite these controls, the link between bilingual intercultural education and a "new social vision" promoting cultural and ethnic identity was explicitly stated at the beginning of most of these training sessions. "Quechua children have Andean culture in their souls," the capacitador at one of the first sessions I observed emphatically argued. "It is they who will develop the language, develop their culture, your culture, and who will lead the Quechua nation that is being forged as we speak through your own efforts. It is for them, then, that you must be here; that you must rediscover your roots. It is for them that you must teach." Such a passionate welcome to teachers was not at all uncommon during teacher training workshops in Cuzco.

Over the two weeks or ten days of the workshops, this new vision is embedded in discussions about language, pedagogy, teaching methodology, culture, and interculturalidad. Consider a discussion initiated by one teacher's question about writing in Quechua. "Why," he asked, "should we spend our time trying to teach children how to write in a language that they use only orally? They want to learn how to write in Spanish or even English instead." The capacitador began his response by stating that Spanish is important and that children must also be taught to read and write in Spanish, but in the proper order (after Quechua). He continued by discussing the pedagogical benefits of teaching reading and writing skills in the child's native language before introducing a second language. "But most important," he emphasized, "the child must develop pride in the Quechua language, because it is the bearer of cultural tradition and history. Besides," he added, "a people who lose their language are no longer a people."

The link between language and identity is one of the key ideological tenets proposed in these sessions. It is used to demonstrate to teachers and parents that if language is lost, then identity, history, and personhood are lost. Even after intercultural education activists began their work with indigenous intellectuals, promoting knowledge of Spanish as part of definitions of Indiannness among teachers in training sessions, the predominance of the Quechua language as essential to cultural and ethnic identity remained. "Spanish is essential for Quechuas," an activist told me during an interview. "But since it's a second language, alien to Quechua communities, it must be taught in the same way — as second to Quechua." Another activist, a capacitador from Urubamba, commented: "Because children are Quechua, they'll learn how to read and write much faster in Quechua than if we tried to teach them these skills in Spanish. But once they know how to read and write, without losing their identity, then we can teach them Spanish, and English and any other language, because they'll already know how to read."

While some parents are temporarily satisfied by these explanations, others, particularly mothers, demand proof of these claims by asking activists to work with them. "If it works so well," a Quechua mother of four from Pacchantata said to me once, "then let them teach us. It would be good." She smiled. "It would be good to know how to write." As we saw in Chapter 3, parents' doubts of the potential results of bilingual education were reflected in their demands for evidence of the benefits of this new methodology.

Teachers were also doubtful. During the first days of the training sessions, they regularly discussed their feeling (usually with one another) that "working toward bilingualism" sounded like "double work." "We'll have to teach these children twice — once in Quechua and then again in Spanish," one of the teachers complained. "They can barely remember anything even after we teach them. What makes these teachers [the capacitadores] think children will remember how to read and write in Quechua when we start teaching them Spanish?" Another piped up, laughing, "What makes them think they'll remember anything, period?" Comments like these, reflecting teachers' attitudes toward highland children, were repeatedly echoed by others in the session, particularly during the first few days.

Activists appeared to be aware of teachers' attitudes toward indigenous children. In part for that reason, most discussions about teaching native and second languages regularly centered on the concepts of shame and pride. An additional benefit of teaching children how to read and write in Quechua, advocates of bilingual intercultural education claimed, was that children would begin to shed the shame associated with speaking a language considered dead by most fellow Peruvians. During one of the training sessions I attended, when teachers asked why Quechua and Spanish could not be taught simultaneously from the beginning, a capacitador explained that "if children see that Spanish is a second language, and second only to their own, they may begin to understand that Quechua is not a backward language, and that it's important enough to teach in school, even before Spanish." I should note here that despite activist rhetoric about the importance of teaching and using Quechua in school, all of the teacher training sessions and most of the interaprendizaje sessions were conducted in Spanish. Teachers, with few exceptions, also spoke Spanish among themselves.

As capacitadores lectured to teachers about how to transmit the importance of indigenous language use and maintenance and the benefits of bilingual education to their students' parents, they were also very much aware that the primary reason for teacher training is the fact that teachers themselves need to be convinced of these ideals. The frequent comments made during sessions linking teachers with indigenous culture and identity form part of activists' efforts to do just that. Explaining interculturalidad to teachers is also a part of these efforts, and probably the most important focal point of all training sessions. "Interculturalidad," explained a capacitador to the forty or so teachers present at one session, "is essential for the construction of a democratic society that aspires to unity in diversity. It is the way to promote interaction, and not simply coexistence, between different cultures." As he continued, however, the capacitador also emphasized the importance not only of cultural interaction but also of the creation of cultural identity. "It is only with the establishment of a strong, unified ethnocultural group that interculturalidad can exist, because only then can we strive for equal relations among equally defined cultural groups."

As part of discussions about interculturalidad, all sessions examined the experiences of teachers who had confronted the parents of school-age children and the leaders of their respective communities about the impending implementation of bilingual education. Most teachers were concerned about the rejection they encountered from parents, especially fathers. Anticipating this problem, capacitadores dedicated an entire day to discussions about "building community awareness." "Parents expect results," said one capacitador. "Quechuas are practical people, and if they let their children go to school, then they want their children to learn in Spanish. We need to convince them that learning Quechua is not a waste of time. That it won't hinder them from learning Spanish. We need to convince them that learning Quechua is best for their children."

At some point during most sessions, trainers asked the teachers present to talk about their most pressing concerns. Invariably comments centered on the tensions between teachers' and parents' views on Quechua and on child labor and the low attendance levels of highland children, especially of girls.

After teachers voiced these concerns, discussion turned to the rift between the social reality of Quechua children and the training imparted by intercultural activists and capacitadores. Without fail, teachers challenged the capacitador's comments about teaching religion, social sciences, or math, or about the techniques that teachers are expected to use as part of their lesson plans, stating that these methods were not compatible with their teaching environments. Just as often as teachers challenged them, capacitadores dismissed their concerns and stated only that teachers should help one another in changing whatever realities did not permit them to implement this educational reform. When asked to demonstrate how to achieve such a change by working alongside them in a real classroom setting, capacitadores almost always said with a laugh that they are too busy for such demonstrations. When a capacitador made such a comment at one workshop, a young, witty, and unusually sarcastic teacher leaned over to me and whispered: "We need to be made competent [*capacitados*]) because we're incompetent [*incapaces*], it seems. And yet [these capacitadores] couldn't begin to do our jobs."

Still, as I noted earlier, during and immediately after workshops, most teachers seemed convinced of the benefits of bilingual education and of the importance of Quechua. It was interesting to hear what teachers chose to highlight when they described intercultural education and what it meant for them as highland teachers and Quechua speakers. The most common responses emphasized the importance of stressing the value of Quechua for children's identity and citizenship. "If Quechua children are to succeed in this new Peru, they need to know that their culture, their language, their identity is a valuable component of the nation," one teacher commented. Another added that bilingual education takes away shame about being Quechua and speaking in Quechua, shame with which most highland children grow up. "But most important," he continued, "it helps these children develop an open mind and to learn that they form part of Peru, and that without them [Peruvians] cannot live in a democracy."

Most teachers claimed they were opposed to the idea of bilingual education before attending teacher training sessions, in large part because of their opposition to the primary place of Quechua in bilingual teaching methodologies. However, after the sessions, many teachers explicitly asserted their role as cultural mediators, citing the importance of teaching children about "the place of Quechua language and culture in the nation." Juan, an elementary school teacher from a community close to Mallqucha, described his own transformation after attending a training workshop in Cuzco for teachers of the Ausangate region:

Before, I didn't agree with the methodology and ideology associated with intercultural education because I felt that children should learn Spanish to better themselves. I thought, "They already speak Quechua." But then during the training, I realized the importance and value of Quechua, our ancestral language. If those of us who speak it don't preserve it, then we let them [the bearers of Spanish culture] win all over again. As teachers, it's our job to make our children understand this.

Miriam, another teacher from a nearby community, stated similarly: "We should be teaching our children in Quechua and Spanish, not just in Spanish. It's easier for us in many ways, because sometimes children who attend our schools have never even heard Spanish before! Besides, if we are Peruvian, we should be allowed to speak both languages, no? We teach our children that today, being Peruvian means being able to speak both Quechua and Spanish."

This support appeared to be short-lived, however. I first noticed differences between the teachers I met during the training and those who had already undergone training. The latter teachers' views were much less positive. Although they agreed with bilingual methodology in theory, they also complained that the reality in the highlands was something else again, and that they didn't feel prepared to challenge this reality, let alone change it. Teachers' comments reflected frustration, fatigue, and often anger: "[Capacitadores] have no idea what we go through. These children we work with, they don't even know what the color of milk is!" Most of these teachers complain that there is much less training in how to teach Spanish as a second language than in teaching in Quechua. Teachers, not capacitadores, face parents who reject bilingual education because, they say, it is only a mask for teaching their children in Quechua and thus denying them opportunities for social mobility. "We need to be able to convince parents that bilingual education works, and that means their children must be able to speak and read and write in both Quechua and Spanish," a teacher commented, "not just in Quechua." The teachers with whom I spoke also expressed much frustration about their attempts at raising awareness among parents of Quechua children with regard to the importance of indigenous identity. "Parents view the school as the only chance their children will get to be different from them," a teacher from the Ausangate told me. "Telling them that their children are indígenas, and that they should be proud of that . . . well, that's just ridiculous to them." The attitude she described was the same I found among parents when I talked with them about their children's education. One father expressed it succinctly: "We are peasants, farmers, and poor. What I want most for my children is for them to become more than just peasants, more than us, so that they can have a better life. Being an indígena, like these white outsiders want us to be, would only be worse." The negative reference to outside imposition of language and identity was common among both parents and teachers in Cuzco. The qualifier "white" was not, though it was appearing more frequently in parents' vocabulary toward the end of my stay in Peru. Marking activists as white could be a reaction to being labeled indígena. By utilizing traditional colonial dichotomies (white/Spanish vs. Indian), this father may have been evoking also the power imbalance determined by perceptions of race, class, and ethnicity.

Just as there were teachers who remained skeptical of bilingual intercultural education, there were those who remained positive, and earnestly tried to implement the methodological changes. Of course, there were many teachers throughout Cuzco who also put forth important critiques of bilingual education, activists, and particularly the designated capacitadores without having undergone the training. Some harsher critics went so far as to say that intercultural education is moving education in Peru backward. "The government wants to impose its ideas, but we teachers are not prepared for the expectations they want to place on us," said the director of a school that had recently been designated a bilingual intercultural school.[2] He did not want to attend the compulsory training sessions, he said, because "those workshops aren't for teacher training, they're for socialization and persuasion. I won't change, though."

When I asked activists about these concerns, their answer was straightforward. One activist noted: "We need to focus primarily on issues of importance, especially since ten days or two weeks is no time at all." Another common response was to emphasize interaprendizaje workshops. In answer to a teacher's request for demonstrations of the implementation of bilingual education in a real setting, the capacitador heading that session answered: "That's why you should go to your interaprendizaje group meeting. We'll let each of you know when your region will have a meeting. You can discuss these things there."

"What Happened to Equality?" Sharing Learning, Reproducing Hierarchies

For the most part, teachers feel they are at a loss when they try to teach, since after training, they have little support. One support structure that does exist, and one that teachers generally look forward to, despite conflicts, is interaprendizaje workshops. These workshops bring together approximately ten to fifteen teachers (in contrast to the forty or so teachers who attend training sessions in Cuzco), all of whom have already undergone training in bilingual and intercultural ideology and pedagogy. One capacitador is assigned to a particular cluster of communities in a particular area, and the meetings, technically held once a month (in reality they usually operate once every two months), rotate from school to school. Sometimes teachers have to walk ten or more hours to the school where the meetings are scheduled. Gatherings are usually held in highland schools, not in the city of Cuzco, like all teacher training sessions. And unlike the lecture style of teacher training workshops, interaprendizaje sessions emphasize sharing, group teaching, and peer evaluations, and capacitadores are expected to act in a nurturing manner toward teachers. Upon arrival at the meeting, teachers are usually divided into groups of four or five, each group member from a different community. Sitting at small tables, teachers share experiences, take notes, then share their notes with the class. They work on assignments prepared by the capacitador, discuss lesson plans, and talk about their attempts to incorporate interculturality in their teaching.

The workshops last for two days, and generally teachers look forward to them as opportunities to share their problems, concerns, and questions and for companionship. As one teacher put it, "At least when I'm here I feel I'm not alone. There are others just as frustrated as I. And sometimes I can even help them." Interestingly, as opposed to what happens in training sessions, teachers usually speak in Quechua among themselves, even if they switch to Spanish when addressing the capacitador. Capacitadores generally tended to be Spanish-language dominant, while teachers were (to varying degrees) bilingual in Spanish and Quechua. Of the seven interaprendizaje sessions I attended, at only one did the capacitador — Antonio — speak with the teachers just as comfortably in Quechua as in Spanish. This linguistic difference between Spanish-dominant instructors and bilingual teachers reflected the same language hierarchies that the program sought to contest.

According to activists, this is where they can see how well teachers have learned the lessons from their training. Capacitadores were usually much more relaxed than at training sessions, and thus more willing to discuss problems of implementation. Although heavily dependent on the personality of the capacitador leading the session, interaprendizaje workshops were structured in such a way that meetings were more conducive to closer and lengthier interactions between the capacitador and individual teachers. Although, as they told me, teachers appreciated the structure of interaprendizaje sessions, they did not think of all capacitadores equally. Virtually all the capacitadores from YACHANA (the NGO working on education in the Ausangate) were seen in a favorable light, or at least so I understood from my conversations with teachers and my observations at these sessions. I had attended interaprendizaje sessions sponsored by other NGOs that had not seemed so harmonious. There the atmosphere had been similar to that of teacher training, fully controlled by the capacitador. Teachers were usually content with capacitadores from YACHANA, however, so I was surprised when I heard that a serious problem had arisen between teachers and a capacitador from this particular NGO.

I disentangled myself from my sleeping bag and rolled off the small piece of plywood that blocked at least some of the chill from the floor. The room in which I usually slept when I stayed in Mallqucha was owned by Marta. She was a woman I met during my first attempt to reach the communities at the foothills of the Apu Ausangate. I paid her three soles, the equivalent of $1 in 1998, and she gave me a piece of plywood, a blanket, and a room. This morning, following routine, I slid on my boots, put on my gloves and coat, and prepared my pack for the return to Ocongate, the next town, where I would wait for a ride back to Cuzco.

It was 5:30 in the morning and freezing. I quickly washed my face with water from a bucket next to Marta's kitchen and sat to join her for coffee, potatoes, and rice. As she poured coffee for both of us, Marta, who knew of my interest in schools and teacher training, casually asked if I had heard that *el professor,* as capacitadores are often called, from YACHANA had angered all the teachers from Ccara, a town about three hours on foot from Mallqucha. I had not, and I asked her how and when she had heard about this incident. "Yesterday," she responded. "Before you returned from Ausangate I saw some of the teachers from the school here and they told me." The incident had occurred two weeks before, she continued, but the same capacitador was scheduled to return that day for a three-day workshop in Ccara. I knew that most of these sessions began at 9:00 a.m., and I had time to eat breakfast and reach the school in Ccara by that time. I also knew the trainer assigned to that region, and thought it would not be difficult to stay in Ccara for the next two days. With that in mind, I set out to explore what had gone on between Ramiro, the capacitador, and the village teachers.

I arrived in Ccara just as the NGO's pickup dropped off Ramiro at the school. Visibly surprised to see me, Ramiro smiled and asked only how long I planned to stay. I told him I was unsure, and we walked into the school to prepare for the day of training. Ramiro, a fifty-year-old man from the highland department of Apurimac, bordering Cuzco, was known for his short temper. He considered himself an enlightened man and often proudly referred to the light skin with which all of his children had been born because he had "married well." He was also known for his fondness for young female teachers, and was feared for that reason. For the next two days, Ramiro was to lead an interaprendizaje workshop.

This was the first time I had attended an interaprendizaje workshop with Ramiro. As he began to write on the chalkboard, I found a spot toward the back of the small, windowless classroom, took out my tape recorder, notebook, and pencil, pulled my coat close around me, and waited. A few minutes later three teachers, two from the school in Ccara and one from Huasipata (about a three-hour hike from Ccara), arrived. All three were pleasant and courteous to Ramiro, whose only comment to them after exchanging good mornings was that as usual, most of their colleagues were late. They were still expecting six more teachers, and Ramiro decided that we would wait for another half hour before beginning. While we waited, David, Clorinda, and Diego, the three teachers present, tried to teach me the Peruvian national anthem in Quechua. Ramiro left the room to pace outside. When the half hour had passed, Clorinda pulled me aside and whispered: "Elena, they're not coming." When Ramiro walked in, Clorinda turned to him and stated flatly, "They're not coming." Ramiro sat down, and the others followed suit. Angry with Ramiro for what had happened during another training session two weeks earlier, the six missing teachers had decided not to attend the rescheduled meetings as a statement against the capacitador and indirectly against the NGO.

According to the three teachers present, two weeks earlier, Ramiro had been angered because most of the teachers took a ten-minute break when he had allowed them five minutes. When the teachers tried to reenter the room, Ramiro closed the door in their faces. A few minutes later he let them in, but, according to the teachers, not before insulting them and using "rude words." Finally, he had not allowed them to explain, which angered them almost more than the insults. As a result, the workshop had ended prematurely and was rescheduled. But the teachers had told Clorinda that until they received an apology from Ramiro, they would not attend the workshops.

I imagine that the discussion that ensued between the three teachers and Ramiro at this time was similar to the one that could have developed two weeks earlier, after the conflict caused by Ramiro's actions. He acknowledged no fault, and felt that he was the one who was owed an apology. This time, however, I was there as a witness, so Ramiro chose his words carefully. After more than twenty minutes of discussion, Ramiro admitted that maybe he shouldn't have used certain words, but he had been exasperated and had lost his temper.

When I discussed the original incident with Diego, Clorinda, and David separately, all three agreed both in their individual accounts of what had happened and in their opinion that the two main reasons for the actions of the six teachers were the lack of "democratic respect" shown to them and Ramiro's racist use of the word *cholo* in his string of insults. "In the teacher training workshops," Diego told me, "capacitadores are always talking to us about interculturalidad, democracy, and respect for cultural and ethnic differences. But if we're expected to act in certain ways, shouldn't the capacitador be an example?" Overhearing our conversation, David added that by definition, interculturalidad implies a horizontal relationship of mutual respect between individuals and cultural groups. "But if this isn't followed by our own teachers," he continued, "then does this thing they call interculturalidad really exist?"

The teachers at Ccara cited the capacitador's hypocrisy as a clear example of why they had trouble believing in the development of social equality through education. As David asked, if the capacitadores don't practice what they preach, why should they? Many of the teachers with whom I spoke asked similar questions. However, some teachers did argue that despite the lack of respect that capacitadores show them, they should try to inculcate the values of interculturalidad and social equality in their students "because we know better." Yet one constant source of strain between capacitadores and teachers is the sense that activists and capacitadores categorize teachers as inferior. The teachers in Ccara, for instance, referred to Ramiro's use of the word *cholo* as proof of what David called a "racist and condescending depiction of who we are." According to them, when Ramiro referred to them as cholos, not only was he insulting them but he was marking ethnic differences between them. "Ramiro's way to mark the difference he sees between us and him — a white mestizo, as he calls himself — is to call us cholos. Well, what happened to equality?"

During a talk I attended in Cuzco by a linguist and proponent of bilingual education, the lecturer made several comments about "the influence of ethnicity" over the effectiveness of teacher training. He argued that since most teachers are either cholos/as or mestizos/as, their "level of identification with indigenous highlanders" was very low. According to him, this lack of identification was the principal reason behind the urgent need for both training workshops and interaprendizaje sessions that would presumably modify "levels of ethnic identification." Additionally, many activists seemed to share the popular prejudices against the capabilities of rural highland teachers. In the same breath, for instance, one activist told me that he thought the teacher was the key to developing highland education, and that he considered that "the existence of ethnocultural discrimination against children is proved by the fact that [children in the highlands] get stuck with third-rate teachers."

While activists and capacitadores advocate social equality, cultural respect, horizontal relationships, and democratic participation at all levels of society, teachers say they often feel that they are being talked down to or treated like children. At Ccara many of these issues converged: the lack of "democratic respect," Ramiro's racist insults, and his threats to cut the teachers' pay in half as punishment for not attending, "all because we were five minutes late," recounted Diego. "It just doesn't seem right." The penalty for not showing up at these monthly workshops is severe for teachers in highland regions. If they attend, the NGO covers the pay they would miss during their two-day absence from school, and in theory provides them with educational materials and training to help them implement the new methodologies that they are expected to use in their teaching. However, if they do not attend the workshops and do not inform the capacitador ahead of time, they are often reported to the regional education authorities, who most often cut their monthly pay, sometimes by half. For teachers, most of whom are already getting short-changed, this kind of punishment not only entails a significant economic reduction but also affects their chances of moving to a less isolated school the following academic year. Diego and Clorinda attended the rescheduled session because they lived and taught in Ccara and could not be absent; David attended because he could not afford to lose half his salary now that his wife was pregnant.

The Contradictions and Conflicts of State Multiculturalism and NGO Advocacy

In Cuzco, as elsewhere in Peru, NGOs represent indigenous highlanders vis-à-vis the state and international funders. International organizations consider them key actors in the effort to strengthen civil society. In light of the ongoing political violence against indigenous populations and of the political instability that plagues Peru, maintaining their place as promoters of social reform policies benefiting indigenous populations would seem crucial. Yet, while NGOs have often provided alternative spaces for discussion of reform and democracy, we should remember that the line between governmental and nongovernmental spheres can get blurry (Jelin 1998).

As we saw in Chapter 3, activists try to engage parents and other community members in conversations about bilingual education and cultural identity through parents' schools and community assemblies. However, if these strategies to garner support for alternative education measures fail, intercultural activists and capacitadores usually fall back on declaring that the educational change in highland schools is not optional, that it comes from the state, and that it will happen with or without community support. In training sessions, teachers are given the opportunity to discuss strategies for achieving parent and community support of bilingual intercultural education, primarily so that it will not be viewed as an imposition from outside the community. When faced with government demands for justifications of intercultural projects and activities, activists argue that the need for education reform comes from community demands for an education better suited to their cultural and linguistic reality. Communities are indeed demanding better education. However, the criteria by which they define a "better education" are often ignored and replaced by the "expert knowledge" of linguists, education specialists, and others who claim to know what is best for highland peoples and their children.

According to capacitadores, one of the best things for Quechua peoples — and crucial to their survival as a people — is the development of cultural pride. As one of the strongest cultural markers of Indianness in the Andes, language has become a central component of this quest for cultural pride. However, the struggle to determine what that language should be is still unresolved. "Education," stated a capacitador, "is the most effective path for learning about one's own culture, and about other cultures. The key is to get children to school. Once there, we can begin to teach them — in their language — about their cultural identity, provide them with self-esteem, and make them aware of their social place in the national sphere." The inculcation of cultural awareness and pride comes with added ideals that stress sharing and mutual respect, and highlight the dangers of individualism. Most capacitadores argue that one of the most valuable aspects of indigenous culture is its communal focus. "By stressing the similarities between our goals and their established way of life," argued an activist present at a teacher training session, "we can try to help them understand that we are on their side." He continued: "We must also make them understand, however, that bilingual education will help their children determine their own course in life as members of the nation." The abstract ideals of interculturality seem secondary to Quechua parents, who see the practical and real needs of Quechua communities very differently than activists do.

This ideological gap is also evident between activists and teachers. Jaime, director of a school in a community near Mallqucha, is a case in point. The walls of Jaime's school were plastered with posters promoting bilingual intercultural education, with writing in Quechua and, according to him, "with everything that a supervisor would like to see if he were to show up for a surprise visit. Not that it would be too likely," he joked, "but it helps because it allows us to work [in Spanish] . . . , the way we feel is best for the children." Jaime did not believe in bilingual education, and argued that learning how to read and write in Quechua is not especially helpful to children in the Peruvian Andes. The two teachers working with Jaime agreed, and supported his decisions regarding the school's adornments, as well as the educational methodologies they implemented in their teaching. "Education is about teaching children," he told me. "It is about teaching children that they must master Spanish, because everything in this country is a racist political game, and they must learn how to play, and how to win." For Jaime, teaching children in Spanish is not a denial of their culture, but rather the recognition that to get ahead in Peru, they need to know how to speak and write in Spanish.

Moreover, as this and other chapters have illustrated, the strongest opposition to intercultural education has come not from teachers but from indigenous highlanders themselves. "Those from the NGOs say they come to help us by teaching our children in our language," a Quechua father told me. "What they really care about is getting paid well enough to send their own children to learn English." While the intentions of activists may be more altruistic than this father seems to believe, there is little doubt that the practice of bilingual education is falling well short of its promises.

My work in Peru among NGO personnel, other promoters of the indigenous cause, and indigenous highlanders themselves points to serious problems and contradictions both within NGOs and between them and the communities for whom they claim to speak. In this chapter I have tried to show that a crucial factor accounting for indigenous rejection of NGO educational and cultural reform programs is the chain of political and social inequalities that reproduce neocolonial distinctions between the "civilizing" forces of enlightened urban NGOs and state officials and "backward" rural actors. These contradictions, along with the ironies of state-led "social movements" and participatory pedagogies uncomfortable with parents' participation, all reflect the lingering legacies of (neo)indigenista projects that simultaneously include and exclude indigenous voices. This is not to say that nothing has changed in Peru. As Chapter 5 shows, the postindigenista ideal of indigenous people speaking for themselves is at work in remarkable transnational ways.

5 Developing Indigenous Spaces

INTELLECTUALS AND

TRANSNATIONAL NETWORKS

> Since their encounter with Atahualpa, the Spanish have
> tried to exterminate us and our culture. For more than
> five hunded years we have survived. Now we do more
> than survive. We reemerge intelligent, eloquent, and
> sophisticated.
>
> — Celestino, Quechua intellectual

> All men are intellectuals. . . . Each man . . . is a philosopher,
> an artist, . . . he participates in a particular conception
> of the world, has a conscious line of moral conduct, and
> therefore contributes to sustain a conception of the world
> or to modify it.
>
> — Antonio Gramsci, *Prison Notebooks*

In an article exploring indigenous ethnicity in Latin America, the anthropologist Michael Kearney argues that "new" indigenous identities, forged in "the global and transnational conditions of the contemporary moment," challenge the limits often imposed on them by the past association of Indians with underdevelopment and tradition (1996: 10). Moreover, he claims that the Latin American indígena today is neither modern nor traditional:

The contemporary indígena is formed out of and merges the numerous fragmented subject positions that are scattered in social and geographic spaces. . . . The ongoing dissolution of . . . dualisms — of which the most general is now the defunct opposition between "developed modern" and "underdeveloped traditional" — . . . is basic to modern thought but now has less and less correspondence to the global and transnational conditions of the contemporary moment, in which . . . identities that are neither modern nor traditional are forming in the margins between the two. It is in these marginal spaces that the new . . . indígena . . . appear[s]. (1996: 10)

The marginal spaces Kearney discusses may seem somewhat nebulous, but they exist in concrete and palpable ways. This chapter explores such spaces by looking at the intellectual and cultural production of Indianness in national and transnational contexts.

Throughout my time in Cuzco, the Center for Andean Studies "Bartolomé de Las Casas" (CBC) was an important and dynamic space for discussion about indigenous identity and mobilization. At the CBC, Peruvian intellectuals gathered with activists, intellectuals, and NGO practitioners from throughout Latin America, the United States, and Europe to talk about education, culture, and indigenous politics. Between 1996 and 1999, discourse about Indianness at the CBC changed quickly and significantly, weaving ideas about modernity and tradition in ways that reflected both the legacies of indigenismo — José María Arguedas's ideas in particular — and the "new" emphasis on global networks.

In 1998 the attention to international networks expanded to include the participation of young Peruvians, selected by both intercultural activists and the UNEBI (now DINEBI), in the Program for Training in Bilingual Intercultural Education for Andean Countries (PROEIB Andes), located in the Universidad Mayor de San Simón in Cochabamba, Bolivia. These young leaders were sent to Bolivia as representatives of a new transnational generation of indigenous intellectuals. All of them received scholarships, funded by grants from the Peruvian UNEBI, the Bolivian PROEIB, and the German Technological Institute (GTZ). Like the CBC, the PROEIB represents an important space for the rethinking of identity. An ethnographic exploration of this institute is also crucial for understanding the impact of local and global debates over representation, and more specifically, the professionalization of indigenous leaders.[1]

The following sections are devoted to an ethnographic exploration of the CBC in Peru and the PROEIB in Bolivia. These spaces illustrate how indigenous identities are being contested and reconstituted. The last section of this chapter moves from these academic contexts back to rural communities to show how local indigenous intellectuals are operating in a variety of spaces and places.

Reconfiguring Indigenous Identity: Intellectuals
and the Politics of Hybridity

> If you ask me what it will mean for us to be Peruvian in a
> few years, well, I think it will mean to be indígena.
> — Andrés Chirinos, Peruvian intellectual

At the end of 1998 I had a conversation with Quispe Huamani, a self-identified Quechua intellectual who worked closely with intercultural activists. We were discussing the advances achieved by indigenous leaders and their movements in Ecuador, Bolivia, and Guatemala, and the potential formation of similar indigenous organizations in Peru. His preferred model, Quispe told me, was CONAIE (Confederación de Nacionalidades Indígenas del Ecuador), the leading national indigenous federation in Ecuador. When I asked why, he answered that indigenous Ecuadorians had managed to achieve recognition as indigenous nations. "Look at their name," he said. "Indigenous Nationalities . . ." he trailed off. After a moment of silence he continued: "[In Peru] we have a long way to go. Before we can organize as indigenous peoples, we must *be* indigenous people. Our brothers and sisters have forgotten their heritage. They call themselves peasants. It's up to us to change that." Quispe was right, identity formation is not the same in Peru as in other Andean contexts. Yet indigenous people were not simply forgetting their heritage. There was clearly, as is always the case, much happening behind that "forgetting."

In 1996, during one of the first classes of the CBC's summer course in bilingual education, several of the students — highland teachers, community leaders, NGO personnel, teacher trainers, and others involved with Andean linguistics and education — began discussing the impact of bilingual education on highland children. When the discussion turned to a negative assessment of the frequent rejection of bilingual education by indigenous parents, Carla, a specialist in rural education who worked in the ministry's Office of Rural Education in Lima, jumped to the defense of skeptical parents. "You have to understand that for these parents, bilingual education means teaching Quechua, not Quechua and Spanish. And I understand their concern. As an ex-indígena and mother, I should know."

I was astonished to hear her call herself an "ex-indígena." Not only had I never heard the term before, but I was intrigued by her choice to identify as ex-indígena, rather than as *mestiza*. Most surprising to me was that no one else in the room seemed at all surprised. Everyone seemed to understand her use of the term. Later I asked Carla why she had used it, and she answered: "I refer to myself that way — as an ex-indígena — because I don't live in my community anymore, I don't wear my polleras anymore, and look," she emphasized, "I speak English and work on a computer in the Ministry of Education building in Lima. My own community calls me a mestiza now. I am not a mestiza. But I'm not a campesina anymore, either." In 1996, to talk about an "educated indígena" or a "computer-literate campesina" was for many people a contradiction in terms. Becoming a professional would somehow move you away from Indianness, a label that evoked — even among intercultural activists — ascribed primordial qualities, such as a claim to territory, Indian ancestry, language, dress, and other markers of "authentic" indigenous identity.

Not long after this discussion I attended a lecture by Antonio, a linguist affiliated with the CBC. The lecture, aimed at both CBC students and NGO practitioners and teacher trainers, addressed the concept of intercultural education as well as the challenges to education reform in Peru. Before talking in general about these issues, Antonio commented on the influence of ethnicity on the effectiveness of intercultural policies and particularly on teacher training. He began his discussion by dividing the population affected by education reform into four "sociocultural" categories: (1) the *runa* (Quechua people), (2) the acculturated indígena, (3) the urban cholo, and (4) the Western mestizo. He wrote these four designations on the board and then proceeded to assign "high" or "low" levels of ethnic identity to each category. The runa was assigned a very high level of cultural and ethnic identification. The acculturated indígena was described as having a low level of ethnic self-affirmation and as being "in search of a new identity." Third, the cholos were defined as children of indigenous peasants (presumably another category still) who, having fulfilled their parents' dreams of becoming professionals, are now politicians, engineers, or teachers who live in urban spaces such as Cuzco, Arequipa, and Lima. Cholos were considered to have an unclear ethnic identity because "their identity combined both tendencies toward acculturation and a marked differentiation from Western culture."[2] Significantly, Antonio claimed that this group (in which highland teachers were frequently included) was noteworthy because of "their powerful political activism," though he did not expand on exactly what this activism entailed. Finally, Antonio described the mestizo as "the type that has traditionally dominated Peru since colonial times." The dominant characteristic of this group, according to Antonio, was Western, and their sense of ethnic identity was ambiguous. An example of this ambiguity, according to Antonio, was that these individuals pointed to the glories of the Inca empire while simultaneously rejecting indigenous identity. At this time, the insistence on implementing bilingual intercultural education among highland peasants was linked to the importance of the rediscovery of peasants' Indian roots, or a return to the high levels of identity held by runas. Like Antonio, other intercultural activists openly stated that only after Indian identity was reestablished among highland peoples—who identified themselves primarily as peasants—could they work toward their inclusion into national society as Peruvian indigenous citizens. The words of one activist in August 1996 sum up the point: "Before our efforts can culminate in the self-determination of indigenous peoples and their participation in national society as legitimate indigenous citizens, highland peoples in Peru have to accept their history and affirm their identity. Only then do a people have the right to self-determination and control over their own future."

Two years later, in 1998, activists' discussions about what it meant to identify as an indígena emphasized different things. I first noticed this change in debates about the impact that bilingual education was to have among high-land Quechua children. Whereas in 1996 and 1997 emphasis was on the importance of teaching in Quechua, by mid-1998 the focus had shifted to the teaching of Spanish as a second language. I should note, however, that although changes were evident in the ideology of intercultural activists, the negative emphasis placed on Quechua instruction among many teachers and parents had not changed. But among activists, discussions about language were no longer dominated by debates about the standardization of Quechua or how many vowels should be included in Quechua orthography. Rather, they now centered equally on the rights of indigenous people to language, education, and technology, and particularly on the importance of elevating the status of Quechua by establishing it as a written language, not only an oral one.

These changes were evident at a conference on bilingual education in Puno in September 1998. During the first day of the conference, a group of indigenous rights advocates from various Andean countries carried a banner that read: "Bilingual Intercultural Education Is Quechua and More: We Indians Have to Liberate Ourselves [Decolonizarnos]." The group included, among others, two Peruvian intercultural education activists, neither of whom identified himself as indígena. I knew both of them well: one had been a teacher in a highland community of Cuzco before becoming a capacitador, and the other was Francisco, a linguist and impassioned advocate of bilingual education. Francisco's presence in particular surprised me. As I watched him weave in and out of clusters of people, waving a banner that associated him with "colonized" indigenous groups, I thought about the many times his views about indigenous representation had changed. A year before this conference, for example, Francisco had told me that "bilingual intercultural education is the principal manifestation of a movement that looks toward reclaiming the spaces from which Indians have historically been marginalized, by first establishing their legitimate identity as Quechuas through teaching in Quechua." At that time, Francisco considered himself a key participant in that movement toward linguistic and cultural validation. By contrast, only a few months before the conference we were currently attending, he had explicitly noted in an interview that one of the most problematic aspects of the development of bilingual intercultural education in Peru was that "the protagonists in defense of the Quechua language and culture are those of us who are alien to the Quechua culture and sometimes even to the language." In that same interview Francisco went so far as to say: "It's not the role of those of us (like myself) who are not indígenas to fight for the survival of Quechua. Our role is to improve the quality of education so that Quechua children can be protagonists in their own development." Despite these recent words, Francisco's emphasis on prioritizing the needs of Quechua peoples by letting them speak for themselves had seemingly changed once again.

When I asked him about the banner later that evening, Francisco answered that although he still upheld indigenous participation in Peruvian education reform as the ideal, he had also decided to work toward that ideal by moving the emphasis in the implementation of bilingual intercultural education away from Quechua and toward the teaching of Spanish as a second language. In Francisco's words:

Quechua is very important, both as a language and for the education of children, but more important than that right now is the emergence of the Quechua as a people with power. Unfortunately, power is defined by Spanish in our country, and in order to change that, we need educated Indians, who can speak not only Spanish but also English, and maybe even French and German. We need to intellectualize Quechua, to promote the development of literature in Quechua; but we need to teach our children to read and write and speak in Spanish. This is the only way that the Quechua Indians of Peru will be respected, as an ethnicity and as members of the Peruvian nation-state.

Francisco's words highlighted the need for educated Indians, but it seemed these educated Indians were not the bulk of indigenous people in the highlands but rather select indigenous intellectuals, chosen by activists to represent highland Quechuas. Educated representatives of oppressed groups have long been central to theories of resistance and struggle throughout the world (Gramsci's organic intellectuals, W. E. B. Du Bois's "talented tenth"). They had also been critical actors in previous movements in Peru for indigenous education and enfranchisement, such as the Comité Tawantinsuyo of the 1920s.

Similar concerns were clearly present in Francisco's new ideas about Quechua power. The significant changes in Francisco's ideas about who the leading activists of education reform should be, and about what they should focus on, is critical to understanding the changes in current discussions about the ethnic and cultural autonomy and identity of Quechua peoples. These changes point to concerns over the representation of indigenous peoples, as well as to continuous disagreements among activists over the goals of bilingual intercultural education: education reform as a way to improve rural education and thus promote indigenous and peasant self-determination, or as a forum for intercultural activists to consciously work toward the development of indigenous identity and solidarity.[3] Moreover, although intercultural activists (despite disagreements) do envision Quechua ethnic and cultural autonomy as an ideal, ideas about what exactly it means to *be* a Quechua Indian have changed drastically among Peruvian advocates of bilingual intercultural education.[4] According to activists in 1999, the key to the empowerment of Peruvian highland peoples lay in their identification as Quechua

Indians. But, as had by then become increasingly clear, Quechua Indians (or at least their leaders) must be educated and well equipped with the tools necessary to assert their place as an autonomous people, "proud of their culture but well versed in the things of this global world." At the CBC I met many indigenous students who shared this concern with the things of the global world.

Entering and Exiting Indigenous Modernity

INDIGENOUS PEOPLES, INTELLIGENCE, AND TECHNOLOGY

Discussions about the use of technology by indigenous peoples — particularly visual media such as television and video — have focused primarily on groups such as the Brazilian Kayapó Indians (Turner 1992, 1998, 2002), the Australian Aborigines (Michaels 1984, 1986, 1991), and the Canadian Inuit (Kuptana 1988; Murin 1988). In an extensive examination of indigenous media, Faye Ginsburg (1991) notes that appropriation of these kinds of technological tools usually occurs in the context of indigenous or minority movements for self-determination and resistance. She notes in particular that indigenous uses of technological tools can "help construct identities that link past and present in ways appropriate to contemporary conditions" (1991: 94). Intercultural activists promote indigenous uses of technology, such as learning how to use computers, as a way to bridge the cultural gap between indigenous highland peoples and Peruvian Hispanic society, and to ease their acceptance by Peruvians as legitimate citizens. At the same time, many of the activists I spoke with denied forcefully that adopting modern technology implied assimilation into the so-called dominant Western culture or loss of indigenous culture. This seemed very different from the "high" and "low" identity designations presented in 1996. Instead, they saw this as another of the contemporary conditions that affect indigenous peoples. As one activist noted, "To be an indigenous person in today's world is by definition to be modern."

One afternoon while I was interviewing an NGO education program director in the lounge area of the CBC, my friend Conejo, an Ecuadorian indigenous activist, walked by. He noticed my tape recorder, and instead of waiting until after the interview was over, he paced back and forth in front of us, listening to what we were saying, until, looking as if he would burst from the apparent urgency of the statement he needed to make, he interrupted to exclaim: "I can't believe you would use *that*," pointing to my tape recorder, "when there are many better ones, like mine, for example." He pulled his recorder (which he always carried with him, along with his cell phone) out of his pocket. Now addressing the interviewee, he said proudly with a big smile: "It looks like this indígena knows a bit more than our traveling friend." We all laughed. I told him he could give me a lesson in technological advances over dinner, and satisfied, he allowed us to continue our discussion.

Alberto Conejo is an Otavalo Indian, one of the leading proponents of bilingual intercultural education in Ecuador. He and I had met at the CBC during my first trip to Cuzco in 1996. There we attended the same seminar on language and education during two consecutive summers, and we spent much time together talking and traveling around Cuzco. I became aware of how important his identity as an Otavalo was to Alberto almost immediately after meeting him. He wore white trousers, white sneakers, and a black felt hat over his long braided hair every day during the three months we spent together. I saw him take off his hat only once, during a moment of silence when we reached Machu Picchu, a site he considered sacred. We spent many long nights dancing to huaynos and drinking chicha, but Conejo was also the person I looked to when I needed help with the CBC's computers or when I needed someone to look over my written work in Spanish.

During the summer of 1997, Conejo, Francisco, and I were sitting on a bench in the Plaza de Armas of Cuzco, enjoying a break from classes and the temporary warmth of a cloudless sky. We were discussing the upcoming assignment in our class about indigenista literature, on which we had decided to work together. Once that was settled, Francisco and Conejo began what appeared to be a continuation of an earlier conversation about the lack (at that time) of indigenous organizations in Peru's highlands. "Runas have nothing they can organize around. No issue [motivo] to bring them together," said Francisco. "But I think education and language can be it," he added. And turning to Conejo, he asked: "Don't you think that once runas realize that their language could disappear, they'll come together and fight for the recovery of their language and cultural practices? I mean, that's what happened in your land, isn't it?" Conejo replied: "In Otavalo, all indígenas can speak Spanish and are economically stable, but they still think of themselves as indígenas. We're very proud of this identity." He paused, and continued: "This happened because years ago our community leaders realized that our language was disappearing, and they acted quickly. First they became leaders in the development of bilingual education policies. Then they got the state to accept their cultural rights. Now we're working on our political autonomy, as indigenous nations. So you see," he said to Francisco, "just keep at it. But," he emphasized, "the one thing you *must* do is show the state that indígenas can be modern and capable, and that bilingual intercultural education will help educate and create the new generation of Quechuas."

By 1999, this vision was apparent among leading bilingual education activists and intellectuals in Cuzco. With discussions about the "resignification [*resemantización*] of the term *Indian*," activists emphatically argued against the common opposition made between *indígenas tradicionales y retrasados* (traditional and backward indigenous peoples) and *el occidente moderno y técnico* (the modern and technical West). According to them, Indian identity had to be broadened to include not just ethnic markers such as indigenous languages and traditional dress, but also elements of the modern nation, such as the use of international languages (English and French, for example) and the use of computers and cellular phones.

I discussed this with Mario, a teacher from Cuzco, in 1999. He was telling me about some of the new developments in the training workshops he attended, and about the latest bilingual education teaching manuals that had just been distributed to various regional education offices. Although he had not yet seen the manuals, Mario was skeptical about their use. "You'll see," he told me. "Some of it will be fine, but most of the drawings will still paint an image of us as *indígenas* stagnant in this world. They don't understand that the children look at those images and see no hope for change." I was surprised by Mario's self-identification as *indígena*. Throughout the three years I had known him, he had always identified as a mestizo, and I wanted to know what had changed his self-presentation. So I asked him, and he frowned and replied:

To be Indian we don't have to be dirty, sleep in the same bed, or eat guinea pig. We have to speak in our language and in Spanish, we have to weave and write, we have to walk with our llamas and fly on planes, we have to retain our traditions and be modern at the same time. Besides, you know I have always been proud of my ancestry. I've just come to realize that to pass that pride on to my daughters, I can't belittle my identity by calling myself something I'm not.

Mario's reconsideration of his identity as *indígena* came with a redefinition of what being *indígena* meant. If, in today's world, being *indígena* included Spanish and modernization, the label, at least for Mario, appeared less problematic than it had before.

Mario's words attest to Peruvian activists' efforts to present a modified image of Indianness; an image of, as Conejo and other intercultural activists have put it, "the Indian as equal to progress, not as the antithesis of it" (Conejo 1998). Since early 1998, their efforts have pushed bilingual education beyond the defense and maintenance of indigenous languages to the additional appropriation of other, more global (as they say) options, as tools to reconfigure Indian identity, and to create a larger space for themselves within the economic and political spheres of their respective nation-states. According to Conejo, Francisco, and others, reframing Indianness within notions of modernity and sophistication was a key step toward the reconfiguration of this identity. In this context, indigenous manipulation of technology became an important aspect of new notions of Indianness.

However, it was not only the actual manipulation of video cameras or of filming that was used to challenge ideas about the place and identity of indigenous peoples in Peru. It was also the ability and the desire to own and use such devices that was verbalized as a challenge to common conceptions of Indians as backward, underdeveloped, or traditional. Moreover, activists and teachers, such as Mario, emphasized that the use of technology, international languages, and other global tools did not de-Indianize or diminish their cultural and ethnic identification as Quechuas. In fact, part of becoming an indigenous intellectual or a professional Indian included knowledge about and ability to use modern technology, and this knowledge was often asserted in public as a reflection of intelligence. Conejo's comment about my obviously uninformed choice of tape recorder (in addition to many other jokes about my computer illiteracy, for example) is a case in point.

Also important was the act of owning, operating, or simply knowing how to operate a camera, a tape recorder, or a computer. Similar to Conejo's emphasis on technological manipulation and knowledge, assertions contrasting indigenous abilities with those of non-Indians were made by Mokuka, a Kayapó leader with whom the anthropologist Terence Turner has worked closely in his efforts to bring video technology to this indigenous group: "Do Whites alone have the understanding to be able to operate this equipment? Not at all! We Kayapó, all of us, have the intelligence. We all have the hands, the eyes, the heads that it takes to do this work" (Turner 1992: 8).

Quispe Huamani struggled with what he saw as a drastic change from earlier ideas about the skills indigenous leaders needed to have in order to be considered leaders. "Just a few years ago, the fact that I spoke Spanish and that I could write in both Quechua and Spanish was considered important enough to mark me as a leader," Quispe told me in Puno during an international bilingual education gathering. "Now that's expected of everyone, and leaders need to speak English and other languages, and use all sorts of electronic gadgets. Remember yesterday when Conejo was trying to get me to buy that recorder? I don't understand what he thinks is wrong with the one I have." The previous day several of us had wandered away from the conference to have lunch by Lake Titicaca. During lunch, Conejo had insisted that we take a stroll down to the *baratillo,* the "cheap little market," where Quispe could buy a tape recorder like his. At least I wasn't the only one our friend Conejo considered technologically challenged. "I didn't feel I needed one," Quispe finished, "but you know, I guess I should at least own one if I want to keep up." Activists in Peru often measured indigenous knowledge against so-called Western concepts of progress and modernization. Much of the discussion about cultural and linguistic preservation was placed next to debates about Quechuas' struggles against the encroachment of Western or Hispanic culture. Yet these same activists just as often highlighted the importance of not only mastering modern technological advances but incorporating them into their daily lives as indigenous peoples. As de la Cadena suggests for indigenous mestizos (2000), professional Indians and indigenous intellectuals expand definitions of indigenous identity to include technological literacy. Contesting the boundaries of both mestizo and indigenous identities is clearly a crucial part of contemporary cultural politics in Peru, yet it is interesting to see how language and education are being used by contemporary activists to redraw the lines between Western ways and local indigenous empowerment.

During an interview with one of the capacitadores from an NGO that had recently become involved with the education reform process in Cuzco, I asked why, in his opinion, questions about language, education, and especially bilingual intercultural education were important to the NGO's work in highland communities. He responded:

Through the preservation of language, what is original, what is traditional, what is ours can be rescued, and once rescued, these [cultural] practices will generate self-validation and identity that the West has tried to take away from us. Today, with all that talk about globalization, men must be able to operate in different contexts; not only in their communities and provinces, but also in other places. For this we need technology, modernity. And when a person has identity, self-esteem, pride, and he also has access to technology and the modern world, he can change not only himself and his people, but also his country.

These kinds of comments were remarkable not only because they came from a nonindigenous activist speaking in the name of an indigenous "us." They were also interesting as they formed part of a discourse of indigenous modernity shared by indigenous and nonindigenous activists alike. In this discourse, essentialized identities began to include ideas of technology and modernity. Still, the ghost of tradition haunted modernizing goals: "rescuing" and preserving "what is ours" was now paradoxically the prerequisite for "access to technology and the modern world."

Cultural Production and the Intellectualization of Quechua

Linked to the merging of tradition and modernity, an important aspect in the modification of the term *Indian* was the emphasis placed on the notion of the intellectual. According to Conejo, Francisco, Quispe, and others, the redefinition of Indian identity was due in large part to the increasing number of *indígenas intelectuales* and *indígenas profesionales*. "These indígenas," Conejo argued at a conference in 1998, "are directly responsible for the change in the meaning of the word *indígena* from ignorance, poverty, dirtiness, and marginality to politics, intelligence, identity, and pride" (Conejo 1998). At this conference, Quispe presented his paper in Quechua. Of at least twenty papers, his was the only one in Quechua. As we have seen, Quispe had considered himself a Quechua intellectual for many years, but his views had recently expanded to include recognition of what he called "the modern needs of our young new leaders, such as the Internet."

When I heard Quispe and other Peruvian activists talk about the significance of indigenous intellectuals, I couldn't help remembering Carla's identification of herself as ex-indígena in 1996. In only two years there had been a shift from a label highlighting a lack of Indianness to one highlighting indigenous identity. This change was significant, for the term *ex-indígena* implied not only a loss of cultural or ethnic identification but also the improbability of an educated or professional indígena. Moreover, ethnicity is seen in Peru as usually corresponding to class (van den Berghe 1975; van den Berghe and Primov 1977; de la Cadena 1995). The transition from indígena to mestizo, for example, is seen not only as a shift in ethnic and cultural identity but also one affecting socioeconomic conditions (Matos Mar, ed. 1970; Spalding 1974). The adoption of labels such as *indigenous intellectual* and the rejection of the term *ex-indígena* among activists and intellectuals pointed to the active reconfiguration of indigenous identity. Although activists did recognize that such labels still stressed differentiation among indigenous peoples and the achievement of a more prestigious status within indigenous communities, many also emphasized that "there is no sense of cultural loss" among these intellectuals. "An indigenous intellectual," explained Quispe, "is an indígena. He may still be treated badly by others, but he is recognized by his community as indigenous, even if he speaks English and uses computers."

According to activists, becoming an indigenous intellectual no longer meant the loss of culture or ethnicity in the way that becoming an ex-indígena or mestizo did. Furthermore, activists claimed that the existence of indigenous intellectuals would encourage parents to accept bilingual intercultural education, since they might see other options for their children. In the case of Ecuador, for example, an indigenous elite had emerged around the development of bilingual education programs. In one of the Ecuadorian indigenous movement's first major victories, the state gave indigenous organizations control of the state agency in charge of bilingual intercultural education. If the promotion of bilingual education programs could lead to similar trajectories in Peru, parents might be more accepting of such programs. If intercultural activists are right, their actions would be of tremendous social consequence, because they could challenge the immutable association between ethnicity and socioeconomic conditions perceived by highland peoples. However, parents are rarely exposed to the ideas discussed here. On a few occasions, children will have a teacher like Mario, who single-handedly demanded computers for his school from the Fujimori government. He received two, an important victory but largely symbolic, as his community had no electricity to power them. When I left, he was in the process of lobbying the state again, this time for the installation of electricity in his village.

The term *professional indígena* encompasses the notion of a politically active individual of indigenous ancestry who can manipulate high-tech communications systems. Most national Indian federations, led by these key actors, have Internet access and use, fax machines, camcorders, and video-cassette players. While in 1999 there were no comparable organizations or federations in the Peruvian Andes (but see García and Lucero 2004), part of the training administered to carefully selected individuals of indigenous ancestry, such as community leaders and a few teachers, included learning how to manage computers, and especially how to work with e-mail. But, as we shall see, learning how to hold intellectual and academic discussions about concepts such as culture and ethnicity and engaging in the cultural production of literature (poetry, short stories, scientific articles) in Quechua also played a role in defining who would become an indigenous intellectual in Peru, and who would not.

The appropriation of tools such as computers can and does affect social and political relations within the communities in which they are used. Turner notes, for instance, that among the Kayapó, operating a video camera and, even more important, becoming a video editor have meant combining a prestigious role within the community with a culturally and politically important form of mediation of relations with Western society. In his words, "It has been one way that people have promoted their political careers" (1992: 7). Similarly, while Peruvian activists provided computer training for highland teachers and teacher trainers, those most closely involved with Quechua literary production or computer keyboard adaptation to the Quechua language were usually activists and a few Quechua intellectuals, but never indigenous parents, community leaders, or children.

Between 1996 and 1999 there was only one seminar that I knew of on computers and indigenous languages. The week-long workshop was advertised (in select local papers and buildings) as an open invitation to all "thinkers" who might have useful insight on the subject. Organized by the CBC and with support from the Universidad del País Vasco (Basque University), this project was designed not only to deal with questions about computerizing Quechua but also to continue debating the standardization and normalization of the language. The group in charge was a team of four Peruvian experts (a linguist, a computer technician, and two research assistants), all CBC personnel, and a Basque linguist (invited by the CBC for the specific purpose of sharing the Basque experience with education activists). Although posters advertised the benefit of the workshop for "all Quechua speakers," during the first day of the workshop the leaders clearly stated that their goals were to develop methodological and technological advances that could be useful to the various linguists and other researchers committed to the preservation and development of the Quechua language. More specifically, by illustrating how Quechua was compatible with computer technology and "cyber-public spheres," the activists involved hoped to advance the process of normalization of written Quechua and the development of a pan-Quechua grammar that spanned Bolivia, southern Peru, and beyond.

While not explicitly exclusive, the seminar was prepared and conducted for individuals who fit specific criteria. It was carried out in Spanish, with references to Quechua only when discussion about the problem necessitated examples of words or sentences to enter into computers; it assumed that all present were familiar with computers and knew how to use them; and, as the workshop entered its third day, the stated goals began to center on the importance of this process for the continued production of literature in Quechua by trained linguists. Some of the teachers present were put off by the technological emphasis of the seminar. "They didn't even ask if we knew how to use those things," one of the teachers said after the first day of the workshop. "And," she continued, "we need to learn how to do this for teaching purposes, not for writing poetry or novels the way they want us to." Frustrated by the gap between the lofty technological goal of the seminar and the harsh realities of resource-poor classrooms, she stopped attending after the second day.

Intercultural activists argued that the computerization of Quechua was a crucial step toward achieving their political goals. If their educational goals were met, they claimed, and children learned how to read and write in Quechua on paper, teachers (presumably all trained in computer skills) would be able to instruct children in Quechua with the help of computers. However, they also stated that they first had to concentrate on preparing those individuals they envisioned as future leaders in the movement toward Quechua political activism, because "they — not illiterate parents or third-rate teachers — will be the ones representing the masses." The distinction between "illiterate parents and third-rate teachers" and "indigenous intellectuals" is clearly marked by activists' statements indicating the importance of "learned" Quechuas for the representation of indigenous demands. Activists claimed that indigenous intellectuals were also important because these leaders needed to think about projecting an image not only nationally but internationally as well.

Activists in Cuzco emphasized that local cultural production was essential to strengthen Quechua identity. This process of cultural fortification, labeled the intellectualization of Quechua, most often referred to the production of literature in and about Quechua. While in some ways reminiscent of the Quechua Renaissance of the late 1600s and 1700s (Rowe 1954; Cerrón-Palomino 1985; Mannheim 1990, 1992) and of indigenista literary currents of the late 1800s and early 1900s (Tamayo Herrera 1980, Itier 1992b), the renewed emphasis on the development of Quechua literature differs from earlier efforts in several ways. Unlike the transference of European literary styles to express indigenista concerns in Amerindian languages (1660s–1780) or the "Inca dramas" written by and for the Cuzco elite (1880s–1930s), the kind of Quechua literary production promoted by activists includes, among other genres, scientific articles about Quechua and in Quechua (Coronel-Molina 1999a, 2000, 2001, 2003), testimonial literature (Escalante and Valderrama 1992), bilingual and trilingual dictionaries, linguistic guides for the study of Quechua (Godenzzi and Vengoa Zúñiga 1994), poetry (Castillo 1998), short stories (Chirinos and Maque Capira 1996), children's stories (Conejo n.d.), and collected narratives about and against the recent political violence (Granda Oré 1990).

The emphasis on literary production, as opposed to the production of textiles, ceramics, and to some extent music, was due primarily to activists' constant struggle against the common misperception (among Peruvians) that Quechua is a dead language or dialect that is restricted to oral use and has no alphabet or grammatical structure. It was also a statement about the perceived importance of the written word versus the spoken word. Textiles, ceramics, and music, all considered aspects of Peruvian folklore, were never spoken about in the same way as writing. Accordingly, one way in which activists tried to elevate the status of Quechua was to legitimize it as a linguistically complex language with a rich literary tradition. To do this, they frequently noted (in radio programs and in local televised interviews) that the existing Quechua literary corpus was a continuation of a tradition of Andean literary production (Itier 1992a: 25). Additionally, activists frequently pointed to foreign interest in the language and cited studies and analyses written mainly by European and North American scholars as evidence of the international significance and reach of Quechua. Activists have begun pointing to the emergence of what they call "transnational Quechua literature." Highlighting the international prestige and diffusion of their language, activists point to the increasing number of Peruvian intellectuals in the United States, self-styled indigenous, Andean, or Quechua, who began writing "self-ethnographies" (Coronel-Molina 1999b), and to develop and examine concepts such as "Andean archipelagos" (Zevallos 2002) and postmodern Andean poetry (Roncalla 1998). Along with local writings on the scientific and linguistic value of the Quechua language (Cerrón-Palomino 1982, 1987, 1988; Godenzzi, ed. 1992; Coronel-Molina 2003) and contemporary analyses of colonial Quechua manuscripts, plays, and other documents (Salomon and Urioste 1991; Cevallos-Candau et al. 1994; Urton

1999), these transnational works have become a symbol, among intercultural activists, of the intellectual reach of Quechua and of Quechua intellectuals.

Faye Ginsburg writes that "indigenous cultural self-documentation tends to focus not on the retrieval of an idealized vision of pre-contact culture but on processes of identity-construction in the cultural present" (Ginsburg 1991: 95). Intercultural activists' efforts toward the intellectualization of Quechua by way of literary production in and about Quechua reflect these sorts of identity-building processes. While many linguists and others continue to stress the preservation of language and of "traditional" cultural practices, they are simultaneously promoting another dimension of Quechua identity through written expression. Through their efforts, Quechua identity is not merely "defended," it is also expanded to include characteristics of the culture they label as dominant. Moreover, activists today also strive to present an image of intellectual and academic indígenas. Distinctions between tradition and modernity, the spoken and the written word, local and global, are no longer starkly opposed, but rather dissolve in the process of defining indigenous ethnicity. Among the activists and intellectuals engaged in these cultural politics of identity, discussions about identity, ethnicity, and Indianness are, in themselves, part of the newly developed vision of who a Peruvian Quechua Indian must be.

Training Indigenous Intellectuals:
Global Spaces, Local Politics

> In the 1990s, the presence and autonomous voice [*voz*
> *propia*] of indigenous peoples mark the end of the century
> and their entry into the new millennium.
> —Luis Enrique López , 1998

The anthropologist Stefano Varese has described the growing empowerment of indigenous movements throughout Latin America as struggles spurred by the link between local thought and global action (Varese 1991). In Peru, the opposite seems to be true. In Cuzco during the late 1990s, ethnic and cultural politics among activists were framed by rhetoric about the impact of globalization on local development and about the "reemergence" of indigenous cultural and ethnic identity as a springboard for local change. Luis Enrique López, leading advocate of bilingual intercultural education, made the following statement at a conference on indigenous education:

Globalization means decentralization, which means regionalism and local space. . . .
Globalization today implies not only economic changes but also cultural processes
of change. . . . We must take advantage of this moment and reclaim local and regional

spaces, and simultaneously use transnational spaces, in order to erase [*desdibujar*] national borders . . . and to better understand our indigenous communities. (López 1998)

The emphasis López placed on local change by working at transnational and international levels rang particularly true for Peruvian activists in the 1990s, largely because of their concerns about political organization in the country. In his analysis of pan-indigenous and popular mobilization in Latin America, the anthropologist Charles Hale says that the Pan-American Indian movement has a transnational identity by necessity (Hale 1994b). He also argues that while the movement is

conditioned by the numerous Indian cultures whose people straddle the boundaries of established nation-states, the well-proven strategy of mustering strength through numbers, and the virtual necessity of meeting outside the purview of repressive states to discuss what is to be done . . . , this identity does not determine the consciousness of actors or the course of events at the grassroots [level], [though] the interplay and influence is pervasive." (Hale 1994b: 14)

Intercultural activists and intellectuals in Peru often said that bilingual intercultural education, as a cause around which indigenous people can organize, could develop a cohesive identity that would serve as a platform for the emergence of an indigenous movement. However, before the fall of Fujimori in 2000, political grass-roots organization in the highlands still held negative connotations for many Peruvians, and government forces maintained strict control over most forms of political organization in the country.

Activists often lamented the limitations on their capacity to organize politically, and with a few exceptions emphasized not the political but the cultural and educational aspects of indigenous organization and identity. Throughout the 1990s, ethnic politics in Peru was characterized by cultural activism. Precisely because of the transnational and global nature of indigenous movements in Latin America, however, as Hale notes among pan-indigenous organizations, activists in Peru were able to assert the political role of Peruvian Andean indigenous leaders, and to take the next step toward the development of a local indigenous organization by training indigenous leaders outside of their country. As John Comaroff comments in his discussion about ethnicity and cultural pluralism in today's world, "it is the very experience of globalism that underscores an awareness of localism — and, in the process, reinforces it" (Comaroff 1996: 174).

Highlighting education reform as one way to reposition indigenous identities and redistribute economic and social resources (López 1998), López and several other intercultural education activists established a regionally specific training program for bilingual intercultural education in Bolivia: the PROEIB

Andes. The center offers a master's program for indigenous leaders from five countries: Bolivia, Chile, Colombia, Ecuador, and Peru. Supported by the Bolivian and German governments, this alternative institute is designed as a training program for bilingual intercultural teachers specifically for the Andean region. To be accepted, a student must be a representative of a recognized indigenous organization and must speak the language of his or her ethnic group.

Although this program is only one of several higher-education centers for Andean indigenous leaders, it is the only one that brings together indigenous representatives from five countries, from approximately twenty indigenous organizations (including three from lowland Peru), and that works with at least twenty Andean universities and is supported by thirty-five state-run and internationally funded organizations as well as two national governments (Bolivia and Germany) (Sichra and López 2003).

The cultural and political implications of this program and the training it offers are striking, especially in the way ethnicity is used as cultural capital to aid the advancement of indigenous ethnic and political autonomy and social reform in Andean countries. For example, upon returning to their communities, students at these centers are expected to use the training they receive, as "agents of change of the sociocultural, sociolinguistic, and socioeducational reality" in indigenous nations (*pueblos*), to develop an awareness of ethnic and cultural identity among individuals in highland regions. Beyond local and regional identities, however, there is explicit mention of the unification of indigenous efforts against ethnic, linguistic, and cultural discrimination, and accordingly, of the development of a pan-indigenous identity and of transnational alliances between indigenous groups.

Part of student training at the PROEIB Andes, for example, includes fieldwork, and students are expected to conduct fieldwork in their home communities.[5] The idea is that as "insiders" they can examine the social conditions there and explore the possibility for work on intercultural and bilingual education or gender roles (i.e., working toward the availability of schooling for girls). Students are then to return to the institute and develop proposals for cultural and educational projects appropriate for their regions. They are also encouraged to form discussion groups and workshops (*mesas de trabajo*) to share their experiences, and to work together toward the development of local and pan-indigenous cultural projects.

The significance of the PROEIB Andes to bilingual intercultural education activists in Peru is tremendous. First, while intercultural activists in Peru continue with their work among community leaders, highland teachers, and parents, some of the activists, capacitadores, and intellectuals already exposed to intercultural ideology and methodology can further their training as future leaders of what activists see as an expanding cultural and education movement. Second, interaction with indigenous leaders, intellectuals, and professionals from at least four other countries and nineteen other ethnic groups is considered an invaluable experience. Indigenous Peruvian students can learn from their classmates about both successful and unsuccessful experiences with grass-roots organizing and negotiations with government agents. Further, sharing several years of training can potentially create alliances with other groups for future benefit. Aware of the international contacts, the availability of technological updates, and other benefits to be gained by participating in the program at the PROEIB, activists in Peru in the 1990s viewed the opportunity for Peruvian indigenous students to attend this center as taking them one step closer to their political goals. While developments among education activists in Cuzco have, from their beginnings, been influenced by many of the leading activists in Ecuador and Bolivia, the links established at the PROEIB bind Peruvian activists even closer to the declared goals of indigenous leaders throughout the Andes.

At the end of 1999, the goals for each class at the institute seemed clear: teach students anthropology, linguistics, and pedagogy; help them develop regionally specific teaching methodologies; and discuss the importance of using this knowledge to expand ideas within local communities about language preservation, cultural revitalization, and, most important, indigenous identity. Because discussions took place in relatively safe political conditions, these forums provided fertile ground for the advancement of original ideas about indigenous politics and for the testing of potentially controversial proposals. This has been explicitly articulated by Peruvian indigenous leaders at the center as a "feeling of potential and hope": "I never imagined that we could be talking to each other in Quechua, as Quechuas," Samuel, a Quechua leader from Ayacucho, told me. "But here, among our indigenous *compañeros* and *compañeras* from Latin America, and among our own Quechua brothers, there is a feeling of potential and hope."[6]

Exploring the politics of Indianness among the Tukanoans in the Vaupés, Colombia, Jean Jackson discusses the ways in which regional, national, and international Indian identity politics influence Tukanoans' local conceptualizations of culture (Jackson 1995a). She notes especially that Tukanoans are in a process of "becoming Indian" (1991) largely as a result of the effective mobilization of what non-Tukanoans consider "authentic" culture and identity. What is significant in this process, and relevant to the Peruvian case, is that notions of culture and authenticity among Tukanoans have changed as a result of actions of indigenous activists, and particularly because of their heightened awareness of the potential benefits and political power afforded to their communities by retaining, preserving, and, most important, asserting their Indian identity (1995a: 12). Similarly, ideas about indigenous identity and citizenship in the highlands of Peru have been shifting for many years. As in Colombia, "becoming Indian" in Peru is a dialogic process that is set within a transnational field of action.

Rediscovering Identity: The Transnational Politics of Indianness

Examinations of the resurgence of indigenous movements address their increasingly global and transnational character (Varese 1988). This internationalization of indigenous politics (Brysk 1994) is considered an important strategy for sustaining and strengthening their organizations. These explorations also address the emergence of indigenous ethnicity in these global and transnational spaces (Nagengast and Kearney 1990; Field 1994a; Kearney 1995a, 1995b; Stephen 1996). As a transnational institution actively promoting the development of localized ethnic identities among indigenous leaders, the PROEIB Andes is an example of such processes. One of the most visible results of interactions among students at the PROEIB is the conscious deconstruction of the category of Indian by indigenous leaders at the center and the construction of an indigenous political identity.

In August 1999 I attended an international seminar at the PROEIB on ethnicity, gender, and education. Participating were approximately forty Latin American professionals, intellectuals, and scholars, including NGO personnel, representatives of the ministries of education of Ecuador, Bolivia, Colombia, and Peru, and international representatives of the German Foundation for International Development, UNICEF-Bolivia, UNICEF-Peru, UNESCO, and the German Technological Institute (GTZ). Among them were five indigenous representatives of indigenous organizations from Bolivia, Colombia, and Guatemala.

For five days the participants sat around a table and discussed, among other issues, their views about social inequality, democratic education, and indigenous autonomy. At the same time, in a room directly below the conference room, indigenous students gathered to take notes about the discussion above, watching the debates about indígenas and education in Latin America on a large television screen. At one point, a discussion about indigenous identity ensued downstairs among several Peruvian Quechuas, Bolivian Aymaras, and Chilean Mapuches. One male student, an Aymara, said calmly that his parents were campesinos-indígenas, but he was now an Aymara professional, not an Indian. A young Mapuche woman replied indignantly that he had a responsibility to his people as an indigenous leader and as a representative of his indigenous organization. "How can you say you're not an indígena!" she exclaimed. "You have a responsibility!" The young Aymara replied: "I still don't understand why they keep calling us Indians. I am a representative of

my people, of my Aymara nation [*mi pueblo Aymara*]. But why do we have
to label ourselves Indian?" Marco, a Peruvian Quechua student, replied:
"We're professionals and we're intellectuals, but we're also indígenas because
we have it in our blood, and because people treat us like indios, whether we're
intellectuals or not. To change that we need to be respected as indígenas and
Quechuas. We need to show them that Indians are also intelligent, capable,
and modern. That's why we call ourselves Indian."

These comments, and many others I heard throughout the seminar,
reflect the multiple perspectives that exist about the ethnic labels used to
depict these indigenous future teachers and leaders. However, what struck
me most forcefully as I sat among these students and listened to their debates
was the enormous variation in their self-representations and in their own
interpretations of indigenous identity. While academic scholars, government
agents, NGO personnel, and representatives of international funding organizations debated development policy geared toward a homogeneous group
of indigenous people, the future leaders of indigenous groups critiqued, challenged, rejected, and in a few cases agreed with the comments made in the
conference room above their small, windowless classroom.[7] Marco's com-
mentary was particularly interesting to me. Given that the Peruvian highlands
have been noted (by scholars and activists alike) for the *lack* of indigenous
identification among their many inhabitants, his self-identification as indígena was significant. Just as important was the fact that he identified others, especially other Peruvian Quechua students at the center, as indígenas
as well. Discussing Indian identity, Kearney says that "the construction of
ethnicity by contemporary indígenas has become and is becoming more of
a conscious, intentional activity than before. . . . The new indígenas are elab-
orating it as political and cultural projects" (Kearney 1996: 10). While
activists have focused primarily on cultural valorization and education
reform, training indigenous professionals as future political leaders quickly
became an important step toward the development of ethnic politics in Peru.

According to Peruvian activists, the principal benefit achieved by student
training at the PROEIB is that indigenous leaders in the movement toward
education reform and cultural preservation will be indigenous. Marco, the
student who commented on the Bolivian Aymaras' concerns about identity
labels, exemplifies this process of "becoming Indian." Before beginning his
studies at the PROEIB in Bolivia, Marco identified himself as a mestizo from
the department of Apurimac, bordering Cuzco. Nonetheless, he felt "a deep
connection" with Quechua, and was proud not only to speak fluent Quechua
but to write it as well. He expressed himself best, he told me, in his poetry,
most of which he wrote in Quechua, although he also enjoyed writing in
Spanish. Marco and I met and became friends in 1996 at the CBC in Cuzco.
At that time, in addition to taking courses on bilingual education method-

ology and Andean linguistics, Marco was a capacitador for one of the first NGOs to work with bilingual education issues in Cuzco. His job was primarily to promote bilingual education and the study of Quechua in workshops specifically designed for highland teachers from communities surrounding Cuzco. He was also in charge of monitoring the performance of teachers in some of these communities.

Because of his involvement with bilingual education policies, his linguistics training in Cuzco, his work with educational NGOs, and his ability to write in Quechua, Marco was accepted into the program in Bolivia.[8] Along with fifty-two other students from the five countries previously mentioned, he began his training in Bolivia in June 1998. I visited Marco and this program that September. After only four months, my friend had transformed himself: now he identified himself as both Quechua and indígena. Whereas before arriving in Bolivia he felt a connection to Quechua, after only a few months with other indigenous students he spoke of the "undeniable commitment" he felt toward "his people" (un compromiso innegable con mi gente).

Fernando, who identified as a mestizo when I first met him in 1997, also spoke of his responsibilities "as a Quechua leader." Talking explicitly about his identity transformation, Fernando told me about his spiritual return (viaje de retorno). "People like us," he said, "who have had opportunities to study, to learn Spanish — maybe English, like Marco — people like us have to lead our people and teach them so they can become free to teach themselves." I asked why he thought he had been selected for the program. He replied:

At first I didn't even believe in teaching in Quechua. Then when I went to training workshops and talked to people, I realized the value of culture and language and identity. People have robbed us of our identity and brainwashed us into believing we're not indígenas. I think [intercultural activists] knew because of my work that I would understand and learn how to be a leader, so they selected me.

While Marco's and Fernando's experiences are only two examples of the consequences of training at the PROEIB (and among activists in other forums), all of the students with whom I spoke verbalized a similar awakening to the importance of indigenous language, identity, and autonomy after "talking to people," or attending bilingual intercultural education workshops and seminars. Adopting or emphasizing indigenous identity was always legitimized by the recognition of indigenous ancestry, and often accompanied by relief at their cultural recovery. Invariably, new indigenous leaders, including community leaders and highland teachers who had recently converted to intercultural education, described feeling guilty because of what they called their previous "cultural loss." A typical comment was a confession of previous rejection of Quechua, or la cultura (the culture). At the same time, however, they also expressed condescension toward their parents and families because of monolingualism in Quechua or "backwardness."

The kind of dialogue I witnessed at the PROEIB, among students as well as between students, teachers, and lecturers (mainly Europeans, North Americans, and Latin American nonindigenous intellectuals), was centered on indigenous rights, ethnic autonomy, power, and the students' self-identification and self-determination as indigenous peoples. As a result of this dialogue, in a short time the various manifestations of cultural and identity politics emerging among Peruvian indigenous leaders at the PROEIB Andes reflected changes in the self-identification of these leaders. Debates about ethnicity and culture among students belonging to at least twenty distinct indigenous groups in the Andes, students' reactions to and examinations of the category of "Indian," and the delicate nature of both theoretical and applied training at the center, all led to visible changes in Peruvian Quechua students' expressions about identity, cultural and ethnic autonomy, and citizenship rights.

Yet despite the intensity of debates about Indianness, politics, and ethnicity (or perhaps as a result of these debates), there has been considerable conflict among students and between students and instructors at the PROEIB, particularly about issues of representation and authenticity. When I first arrived in Cochabamba, I overheard a conversation that some of the students — among them Fernando — were having about what he called a "political counterdiscourse" among the students during the first four months of the program. After the gathering of students broke up, Fernando shared with me some of the initial malaise at the center, due (according to him) to conflicting interests between the various indigenous representatives, all of whom had certain expectations about the training they were to receive in Bolivia. This conflict arose as much among students as between students and instructors, and it revolved around differing interpretations of concepts such as Indian identity, ethnicity, culture, and political activism. When I asked him to explain what he meant by a "political counterdiscourse," he replied: "Some of the instructors and especially some of the students regurgitate jargon about Indian rights, the environment, globalization, because it's in fashion. But what do all these words and theories have to do with us? With our people? With indígenas? That is what we need to debate."

As indigenous leaders increasingly participate, as presenters or experts, in forums such as the conference I described earlier, and as they collaborate with U.S. or European scholars and representatives of international institutions, other people sometimes see them as Westernized.[9] During a panel at this particular conference about gender discrimination, for example, one Aymara intellectual presented her ideas about gender roles in Aymara society. Being Aymara herself, she consistently claimed authenticity throughout her talk, which emphasized the inequality of men and women in Aymara homes, and ended by stating that her position, as representative of the Aymara community, gave her the authority to say such things about "her people." Her presentation caused an uproar in the classroom below (where I sat with the students watching the presentation), particularly among the women in the room. According to most of their energized reactions and comments, the woman who claimed Aymaraness was clearly an impostor. "How can she *really* be Aymara if she uses concepts and words like 'gender'?" one woman asked, exasperated. "That's nothing but a Western imposition," she said forcefully as she picked up her copy of Fredrik Barth's *Ethnic Groups and Boundaries* and walked toward the door. "I don't think we should stand for that."

Interculturalidad, Globalization, and Citizenship: New Terms for Indigenous Struggle

Examining the work of scholars writing about globalization and nationalism, the anthropologist Robert Foster asks: "Are the globalization and localization of cultural production two moments of the same total process . . . ?" (Foster 1991: 236). López, the leading activist I mentioned earlier, would say yes. In his opinion, globalization allows for the expansion of local spaces and the development of localized identities that are simultaneously globally constituted. Significantly, this term crept up during most of the conversations I had with activists from Peru. The effect that the concept of globalization and its various interpretations has had on the actions of indigenous leaders should not be underestimated. The actions of indigenous leaders and activists have been portrayed as examples of the many ways in which marginal groups challenge and expand our understanding of democracy in Latin America by broadening existing definitions of citizenship and popular participation (Alvarez, Dagnino, and Escobar, eds., 1998). Additionally, scholars have illustrated how international discussions about indigenous rights and globalization can and do affect indigenous activists' particular concerns about representation, identity, and the kind of change desired for their communities (Brysk 2000b, Edelman 1999). Marco's concern with the image of indigenous peoples as "intelligent, capable, and modern" also reflects activists' almost constant references to indigenous peoples as "global peoples."

I met Marco, Fernando, and several of the other Peruvian Quechua students now at PROEIB Andes two years before their admission into the program because of my contact with them in Cuzco. Since their entry in mid-1998, interactions among these indigenous leaders, as well as with representatives of international funding agents, NGO personnel, and social researchers at the center, are changing the ways in which Peruvian Quechua leaders can and do represent themselves. These self-representations are tied to new ideas about citizenship rights, democracy, and human rights, and to the expansion among Quechua leaders of notions of a Quechua community, at both local and transnational levels. Yet even before the start of PROEIB, one could feel the sense of possibility that ideas about education and identity carried.

Since my first encounter with education activists in Peru in 1996, there has been a significant expansion of dialogues about language and identity. When I asked Quispe what democracy meant to him, he responded: "Democracy in Peru has often meant forgetting we exist; erasing us from the map. What we need is a revolutionary democracy. We want to be included, to be part of this global process that people talk about; of globalization. But we want to do so as Quechuas and as Peruvians, because we are members of two nations." As Quispe's comments reflect, the ways in which these concepts are interwoven demonstrate a re-visioning of national belonging and cultural citizenship in Peru today. The mention of a "revolutionary democracy" was also common among activists, though in all cases they stressed a peaceful revolution, or, in the words of one activist, a "revolution of words, education, and culture" that would help Quechuas demand rights as indigenous Peruvian citizens. Intellectuals in centers such as the CBC in Peru and the PROEIB in Bolivia are clearly playing an important role in challenging the boundaries of dominant identities and orthodoxies. Yet indigenous intellectuals also exist outside of academic centers. In communities, local indigenous intellectuals are also engaged in contesting the relations of representation.

In September 1998 I was sitting on the dirt floor of a classroom in a highland school about two days' travel from the city of Cuzco. Paola, the nurse appointed to the nearest medical center, was sitting next to me. In the classroom about twenty Quechua men and women, all parents, gathered and waited for the arrival of the school's director. This day was important for Clotilde, the director. On this day, she had told me a few hours before, she would inaugurate the community's first escuela de padres. Everyone would be there, even the capacitador assigned to her community. As Paola, the parents, and I silently waited for Clotilde and the capacitador to arrive, Pablo, one of the most outspoken men in the community (and one of the most outspoken I ever encountered in the area), suddenly stood up and addressed the gathering. "Why are we here?" he asked. "Is it because we want to know about this educational change that's happening? Because you know, they don't care about education. They want us here so they can brainwash us. They call it consciousness-raising [concientización]." Heraclio, president of the community, visibly annoyed by Pablo's comments, responded:

What do you care why they want us here? What's important is what we can get out of it. Look, first we were indios and had no rights. Then we were campesinos and we received some benefits. Now they say we're indígenas, and that being indígenas

and Peruvian means that we'll get more benefits, like better education for our *wawas*
[children]. Until now, being Peruvian campesinos hasn't given us a thing. Maybe being
indigenous citizens will.

This was the first time I had heard the concept of indigenous citizenship
verbalized by a community leader. It was also the first time I had heard so
many identity labels being thrown around at once by Quechua parents.
Heraclio's awareness of activists' identity politics was not unusual, however.
As noted in earlier chapters, parents were conscious of activists' desire to
develop indigenous identification among highlanders. What was distinct from
my experience in other communities, however, was the open use and manipulation of ethnic labels for very specific ends.

International attention to indigenous rights has focused not only on the
collective rights of indigenous groups but also on the expansion of the individual rights of indigenous citizens as new actors in civil society (Alvarez et
al., eds., 1998; Brysk 2000a). This "re-Indianization," as the anthropologist
Charles Hale (1997) describes it,[10] can be partly understood as a response —
both by indigenous groups in the region and by organizations and individuals sympathetic to the indigenous cause — to the pervasiveness of neoliberal
economic policies and increasing global networking.

Discussions about essentialist presentations of ethnicity focus on "who is
utilizing essentialism, how it is deployed, and where its effects are concentrated" (Fuss 1989: 20; see also Foster 1991; D. Scott 1991). With regard
to indigenous peoples specifically, cultural essentialism has been examined
as a political strategy to attain benefits in the face of political and social exclusion (Warren 1992, 1998a; Cojtí Cuxil 1996). This does not mean, however,
that Latin American indigenous leaders invent, create, or mobilize ethnicity
solely for political purposes. Though in some cases the adoption of Indianness or indigenous identity is analyzed as a direct result of the link between
ethnicity and the right to land, education, language, or development aid
(Roosens 1989), most examinations of the relationship between ethnicity
(particularly indigenous ethnicity) and political action in Latin America provide a more nuanced analysis of the "range of ways that essentialist precepts
are woven into political consciousness and practice, and the highly variable
material consequences that result" (Hale 1997: 578).[11]

While Hale and others argue that the intersection of local, national, and
global forces in Latin America has led to the emergence of the indígena as
a "new subject position," I would hesitate to say that Heraclio's comments
about indigenous citizenship indicate the repositioning of highland peoples
at all levels of Peruvian civil society. Yet my observations in Peru lead me to
agree that "indigenism," as the anthropologist Alcida Ramos (1998) labels
the dialectic relationship between indigenous peoples and national society,
has (re)emerged in Peru as the basis for renegotiating identity politics and

citizenship in the country. The intersections of local (grass-roots), national, and global forces have opened the possibility for indigenous peoples in Peru to become indigenous citizens. However, indigenous highlanders are still defined by their difference from those in power, and most parents and community leaders with whom I spoke were aware of the existing ethnic and cultural hierarchies in their country. They also stressed their awareness of the fact that activists mobilize around notions of valorization and preservation of Quechua culture, although most of them are not Quechuas themselves. Would the return of indigenous Quechua leaders to highland communities change this? Further research is needed to explore the dynamics of this process.

Indigenous leaders who graduate from the PROEIB Andes will have had two years of interactions with other indigenous leaders, with instructors from North America, South America, and Europe, and with representatives of international aid organizations. Moreover, they will have immersed themselves in works of political theory, social thought, and radical pedagogy. Holding a master's degree in education and linguistics, these new social actors are well positioned to occupy unique spaces in civil society. One of the most significant outcomes is simply the challenge to the links among Indianness, class, literacy, and poverty, so often assumed in Latin America to be unbreakable. Much like the middle-class Mayas of Guatemala, who as a result of pan-Maya activism are now a legitimate social group (Warren 1998a), Quechua intellectuals, because of the status they have gained through education (de la Cadena 2000: 9), represent a new social category. Whereas a few years earlier learning English and using computers were enough to designate cultural loss and identify someone as an ex-indígena or mestizo, today these skills do not necessarily imply a loss of identity. Rather, they are expected attributes of indigenous intellectuals and professional Quechuas, and crucial components of current definitions of indigenous ethnicity. Following precedents set by leaders of the broader Indian rights movement, indígena leaders must speak their indigenous language, must have indigenous ancestry, and should wear (or at least own) clothing representative of their community or region, but must also master Spanish, know how to operate a computer, be capable of navigating among international donor agencies, and know how to negotiate with both state and foreign development agents for funding for their communities. In short, indigenous leaders are increasingly defined by their ability to move in both local and global spaces (Brysk 2000).

The emergence of these indigenous intellectuals also raises interesting questions about the nature of ethnic politics and representation. Indigenous leaders leaving the PROEIB have all been trained in bilingual intercultural education methodology and are expected to disseminate this kind of education among highland communities. For these leaders, speaking, reading, and writing in Quechua has become a status symbol. Beyond verbal fluency, written fluency in an indigenous language, along with the manipulation of other cultural markers such as dress, qualifies these intellectuals as indígenas. As such, they form part of the increasing number of individuals throughout Latin America who are seen by states, international donor organizations, and NGOs as representatives of indigenous peoples, and their social status is elevated accordingly. The elevation of status of these individuals, due in part to their manipulation of vernacular languages as languages of authenticity and Indianness (Anderson 1990), is also a consequence of their ability to manage global tools, technological innovations, and international languages (e.g. computers, the Internet, and English). Their unique position as bilingual (in many cases trilingual) mediators between the traditional and the modern, also bears on the notion of bilingual intellectual elites as crucial actors in emerging nationalist movements (Anderson 1991 [1983]), a fact that may have served as incentive for activists' emphasis on training indigenous intellectuals. Until now, activists and capacitadores have almost always acted as mediators between indigenous Quechuas and teachers on the one hand and the state on the other. They have also acted as mediators between the state and international funding agencies interested in social development projects aimed at indigenous groups. What have usually come to the surface, then, have been activists' interpretations of local developments among indigenous highlanders, which, as I have discussed throughout this book, are not the same as those that Quechua highlanders might highlight. Regardless of parental challenges to bilingual intercultural education, activists have been the primary representatives of indigenous highland Peruvians, and usually they voice their own opinions—not those of parents or teachers—about the needs of indigenous peoples in the country. In part because of questions (from indigenous leaders in neighboring countries as well as from parents themselves) about their capacity to represent highland Quechuas, activists focused on selecting and training individuals who would fit better as leaders of an indigenous organization. Yet, as Les Field suggests, "the term [*indigenous intellectual*] does not connote that either genealogically or culturally marked Indianness naturally endows indigenous intellectuals with the capacity to represent the ideas and interests of indigenous peoples" (1996b: 141). Again, the distinction between literate, bilingual indigenous leaders and frequently illiterate Quechua farmers critically separates the realities of these two groups of people. Yet, as Gramsci would observe, both community members and Indian professionals are intellectuals, as they each contribute "to sustain a conception of the world or to modify it" (1971: 9). Their contributions and conflicts are central to reimagining and reforming Peru.

The Ausangate, 1998. This and the following photographs all by the author.

Children line up for school in a community in the Sacred Valley, 1998.

Inauguration of the parent school in the Ausangate, July 1998. Parents were able to use forums like this to influence the actions of EIB proponents.

This poster promoting bilingual intercultural education was distributed by the
UNEBI throughout the Ausangate region in 1998.

A man helps his son with schoolwork outside the main building of a school in the Ausangate region. Though it was unusual for men to be so publicly involved with their children's education, parents did play an active role in shaping the content of bilingual intercultural education in the region.

Part **III**

CONCLUSIONS

6 Articulating Indigenous Citizenship

INTERCULTURAL IDENTITIES AND POLITICS

> If we [Peruvians] are to transform this country into a
> more democratic place, the concept of a multicultural
> and plurilingual nation must go beyond the paper [the
> constitution] and into our schools and our reality, so
> that our children can feel that to be Quechua is to belong,
> not to be strangers in their own country.
>
> — Rodolfo, schoolteacher in Cuzco, 1997

As I near the end of this book, I feel that it is important to share some of my thoughts about why I decided to write it in the first place. After all, there are certainly many good scholarly works on multiculturalism, development, and indigenous politics. Why one more? One reviewer offered a possible answer in suggesting that this book didn't really belong among those subject headings; rather, at the end of the day, the "real topic" of the book was education. While I agree that this book is certainly about the debates over the ideas and implementation of new educational programs in the Andes, the voices in these debates speak to the broad questions of development and democracy. This should not come as a great surprise; education has never been far from either the emancipatory Marxist challenges to oppression (as demonstrated in the embattled prose of Gramsci and Paulo Freire) or the liberal promise of freedom and democracy (as illustrated by the hopeful pragmatism of John Dewey). As the previous chapters have tried to show, the politics of indigenous education in local communities and transnational institutes have profound implications for the ways in which scholars think about not only Peru but the large questions of identity, citizenship, and social movements in many parts of the world.

Resituating Peru

As the Introduction explained, the case of Peru has occupied a peculiar but critical place in scholarly discussion of the latest wave of indigenous politics in Latin America. It is peculiar because for the country that was the center of the Inca empire, and where roughly 40 percent of the people are officially categorized as "indigenous," indigenous mobilization has not taken the explosive forms that have attracted so much attention in Ecuador, Bolivia, Guatemala, and Mexico. It was critical, however, in many academic discussions largely because it represented absence. Peru, in the vocabulary of social science, was a "negative case."

Yet if we step back and look anew at these writings in an anthropological spirit, it becomes clear that the very characterization of indigenous "absence" is itself a representation of indigenous politics in need of careful examination. Built into these characterizations of Peruvian indigenous politics (implicitly or explicitly) are certain models of what count as political and social movements: they should be national, they should be organized around recognizable banners of identity, and their tactics should resemble the familiar forms of coordinated marches, strikes, and street protests.[1]

Like all analytic constructs, these models have advantages, but they also have clear limitations. Most serious, once we accept the claims of absence, there is less urgency to the question of what is taking place on the ground. Rather, the question becomes "Why is what is happening elsewhere not happening here?" When the question is framed this way, it becomes harder to see the profound importance of indigenous parents negotiating and contesting the programs of NGO workers and state agencies. It is also less clear how a transnational indigenous institute matters to the dynamics of the new subject-making politics of indigenous movements and their advocates in Peru and elsewhere.

In the place of the language of failure, I suggest that we move toward the language of articulation (Hall 1996 [1986]; Clifford 2000, 2001; Li 2000). The theory of articulation, as has been mentioned, refers to the double meaning of the term: the act of expression as well as the process of joining together distinct elements and positions. Identity politics is, as Clifford puts it, a "political cobbling together," as ideas, interests, and agendas come together in powerful yet always provisional ways. "Instead of rigid confrontations . . . one sees continuing struggles across a terrain, portions of which are captured by changing alliances, hooking and unhooking particular elements . . . crucial political and cultural positions are not firmly anchored on one side or the other, but are contested and up for grabs" (2001: 477).

As Li demonstrates in her insightful ethnographic study of Indonesian indigenous politics, in order to understand how this "hooking and unhooking" actually happens, anthropologists must pay attention both to the agency of subaltern subjects in repositioning themselves politically as well as to the "unevenness of conjunctures and conditions of possibility" that are often presented by states and NGOs (2000: 153). In a similar spirit, I seek to show how indigenous politics in Peru offers additional insights into the politics of articulating indigenous identities and forging alternative conceptions of citizenship and social movement.

Indigenous Citizenship: Theory and Practice

Citizenship, as concept and category, has a long history. With roots stretching back to Aristotle, liberal conceptions of citizenship describe the relationship between the state and its political subjects. Citizenship expresses ideals of belonging, equality, and participation in public life. In some demanding versions, citizenship also invokes a sense of duty to the state and fellow citizens. All of these visions, however, have in common the premise that cultural or racial difference is not a morally relevant consideration for the exercise of citizenship. When racial oppression has threatened citizenship, the liberal response has been to attempt to eliminate the legal structures that enforce that oppression so that race can again be taken out of the mix of politics; citizenship becomes once again "color-blind." José de San Martín, at the moment of Peruvian independence, articulated precisely this kind of view when he declared that "in the future the aborigines shall not be called Indian or natives; they are children and citizens of Peru, and they shall be known as Peruvians" (quoted in Lynch 1973: 276).

Notions of indigenous citizenship clearly go against the grain of this tradition, as a particular notion of indigenous identity is hitched to a supposedly universal category of citizen. Yet, as we have seen, many intercultural activists, indigenous intellectuals, and state officials have sought to advance precisely this hybrid notion — the idea that one can be Quechua and Peruvian, or more strongly, become Peruvian by being Quechua. This strategy seeks to rework the concept of citizenship so that cultural difference is no longer a criterion for exclusion, but one of inclusion in a multicultural political community. As many scholars have noted, the recasting of citizenship in postliberal ways is emerging throughout Latin America, and indeed the world (Yashar 1998 and forthcoming; Stavenhagen 2002; Kymlicka and Norman, eds., 2000). Even if we limit our discussion to Peru, it is clear that the cultural politics at the turn of the millennium are forcing scholars to refashion the conceptual tools with which we have apprehended questions of belonging in the modern world.

One scholar who provides some possible conceptual starting points is the anthropologist Renato Rosaldo. In Cuzco, activists have used the idea of indigenous citizenship for motives similar to those behind Rosaldo's concept of cultural citizenship. Rosaldo argues that "cultural citizenship operates in an uneven field of structural inequalities where the dominant claims of universal citizenship assume a propertied white male subject and usually blind themselves to their exclusions and marginalizations of people who differ in gender, race, sexuality, and age" (Rosaldo 1999: 260). Rosaldo calls for "full citizenship" and cultural recognition for those who occupy "subordinate positions" in society.

Yet this view of cultural citizenship — even for those sympathetic to its politics — has certain analytic drawbacks. Aihwa Ong describes some of the problems with Rosaldo's view when she suggests that he "tends to only one side of the unequal relationships." Rosaldo, she suggests, "gives the erroneous impression that cultural citizenship can be unilaterally constructed" and that disadvantaged groups can "escape the cultural inscription" of state and social forces that "define the different modalities of belonging" (Ong 1999a: 263–264). In place of Rosaldo's conception, Ong provides an alternative view of cultural citizenship that is very much in the spirit of the theory of articulation described above, one that emphasizes agency as well as broader power relations. "Cultural citizenship is a dual process of self-making and being-made within webs of power linked to the nation-state and civil society. Becoming a citizen depends on how one is constituted as a subject who exercises or submits to power relations . . . in shifting fields of power that include the nation-state and the wider world" (Ong 1999a: 264). This view has several important advantages for our understanding of the politics of indigenous citizenship in Peru.

First, it does not limit discussion of citizenship to the state but rather, following Foucault, looks to "civil institutions and social groups as disciplinary forces in the making of cultural citizens" (Ong 1999a: 264–265). State agencies, NGOs, and rural communities are thus all connected in the webs of power that run through Peruvian society and shape Peruvian identities. Second, Ong opens the door to moving theorizing citizenship beyond the boundaries of the nation-state (see also Basch, Glick Shiller, and Szanton-Blanc 1994; Glick Schiller and Fouron 2001). Elsewhere, in the context of her ethnographic work on Asian migration, Ong argues that transnational resources and networks are integral parts of the ways in which subaltern subjects (migrants in her case) can flexibly reposition their memberships in multiple political communities (Ong 1999b). Her notion of "flexible citizenship" is useful in understanding how local identities (Quechua, Aymara, Asháninka) also become part of international identities (indigenous) through the transnational reach of movement activity, development agendas, and international law. With these more flexible, articulated notions of citizenship in mind, we can now return to the ways in which states, NGOs, and communities construct (deconstruct and reconstruct) indigenous citizenship in the Andes.

Interactions Among Communities, the State, and NGOs

As Chapter 3 demonstrated, rural Quechua-speaking people do not universally accept the concept of indigenous citizenship. Over the centuries, the highland peoples of Peru have uneasily and unevenly taken the terms *Indian, Peruvian,* and *peasant* (among others) to describe their reality and their relations with colonial, republican, and populist states. Now these same populations are being encouraged to think of themselves in a new (but old) way, as members of both Quechua and Peruvian nations. One parent saw this as an opportunity that his community should seize. Perhaps this would finally help bring in desperately needed resources to the community, if not from the state, then perhaps from NGOs. But as we have also seen, many resisted the idea of indigenous citizenship that came with the new intercultural education. Quechua parents worried that instruction in Quechua, rather than opening the door to a new era of indigenous citizenship, would simply lead to the same dead end of being Indian in a racist society. The only road to citizenship they saw was one that went through Spanish-language education. Yet, ironically, in hopes of moving along that road, some Quechua mothers sought to gain access to intercultural education themselves in the hope of being able to teach their children the Spanish they could acquire.

Although there is no single unified response to intercultural education, I would argue that in all these acts, citizenship is being articulated in dynamic ways. As members of local communities, parents invoke their right to have a say in the education that their children will receive. As target populations of NGO programs, they negotiate with development workers the terms of programs that expand from a focus on rural children to an emphasis on work with indigenous parents through parents' schools.

As survivors of a long war waged often indiscriminately in their lands, rural Andeans receive skeptically the promises of inclusion that come from outside their communities. Through all these responses, indigenous people are engaged both in the "self-making" Ong described and in negotiating the various currents of power that flow through the discourses and resources of international donors, local NGOs, and the state. In all these interactions, indigenous people are very much aware of the unequal power relations that characterize development encounters (Escobar 1995). Yet they navigate these inequalities through performative tactics that acknowledge the authority of outside officials and agents while simultaneously transforming and adapting outside forces to local contexts.

The fact that some rural Andeans have performed indigenousness strategically while others have not demonstrates that local–global currents do not always converge in ways that make such performances likely. In her study of Indonesian rural people, Li (2000) argues that the discourse of indigenousness took hold more explicitly in some communities than in others because global and local agendas become conjoined and create specific "slots" that rural people sometimes can and choose to fit into and sometimes do not. "Complexity, collaboration, and creative cultural engagement in both local and global arenas," suggests Li (2000: 173), "best describe these processes and relationships."

As Li suggests, and as I have tried to do, we must pay close attention to both local and global arenas. According to Michael Kearney, globalization consists of "social, economic, cultural, and demographic processes that take place within nations but also transcend them, such that attention limited to local processes, identities, and units of analysis, yields incomplete understanding of the local" (Kearney 1995a: 548; see also Basch et al. 1994). Limiting analyses to local developments can provide us only fragments of the picture. It is also important to note, however, that this means not only that all our local studies must be more global, but also that our multisited investigations must be more local. Local demands and expressions of identity inform developments at transnational levels. While the internationalization of the movement for indigenous rights has certainly influenced ideas about who indigenous peoples are and what being indigenous means, local modifications in notions of Indianness among those who had not previously identified themselves as Indian, such as some Quechua community leaders in Cuzco, can also affect national and international notions of what "target populations" should look like and where to find them. Increasing international aid for indigenous education, health care, and other social development programs directed at indigenous peoples has only recently become an incentive for Quechuas in Peru to rethink identity and learn how to manipulate their position to gain access to such aid. However, such instrumental thinking takes us only so far. Multiple understandings, misunderstandings, and conflict make political identity formation an unpredictable dynamic and transnational process.

Transnational Indigenous Citizen-Making

Outside of the national space of Peru, indigenous subject-making occurs in extremely important ways. With an international indigenous movement carving out spaces for encounters of indigenous people throughout the world, the transnational nature of identity formation becomes especially clear. As Chapter 5 illustrated, in places such as the PROEIB in Cochabamba, indigenous students from throughout South America join in debates about their own sense of belonging in their home countries and communities while simultaneously inhabiting a transnational community of indigenous youths who are creating their own sense of identity, action, and obligation.

The duties of these new leaders are echoed in the remarks of the young Mapuche who reminded her Aymara classmate that he owed something not just to his people, the Aymara, but to all those nations and peoples that had been swallowed by the label of Indian. These new ties of solidarity serve not only to strengthen local expressions of indigenous politics but also to create a common set of expectations and goals for what the future generations of indigenous leaders will achieve. In spaces such as the PROIEB, students accumulate valuable symbolic and cultural capital that will allow them to return as robust indigenous citizens, often with jobs awaiting them at ministries of education.

With this in mind, researchers must explore the outcomes of indigenous professionals' planned return to their communities as leaders, as well as Quechua highlanders' perception and acceptance (or lack thereof) of these new indigenous elites. This return poses yet another challenge for indigenous citizenship. In becoming professionalized and legitimized by the new networks of transnational Indianness, cultural difference is not only made safe for the new democratic, multicultural state, it seems to be effortlessly absorbed by it. Quite apart from the contestation and negotiation that take place in rural communities, this separate sphere of indigenous intellectual production has the potential either to change state-indigenous relations generally or to make radical change less likely as neoliberal regimes attract visible and "authentic" indigenous peoples into the distant and isolated halls of governance. In order to understand this potential danger more fully, it is worth briefly going back a few centuries.

LOOKING FOR INCAS, AGAIN: THE NEW POLITICS OF INDIANNESS AND MULTICULTURALISM

Despite the many new ways in which rural and indigenous identities are being negotiated, it is clear that the state continues to wrestle with the legacies of earlier efforts to solve the "Indian problem" that seemed to stand in the way of national development. Among the most perceptive students of the long history of these efforts was Alberto Flores Galindo, whose classic book *Buscando un Inca* (Searching for an Inca [1987]) revealed both the dangers of and need for Andean utopias and identities. In that work, he tells the remarkable story of two early-nineteenth-century criollos who, mesmerized by the idea of an Inca revival, tried to begin an Indian insurrection that would restore the Inca. They did so, however, without ever consulting any Indians. They assumed that Indians would of course participate in the restoration of their past. Perhaps not surprisingly, their insurrection failed and the non-Indian revolutionaries were hanged in the central plaza of Cuzco before a large crowd of indigenous spectators.

Flores Galindo's story of an ill-fated Andean utopia is a useful one for thinking about the Peruvian government's more recent attempts to come to terms with Peru's Andean and Indian legacies. These efforts came, perhaps appropriately enough, under the administration of Alejandro Toledo, a man of Andean origins whose rags-to-riches story served him well in his campaign for president. Toledo's wife, Eliane Karp, also made much of indigenous symbols and identity during her husband's campaign. In one memorable campaign stop, she suggested that her husband was not only a man of the people but the choice of the mountain spirits themselves (*apus*): "Listen to me carefully, Miraflores yuppies [*pituquitos miraflorinos*],[2] the apus have spoken: my cholo is good [*sano*] and sacred." She even went so far as to say that Toledo represented the reincarnation of the Inca Pachacuti (Centurión 2002). Whether Toledo was ascribed the "impure" label *cholo* (in Erving Goffman's [1963] phrase, a "spoiled identity" ascribed to indigenous people who migrate to the cities) or described in the more "pure" language of Inca revival, the Toledo/Karp discourse was meant to Peruvianize his campaign against both the Japanese-Peruvian Fujimori and the elite, white political class of Lima.

As Chapter 1 detailed, the strategy proved successful: Toledo managed to capture the presidency and inaugurated his term at the very heart of "deep Peru," in a ceremony at the ruins of Machu Picchu. Symbolism was to give way to substance as Toledo, along with other Andean presidents, signed the Declaration of Machu Picchu in support of indigenous rights. Karp took an increasingly visible role in the institutionalization of the principles declared in that document. There are now new opportunities for the inclusion of indigenous issues in national agendas, but Toledo and Karp have also shown the dangers of the recurring manifestations of an Andeanism that risks marginalizing the many concerns and voices of Andean peoples.

As was mentioned above, the most important (albeit controversial) governmental space that has opened up is the National Commission of Andean, Amazonian, and Afro-Peruvian Peoples (CONAPA), formerly headed by Karp. The visible role of the commission and the inclusion of indigenous leaders certainly represents a break from earlier assimilationist efforts to integrate the nation. It seeks to advance an alternative project of multicultural state-building, inspired by the often-invoked description of Peru by José María Arguedas (1993 [1968]) as a country of "all bloods," Indian, black, and European.

However, this official multiculturalism carries new risks. First, as many have noted, the personal leadership style of Karp, as the protector of indigenous people, calls forth paternalist ideas of previous periods of populism and indigenismo. The commission, in this view, is a threat to the autonomous spaces of representation in civil society. Co-optation becomes the price of inclusion. As Hale (2002) has noted, these kinds of official recognition of difference have the effect of distinguishing the "legitimate" from the "radical" elements of movements, thus redirecting the energy of cultural activism. "A principal means to achieve this redirection is the strategic deployment of resources, which rewards organizations that promote acceptable cultural rights demands, and punishes the others" (Hale 2002: 498).

Second, by bringing indigenous and Afro-Peruvian groups into the same framework, the commission, paradoxically, homogenizes difference, ignoring the distinct histories and places that these groups occupy in what Peter Wade (1997) terms the "structures of alterity." These differences are often explicit in the ways in which some organizations describe their communities vis-à-vis others. In an interview in 2002, a prominent Amazonian leader described the differences between Andean, Amazonian, and Afro-Peruvian pueblos or peoples in the following terms: "We, the Amazonian peoples, are a nation, we have identity, we have culture. The Andean peoples have been a nation, have had identity, have had language and culture. The black peoples are not a people, do not have identity, do not have language [and culture]."

These tensions are not unique to Peru or to the commission, as similar projects exist in Ecuador, among other countries. In various multicultural projects, there exists a tendency to gloss over different histories and asymmetries in an effort to form a united subaltern subject or, in the register of the World Bank, identify specific target populations. This does not imply that these spaces are not important or that indigenous and Afro-Latino populations cannot use them for transformative purposes. All attempts at inclusion, however, carry with them the possibilities of new forms of exclusion.

Whether one sees Toledo and Karp as supporters of indigenous peoples in their struggles for autonomy or as a reflection of the dangers of the "menace of multiculturalism" (Hale 2002), it is clear that the political context for indigenous movements has changed remarkably in the last few years. While the dangers of co-optation and the erosion of autonomous indigenous representation are real, indigenous people are clearly constructing their own autonomous spaces of representation. They are not waiting for others to construct utopias for them. Instead, they are building their own organizations, advancing their own struggles, and leaving the search for Incas to others.

Indigenous Social Movements: Articulating Local and National Struggles

Finally, it is instructive to come back one last time to the question of whether we can use the language of social movements to describe what is happening in Peru. As we have seen, the consensus among scholars has been that indigenous social movements have been lacking in Peru, while they have been all too noticeable in the nationwide marches and protests of neighboring republics. As new organizations have started to form on the national stage in Peru, coordinating protests and making demands on the state in ways reminiscent of activities in Bolivia and Ecuador, some observers are tempted to say that at long last Peru is catching up with the rest of the region.

This kind of framing, however, involves some problematic binary conceptions of the success or failure of a social movement. At best, it implies that in the Andes we are confronted with a choice between studying either a full-blown social movement, with its public displays and performances, or situations of what James Scott (1985) famously dubbed "everyday forms of peasant resistance." Although these are both important framings for social struggles, I think we should resist the temptation to characterize entire countries as "cases" of one or the other. To some extent, that is what has happened in the conversations over indigenous movements in the Andes. Ecuador and Bolivia, for instance, are cases of strong social movements struggling against states before the eyes of the entire world. Peru, in contrast, becomes a case of disarticulated struggles yet to converge and become unified. I would suggest that there are costs to thinking about indigenous struggles in these clear-cut ways.

The more visible politics of national protest and marches draws scholarly gazes toward the dramatic showdown between dominant power and subaltern agency in capital cities and public plazas; underexplored, however, are the less obvious daily confrontations between states, NGOs, and indigenous agents in rural communities and schoolhouses. Marches that end in capital cities are clearly important to advancing indigenous struggles, but so are the micropolitics of contention that shape state policies and community politics.

Rather than think in terms of one or the other, either national or local tactics, one might, in the spirit of articulations, consider how these multiple examples of contestation and negotiation can shed light on each other. Certainly local-level contestation occurs throughout the highlands of all Andean countries, but fixing our gaze on the peaks of social-movement activity obscures the valleys of contention that sometimes are linked to national social-movements and sometimes are not. This suggests that we should heed the advice of social-movement theorists who stress the importance of a multiplicity of subject positions and spaces for struggle (K. Warren 1998b; Edelman 1999, 2002; Li 2000). Ethnographically thick discussions of this diversity on the ground are too rare. If social movements are exercises of indigenous representation, it would make considerable sense to think more about the people and communities in whose name social movements act. Contestation does not simply occur vertically between monolithic dominant and subaltern actors, but also horizontally as tension in hegemonic and counterhegemonic projects makes new political positions possible in a variety of ways. Local actions by rural Quechua communities against intercultural activists paradoxically count as an example of indigenous mobilization, since Quechua-speaking peoples are compelling outside forces (NGOs and state) to take seriously the demands they have formulated collectively about the place of schooling (and more) in their communities.

Previous chapters have tried to show how important local spaces are for defining the terms of indigenous citizenship. Rather than rehearse events already described, I would like to share one more recollection that helps make the point. After a gathering at the house of a linguist (and advocate of intercultural education) from Cuzco, some of those who had attended the get-together meandered over to the Plaza de Armas, where we would continue talking over some coffee. We went into the Café Varayoc, a small coffeehouse known (sometimes mockingly) as *el café de los intelectuales* (the intellectuals' café) and ran into several other friends, who were engaged in what looked like a serious debate about bilingual education. "Can you really talk about interculturalidad and Quechua literacy," argued a professor from the university in Cuzco who opposed the implementation of bilingual intercultural education in the highlands, "when everyone else in the country cares about learning English and eating at McDonald's? How is learning how to read and write in Quechua going to help them develop economically? It's a nice thought, maybe even ideal. But what I'm concerned about is your motivation," he continued, pointing to the young man opposite him. "Do you want education or revolution?"

At this question, Carlos, the other participant in the debate, laughed and lightened the mood around the table. "You just don't understand. You cuzqueño intellectuals, you have so much cultural richness, and yet you look to Lima, and to the imperialists. If we *did* have a revolution," he continued jokingly, "you'd be the first to feel it."

Most of those at the table laughed, and the discussion seemed to have ended. The professor did not seem angry in the least. He placed a few *soles* on the table to pay for his beer and got up to leave. By way of goodbye, he turned to Carlos one last time and said, "I'll see you in class next week, but be warned. Before you know it, the people will mobilize. But they will mobilize against you criollo indigenistas."

In challenging the curriculum that was coming from the ministry and NGO programs, Andean communities were proving the professor right. Pursuing a variety of actions both within the community and across communities, Quechua parents were articulating a collective response to ideas and actions perceived as coming from outside. Surely, then, they were involved in the politics of social movements even if their struggles did not reach national proportions. And these are not the only sites of indigenous struggle in Peru.

RONDAS CAMPESINAS

Although it often goes unmentioned in reviews of Peruvian "failure," social-movement scholars *have* given consideration to local politics, specifically the constitution of civil defense patrols, or rondas campesinas, in the highlands (Starn 1992, 1999; Yrigoyen Fajardo 2002; Degregori et al. 1996). Originally organized in the northern Andes as a response to livestock theft and the inadequacy of state protection, the rondas acquired new significance in the southern Andes in the context of the war between the state and leftist guerrillas. The rondas have been particularly important and controversial for their connections to (and disconnections from) military strategies to defeat Sendero Luminoso. The ambivalent place of the rondas and the questions they raise are useful for highlighting the complex layers of meaning and practices in rural Peru. The rondas, like other forms of community contention, raise important questions about both ethnicity and social movement.

First, some could ask if the rondas, like the other community practices explored in this book, can be seen as truly indigenous. Indeed, their status as campesinos would seem to signal a reluctance to link their activities to the "return of the Indian," so celebrated elsewhere in the region. This effort to separate the Indian from the peasant, however, has the effect of suggesting that a clear line exists between them. Additionally, it seems to imply that analysts have the final word in deciding what is indigenous and what is not. In the context of highland Peru, both *indigenous* and *peasant* are highly racialized terms, reflecting old (neo)colonial cartographies of civilization and barbarism, modernity and backwardness. Rather than take *Indian* and *peasant* as static labels, we would do better to follow Starn (1992: 95–96) and others in seeing them as "partial markers" that are part of many layers of subjectivity. Finally, it is important to note that, given new multicultural legislation that recognizes the power of "peasant and native communities" to administer some forms of communal justice (in accordance with international agreements on indigenous rights, such as ILO 169), ronderos are being woven into the fabric of new multicultural states (Yrigoyen Fajardo 2002).[3]

Second, an additional ambiguity regarding the rondas, again like the *comuneros* working against intercultural education, is whether they can be classified as social movements. As suggested above, this contested concept raises questions about the oppositional character assumed to be a defining characteristic of movements and about the models of organizing that scholars use to understand them. Rondas, after all, often worked in close consultation with state military forces, if not under their direct supervision. At other times, however, they emphasized their distance from the state. Rather than require strict definitions of counterhegemony, it is better to interrogate the complexities of specific situations. As Starn notes, "it is more fruitful to approach each new movement as unique and dynamic with multivalent implications for relations of power and inequality" (1992: 95).

RESOURCE MANAGEMENT AND DEVELOPMENT

Another example of the complex dynamics of local indigenous politics can be found in the context of state–community interaction over the management of local natural resources, such as water. With impressive historical and ethnographic skill, Paul Gelles (2000) sketches a vivid picture of the cultural politics of water management in the "transnational community" of Cabanaconde, in the southern Peruvian highlands. Despite the pushes and pulls of globalization that have affected Cabanaconde, Gelles argues that to understand the cultural and political forces that have forged this community and the collective identity of its members, one must not lose sight of the importance of local landscapes and long-existing Andean political institutions. In particular, Gelles demonstrates how despite state efforts to "rationalize" irrigation through Western technology and bureaucracy, Cabanaconde has continued to use the Andean forms of dual spatial organization (upper and lower moieties or *sayas*), and relies on systems of symbology and authority based on Andean sacred landscapes. Water mayors, for example, perform rituals for Mount Hualca Hualca, the Earth Mother, and other deities as part of a highly ritualized system of resource distribution among the upper and lower sayas of the community. In line with previous studies of resistance and adaptation in the Andes (Stern, ed., 1987), Gelles explains that such indigenous institutions and practices persisted over centuries because some "were appropriated and used as a means of extracting goods and labor" by Spanish and Peruvian authorities, while "others were used to resist colonial and post-colonial regimes" (2000: 11). Gelles uses irrigation systems to examine the conflict between Western states and local Andean ways of life, and emphasizes the hybrid and dynamic nature of Andean culture itself.

Interestingly, in a separate essay Gelles (2002) joins the chorus of scholars who think it "inconceivable" that indigenous movements such as those in Ecuador will emerge in Peru. Leaving aside the fact that as his article went to press, national indigenous organizations in Peru were protesting in the streets of Lima, the more serious issue at hand reflects Gelles's decision to overlook the importance of the local contestation he has so richly documented as he seeks an explanation for the seeming absence of collective action at the national level. While scholars recognize that national-level mobilization may galvanize international support more urgently than less visible community contention, there is no clear reason why they should see one level of struggle as necessarily more consequential than the other. One can imagine national-level protest being full of sound and fury but leading to disappointment, while local-level action may silently change the terms of programs that policy makers design at their desks in Lima or Washington.

Whether we examine the politics of intercultural education, civil defense patrols, or water management, community politics are never simple local stories. Indeed, they are connected, in often messy and uneven ways, to national and international forces. Indigenous organizing does often occur across communities and regions, and takes the form of regional or national federations. These kinds of organizations in Ecuador and Bolivia have been taken to be the very models of indigenous movements. "The label 'grassroots movement' holds an assumption about the likelihood of growing taller and stronger" (Starn 1999: 256). Yet we should not assume that this kind of community politics will always tend to move toward political activity at a larger scale. As Starn has insightfully noted in the case of the rondas, local community politics

force us to recognize that there is nothing natural at all about a movement going regional, national, or global. A collection of tribes in the Amazon in Peru, a neighborhood association in the United States, or any other movement may join together as a force for change, or they may not, depending on many factors, as occurred with the rondas. . . . The failure of the rondas to grow into strong federations offers confirmation that even mobilizations for change can proceed in many ways besides up. (1999: 256)

Conclusion

While we must acknowledge that the patterning of indigenous politics varies in many ways, the Peruvian case is clearly not a matter of absence; rather, it raises important questions for indigenous movements throughout the continent. First, peasant organizations, indigenous intellectual movements, nongovernmental organizations, and ethnic federations have been important elements of indigenous contention in Peru, as they have been in neighboring republics. Although leftist movements in the highlands, especially the nightmarish Maoism of Sendero Luminoso, had an adverse impact on indigenous peoples and their communal organization, Indianness never disappeared from highland Peru. In a long history of indigenous resistance (Stern 1982, 1987), strategic adaptation has often been mistaken for silence or absence.

Indigenous resistance has been more visible and perhaps more influential in the Amazon, especially in shaping indigenous movements throughout the region. The Amuesha Congress of the Peruvian Amazon can claim to be among the pioneers of the ethnic federation models that have shaped latter-day indigenous organizing in Ecuador and Bolivia. As indigenous organizing goes global, Peru has hardly been on the sidelines. Amazonian and (more recently) highland peoples have contributed significantly to the internationalization of indigenous politics through the creation of transnational alliances (such as the Coordinadora de Organizaciones Indígenas de la Cuenca Amazónica, or COICA) and participation in transnational networks (such as PROEIB).

Second, as "development with identity" has become a watchword for state and international policies, indigenous people continue to negotiate notions of Indianness and citizenship in ways that states and NGO activists had not expected. The case of intercultural activism has been especially illustrative of the ability of indigenous communities to shape the kinds of policies that have often been designed for them but not with them. Moreover, as the Fujimori regime came to a close, new possibilities began to emerge on the horizon. CONACAMI has shown its ability to create a powerful highland movement around urgent environmental and cultural questions about the problems of mining, an indigenous issue since the sixteenth century. Additionally, it and other organizations have challenged First Lady Eliane Karp's perhaps well-intentioned but problematic efforts to structure indigenous representation from above. Although the Toledo administration has hardly been the indigenous opening he promised during his campaign, indigenous actors have emerged in unprecedented ways during a critical juncture in Peru's political history.

Finally, given the range of local, regional, national, and transnational activities explored in earlier pages, how should we think of Peru in the context of regionwide indigenous politics? One possibility might be to celebrate the idea that Peru is catching up with neighboring Bolivia, Ecuador, and other countries in spawning powerful movements. This approach, however, rests on a teleological view of the trajectory of indigenous politics, in which local communities must grow into national and international ones in order to be considered successful. This way of seeing indigenous politics obscures and limits our understanding of the always dynamic, multiple, and contradictory ways in which collective action occurs. Rather than explaining the absences in Peru, we might begin to ask about the absences elsewhere. When the emphasis is placed on specific national and international organizations as *the* social movement, what kinds of organizing and politics go unseen, unexplored, and undervalued? I suggest that we should not look only for everyday forms of resistance, but rather interrogate the everyday categories of scholarship that privilege certain political and cultural forms to the exclusion of others. Local activisms become invisible in a sociology of movements that sees only the peaks of mobilization and neglects the valleys of local contention. We should seek various views of the landscape of politics and culture, being attentive to its various scales. While the current moment of globalization should prompt us always to look for international connections, it is important to recall that the precise nature of those connections will always challenge the old maps and models that scholars have used to understand them.

Inevitably, social scientists will have to choose how best to view the rugged terrain of indigenous politics in the Americas. As Néstor García Canclini has suggested, different social sciences have acquired their perspectives in distinct ways: the anthropologist on foot, the sociologist via the highway, the communication specialist by plane, and the historian "not by entering but rather by leaving" (1995: 4). I would add that indigenous people themselves are traveling the same routes of community, technology, and transnationalism. Their struggles take place inside their communities and far beyond them; they involve their neighbors and the World Bank; their children learn in local schools and international institutes. As my friend Mario told me, indigenous people "walk with llamas and fly in planes." Anthropologists would do well to try to keep up.

Notes

1. Although, as Ramos (2002), Warren and Jackson (2002), and others suggest, we must not forget that this "recent" trend in indigenous mobilization can be traced back to earlier moments of struggle in the 1960s and 1970s (2002: 1). One could also take a longer view, following Stern (1987), and examine patterns of resistance and rebellion from the eighteenth century to the present.

2. Although dynamics in the Amazonian regions of Peru would shed additional light on the broad mosaic of indigenous politics in the country, they are beyond the scope of this book (but see Dean 2002, 2003; Smith 1996, 2001; Varese, ed., 1996).

3. I do not mean to draw a bright line between Peruvian and Ecuadorian (or Bolivian) forms of contention. There are bound to be commonalities in the strategies and tactics of indigenous organizations that are increasingly in contact with one another. Cocalero organizations in both Peru and Bolivia, for example, have engaged in very visible marches and protests.

4. AIDESEP and CONAP are two indigenous organizations that have existed for decades despite and often in response to the violence. While the war is largely seen as a thing of the past in the highlands (despite recent concerns over the resurgence of Sendero Luminoso), it continues in the jungle. In fact, some Asháninka communities report living in "slave-like" conditions under Senderista control (SERVINDI 2002a, Hidalgo 2002).

5. For reviews of this work see Edelman 2002, Lucero 2000, and Tarrow 1994.

6. Some Web sites and electronic newsletters focusing on Peruvian indigenous issues are Quechua Network (www.quechuanetwork.org), Correo Indígena and SERVINDI (coppip@amauta.rcp.net.pe), Comunidad Indígena Asháninka Marankiari Bajo (ciamb_peru@hotmail.com), Coordinadora Nacional de Comunidades del Peru Afectadas por la Minería (http://www.conacami.org), (Conferencia-COPPIP (http://coppip.rcp.net.pe), Coordinadora-COPPIP (http://www.laneta.apc.org/rci/organinteg/coppip.html), CONAPA (http://www.conapa.gob.pe), and Ciberayllu (www.ciberayllu.org).

7. As the rest of this book makes clear, in time my research developed into critical interpretations of what I saw as gaps between rhetoric and practice, but which many activists were quick to debate, refute, and contest.

8. Preliminary research grants from the Watson Institute for International Studies at Brown University and a Foreign Language and Area Study Summer Fellowship allowed me to spend the summers of 1996 and 1997 in Cuzco conducting language study and preliminary research. Thanks to a dissertation grant from the Fulbright Commission for International Educational Exchange, I conducted the majority of field

research in Peru between October 1997 and November 1998. I returned to the Andes (Cuzco and Cochabamba) for a month of research in August 1999.

9. Unless otherwise noted, all translations are my own.

10. For critical examinations of the Academia Mayor de la Lengua Quechua in Cuzco, see Godenzzi, ed., 1992; Itier 1992a, 1992b; Niño-Murcia 1997; Marr 1999; and Coronel-Molina in progress.

11. While activists passionately debate the importance of revitalizing Quechua, of teaching in Quechua, and of writing and reading in Quechua, invariably they debate these issues in Spanish. For this reason, with one exception, all of my conversations with activists were in Spanish.

12. For the privacy and safety of the people I mention in this book, I have changed the names of most people and communities. Some public intellectuals, however, wanted me to use their real names.

13. In her work on gender and ethnicity in the Andes, Marisol de la Cadena explores some of the reasons why, as she says, "women are more Indian" (1995, 1996). The anthropologist Penelope Harvey has also examined the ways in which language patterns in the highlands, particularly bilingualism, are conditioned by gender (1989, 1994).

14. Interaprendizaje workshops are gatherings of highland teachers from several communities who come together, under the supervision and guidance of an NGO representative, to share their experiences with EIB in the classroom.

15. Most Peruvian and foreign intellectuals working in Cuzco repeated this phrase often.

16. The quote is from testimony cited in Deusta and Rénique 1984: 78.

17. The words *cholo* and *chola,* especially in their diminutive forms (*cholito, cholita*), are also frequently used as terms of endearment, though only among friends or relatives.

CHAPTER 1. IN THE SHADOW OF TERROR

1. *Compadrazgo* or *comadrazgo,* a fictive kin relation, is usually established in the Andes through the symbolic adoption (or sponsorship) of one person's child by another during certain life-cycle rituals (such as baptism or the hair-cutting ceremony). Such a social tie involves material support of the child, such as the provision of food, clothing, or other gifts, as well as money for the child's support, including education or health-related expenses.

2. The charango is an instrument similar to the mandolin.

3. In Peru, as in most of Latin America, social scientists, university students, teachers, artists, and other intellectuals and academics are frequently associated with the political left, and in many cases with revolutionary movements, usually labeled "subversive" by Latin American states. In the early to mid-1990s, as the country emerged from civil war, Peruvian intellectuals were particularly cautious about their work. Until 2001, many of the highland and lowland departments were designated by the state as "emergency zones," where police and the military had complete control. For instance, the law stated that any individual could be arrested and held for thirty days if he or she was considered "suspicious." Also by law, authorities were under no obligation to disclose the person's whereabouts during the period of "interrogation."

4. Much has been written on Sendero Luminoso by both Peruvian and North American social scientists. For examinations of the origins and organization of Sendero Luminoso, see Degregori 1990, Gorriti Ellenbogen 1990, Palmer 1992, and Poole and Rénique 1992. For detailed explorations of social relations during this time, as well as insightful case studies of the political, cultural, and social upheaval created by Sendero, see Stern, ed., 1998.

5. Guzmán also considered himself the "fourth sword of Marxism." He was known by his followers as "Presidente Gonzalo," and his writings and discourses were the basis for what Senderistas called "Gonzalo thought."

6. Sendero also had important geostrategic reasons for choosing to begin its armed struggle in the Ayacucho and Central Jungle regions. The closeness of both regions to Lima, the capital, emphasized their significance as bases from which to launch the "popular war."

7. Guzmán was a philosophy professor at the University of Huamanga. Sendero's second in command, Osman Morote, was an anthropologist.

8. Gorriti is a leading analyst of Sendero Luminoso. His history of the organization is considered one of the most detailed examinations of the movement and of the ideology behind Sendero and its leader.

9. Many Peruvians blame Belaúnde for the devastation brought by Sendero Luminoso, citing his failure to act against the insurgency in the initial years of their struggle.

10. Although the military was activated in full force at the end of 1982, by early 1981 Belaúnde had already begun to deploy special counterinsurgency units to Ayacucho. While he concentrated on Ayacucho, however, Sendero was able to expand into the rest of the country. See Poole and Rénique 1992 for a detailed political history of Peru's "time of fear."

11. Though the Movimiento Revolucionario Túpac Amaru (MRTA), an urban-based guerrilla movement, was also active during the 1980s and 1990s, it was never considered a national threat in the same way as Sendero Luminoso (Basombrío Iglesias 1998). The MRTA was less fanatical than Sendero and more likely to negotiate with official political forces. They received international attention when they held prominent politicians and diplomats hostage at the Japanese embassy in Lima between December 1996 and April 1997, an act widely acknowledged to have led to their dissolution after government forces retook the embassy.

12. For a detailed examination and critique of the journalists' massacre and the Vargas Llosa report, see Mayer 1992. The 1985 documentary *Fire in the Andes* also critically examines the massacre and the Vargas Llosa report, and documents the efforts of the journalists' families to challenge the government's version of events.

13. The topographic boundaries between the coast, the highlands, and the jungle of Peru not only separate indigenous populations geographically but mark them as culturally and racially distinct from one another. Despite current debates about the fluidity of ethnicity, the social construction of "race," and the ever-changing pathways of "culture," most Peruvians still envision a white European coast, an Indian jungle, and a highland of dark-skinned peasants.

14. The anthropologist Guillermo Bonfil Batalla (1987) adopted this phrase and applied it to his discussion of Indian identity in Mexico.

15. Ponciano del Pino (1998) provides a view of the contradictions of everyday community life with Sendero and the unevenness and ambiguity of indigenous "support" of Sendero Luminoso. He illustrates the varied strategies that indigenous peasants used to negotiate Senderista "hidden scripts" of racism and totalitarianism.

16. It was never clear from the investigation into the journalists' murder whether the peasants of Uchuraccay (and of Huaychao) acted on their own initiative or collaborated with the military stationed in the region. In either case, resistance to Sendero — with or without military complicity — was very much a part of peasant life in the early stages of the war.

17. Accounts and explorations of highland peasant militias and their connections to government forces appear in Degregori et al. 1996 and Starn 1998, 1999.

18. Because of their ambiguous status, the rondas did not figure prominently in these discussions, even though many of their members and families were directly affected by the violence.

19. Although violence diminished significantly after Guzmán's capture, Sendero's violent presence is still very much a part of life for many indigenous peoples, particularly in the Central Jungle region (SERVINDI 2002a). Debate over the effectiveness of the Truth and Reconciliation Commission has highlighted the plight of many indigenous groups still living under slavelike conditions in isolated regions of the Peruvian jungle. Moreover, the explosion of a bomb across from the U.S. embassy on the night of March 20, 2002, which left nine dead and dozens severely injured, highlighted the fact that the threat of violence is still real. More recently, reports — in sources as varied as *The Economist,* NACLA (the North American Congress on Latin America), and the Lima newspaper *El Comercio* — of Sendero Luminoso's resurgence and of clashes between government and opposition forces have emphasized this threat.

20. *Serrano* is a derogatory term designating a person from the sierra or highlands. Although it can also be used as a term of endearment, it is often at best a patronizing and demeaning designation. However, in recent years some people have begun to reclaim the term as one of strength and pride.

21. Violence certainly shaped political possibilities. However, the violence itself provided a motivation and cause around which to organize, thus creating conditions for later periods of indigenous politics even in the Central Jungle, where violence is very much part of the region's present.

22. Chapter 4 takes a closer look at the "menace" (Hale 2002) posed by the alliance between neoliberalism and multiculturalism.

23. It is also worth emphasizing that transnational politics predates the fall of communism. The 1970s saw several attempts to organize international working groups for the defense of indigenous peoples. A brief list of these meetings includes the First and Second Encounter of Indigenous People in Barbados (1971 and 1977), the U.N. World Conference to Combat Racism and Discrimination (1978), and the establishment of the International Working Group for Indigenous Affairs in the late 1960s.

24. By 1999, Fujimori and his government were increasingly accused of authoritarian and repressive actions. The media were one target. From one day to the next, for example, *Hildebrand,* a TV news show (similar to *Dateline* or *60 Minutes*) an-

chored by a radical journalist from the political left and openly opposed to Fujimori's government, was suddenly taken off the air. Fujimori also seized control of a Lima-based television station (Frecuencia Latina) after it broadcast reports exposing government wrongdoings, and revoked the citizenship of the station's majority owner, Baruch Ivcher, an Israeli-born businessman.

25. The Inca empire was divided into four regions or *suyos,* with its capital, Cuzco, at its center.

26. Toledo also highlighted the controversy over Fujimori's citizenship. Although Fujimori maintained that he had been born to Japanese immigrants in Peru, reports surfaced that he had actually been born in Japan and therefore had not been eligible to occupy the presidency.

27. After Fujimori left the country, the Peruvian press reported that during the protests the National Bank had been burned and several people killed by government forces in an attempt to paint Toledo as a violent leader and to discredit the opposition.

28. From Japan, Fujimori launched his own Web site, where he maintains his innocence. He has hinted at the possibility of running for president once again in 2006.

29. A significant problem with the makeup of the commission was the fact that while there was no indigenous representation, one of the five members added after Toledo took office was a former army general.

30. Because the testimonies were delivered primarily in indigenous languages, TV broadcasts had Spanish subtitles.

31. This also reflects the tendency to marginalize various kinds of subaltern concerns (women's issues, indigenous rights) and place them all in the same space.

32. Since Toledo's inauguration, Karp has been the one to emerge as a staunch supporter of indigenous cultural, social, and political rights. Her support for indigenous rights, however, is imbued with dangerous paternalism. Her romanticized notions of indigenous identity and politics are increasingly questioned and challenged by both new and old indigenous organizations and by indigenous rights advocates and intellectuals (SERVINDI 2002c; 2003). See García and Lucero 2004 for a more in-depth discussion of indigenous politics in Peru, and of Karp's problematic role as indigenous-rights spokesperson.

33. The consolidation of the CCP in the 1950s was led by the Moscow-line Peruvian Communist Party (Smith 1983, Degregori 1993, Remy 1994), making Arpasi's selection as congresswoman especially striking.

34. For an example of these lingering racial hierarchies, see Vargas Llosa 1990. For an examination of Toledo's mestizaje and the deployment of both popular and neoliberal symbols, see de la Cadena 2001.

35. Though Karp is often referred to as an anthropologist, her graduate studies at Stanford, where she and Toledo met, were not in anthropology but in French literature and economics. Thanks to Patricia Oliart for this observation.

36. Unless otherwise noted, all quotations from Miguel Palacín are taken from an interview José Antonio Lucero and I conducted in Lima on June 4, 2002.

37. This requires further investigation, as the autonomy and independence of each organization has been questioned by the other.

38. *SERVINDI* can be obtained by writing to servindi@hotmail.com. News from the Conferencia can be obtained by writing peruindigena@yahoo.es.

CHAPTER 2. RACE, EDUCATION, AND CITIZENSHIP

1. It is worth noting that despite his passionate oratory about indigenous social-ist revolution, Mariátegui never traveled to the Andes (at least in part because a crip-pling bone disease confined him to a wheelchair).

2. The essay is titled "El proceso de la literatura" (The literary process).

3. Commenting on French peasants in his *Eighteenth Brumaire,* Marx said, "They cannot represent themselves, they must be represented."

4. There is some disagreement over whether González Prada should be called an indigenista (Kristal 1991). Some scholars also place different degrees of emphasis on the place of indigenous education in González Prada's thinking (Zúñiga et al. 2003).

5. It is important to note that indigenista visions excluded Amazonian "savages."

6. For alternative views on peasant and indigenous participation in the War of the Pacific, see Mallon 1995.

7. Túpac Amaru II, a merchant by the name of José Gabriel Condorcanqui, claimed direct descent from Túpac Amaru I, who led a revolt against the Spanish administration and was the last Inca murdered by the Spanish. Although the revolt was brutally crushed less than a year after its inception in 1780, it is often cited as the precursor to Peruvian independence (O'Phelan Godoy 1988). Túpac Katari led an Aymara rebellion in Upper Peru (now Bolivia), which was also put down by the Spanish in 1781. In what is now Peru, because of Túpac Amaru's proclamation of the return of indigenous governance, colonial authorities associated the cultivation of Quechua cultural practices with political nationalism and revolution. After the rebellion failed in 1781, the Quechua language, cultural practices, theater, and other literary expressions were explicitly banned. The prohibition remained in effect for almost two hundred years. Both Túpac Amaru and Túpac Katari were drawn and quartered.

8. Steve Stern (1987) suggests that Haitian and Andean insurrections were part of an eighteenth-century pattern that petrified the ruling elites. In the 1990s, these kinds of proclamations have resurfaced in newspapers and journals throughout the Andes in response to indigenous protests over neoliberalism and other policies affect-ing them (see, e.g., Gustafson 2002).

9. For a more detailed examination of Leguía's indigenismo, see de la Cadena 2000.

10. The Asociación Pro-Indígena (1906–16) was an organization of urban and rural intellectuals and leaders from various provinces. For more information about it see Kapsoli 1980 and Kapsoli and Reátegui 1972.

11. Leguía's support for the committee was not only a way to increase political support for his administration; it was also, as some have noted, a way to manipu-late and control the peasant movement that had been growing in the southern high-lands (Francke Ballve 1979: 130–131).

12. For more on the complexity of the relationship between some cuzqueño indi-genistas and landowners, see de la Cadena 2000.

13. However, the reclassification of indigenous peoples as peasants or natives was clearly still imbued with racial, glossed as "cultural," overtones.

14. Particularly important were rural rebellions and land invasions during the 1960s, many of which were led by Hugo Blanco; see Montoya 1986.

15. The National System to Support Social Mobilization, or SINAMOS, was the agency launched by the government to mobilize populations — especially in rural areas, urban shantytowns, and the labor movement — and to channel their energies into the national political process. In Spanish *sin amos* means "without masters," a phrase evocative of the sweeping agrarian reform also implemented by Velasco, which attempted to redistribute land to highland peasants by taking it out of the control of a handful of elite landowning families.

16. The 1974 Law of Native Communities also recognized indigenous territorial rights and, significantly, subsoil rights. However, Francisco Morales Bermúdez (with the constitution of 1979) dismantled many of Velasco's policies, promptly taking away subsoil rights and further restricting territorial and other rights (Yrigoyen Fajardo 2002).

17. Throughout the colonial period and into the late 1960s, haciendas were estates owned by Europeans and worked primarily by Indian laborers. The hacienda became a hallmark of colonial Peru and Mexico, though it developed into a powerful economic institution that would last long into the twentieth century.

18. For diverse perspectives on the limitations of the economic and agrarian reform goals of the Velasco government, see Eckstein 1983 and Lowenthal 1983.

19. The negative reaction evoked at this time by the possibility of the implementation of bilingual education among all sectors of the population was cited by intercultural activists in the 1990s as the primary reason for *not* actively demanding the compulsory teaching of indigenous languages in nonindigenous areas. However, a few urban schools in Cuzco (such as Pukllasunchis, in the barrio of San Blas) with links to bilingual intercultural education activists have begun teaching indigenous languages as second languages to children monolingual in Spanish.

20. Because Sendero originated in the highlands, government forces often presumed that indigenous peoples were subversives or Sendero sympathizers. See Chapter 1 for a more detailed discussion.

21. Throughout Latin America, bilingual education aimed at indigenous populations has often been linked to national integration policies (Torres and Puiggrós, eds., 1997). However, in July 1980 a group of bilingual education specialists met in Pátzcuaro, Mexico, and recommended a change of focus from bilingual education alone to education that was both bilingual and intercultural (Pozzi-Escot 1992: 297). Although in the 1990s advocates of intercultural education in Peru pointed to the Pátzcuaro meeting as the first real discussion of intercultural education, intercultural and bilingual education proposals in Latin America date back to indigenista and indigenous projects in the early to mid-1900s.

22. Inasmuch as education had become politically charged since the 1970s, proponents of EIB had to be careful in their discussions about intercultural education, emphasizing their cultural and linguistic concerns and not, as they often said, the "potentially subversive" consequences of education.

23. I met Juan Carlos Godenzzi in June 1996, when he was acting program direc-

tor of the Centro de Estudios Andinos "Bartolomé de Las Casas" (CBC). When I returned to Cuzco in June 1997, Godenzzi had just left to head the UNEBI in Lima, and there was much (and very heated) debate among other intercultural activists about why Godenzzi had been offered the position and why he had accepted it. This debate formed part of a larger one (which continued throughout my time in Cuzco) about working against or within the state.

24. As I discuss more fully in Chapter 4, the reality of intercultural schools in the highlands does not often match the optimistic statements made by either intercultural activists or state representatives.

25. In fact, most of the staff with whom I spoke at the UNEBI in 1998 emphasized the difference between the Peruvian intercultural education project, one that (according to them) was about promoting national unity, and the Ecuadorian intercultural project, which they claimed promoted a "separatist" environment.

CHAPTER 3. COMMUNITY POLITICS AND RESISTANCE

1. For a discussion of indigenous and peasant expressions of the connections between reading and writing and being able to see, as well as the link between darkness or blindness and illiteracy, see Montoya 1990, especially 85–109.

2. This chapter draws heavily on an article published in *Latin American Perspectives;* see García 2003.

3. According to Albó, Quechua, along with other indigenous languages, is oppressed because it is spoken by a large percentage of the population in Peru but is of little if any official importance. He considers its oppression to derive from the domination and exploitation of Quechuas by Hispanic Peruvian elites.

4. It would also be interesting to explore community mobilization around bilingual education policies in the 1940s.

5. A reason for the apparent stronger parent participation in the Ausangate than in the Sacred Valley may be related to the greater economic opportunities that tourism provides in the Valley, which pull parents (fathers in particular) out of daily community life.

CHAPTER 4. CONFLICTED MULTICULTURALISMS

1. For discussion of the potential "menace" of neoliberal multiculturalism see Gustafson 2002, Hale 2002, and Wade 1997. On the "non-coincidence" of civil society and community in the Andes, see Beverly 1998.

2. As I discussed earlier, the line between the work of education activists with NGOs and international funds and their involvement with the state is ambiguous at best, especially for teachers and parents who view intercultural activists as regional and local extensions of the Ministry of Education in Lima.

CHAPTER 5. DEVELOPING INDIGENOUS SPACES

1. I have used the real names of both the Centro de Estudios Andinos "Bartolomé de Las Casas" (CBC) and the Programa de Formación en Educación Intercultural Bilingüe para los Países Andinos (PROEIB Andes) because they are both recognized

public spaces. However, unless I provide full names, the names of intellectuals and of the young indigenous students at the PROEIB have been changed.

2. As the anthropologist Mary Weismantel demonstrates (2001: 90–92), similar attempts at defining the term *cholo/a* abound in the anthropological literature on Peru.

3. These concerns are most often responses to criticisms coming from parents of Quechua children who ask why they should follow imposed changes in their children's education. Other concerns stem from increasingly frequent accusations by leading members of other Latin American indigenous organizations against indigenous rights advocates they see as using "the Indian cause" to obtain funding for individual projects without "being Indians" themselves.

4. I should emphasize here that there is a marked difference between activists' attitudes toward working with parents and teachers and working with indigenous intellectuals. All of the discussions about the use of "global tools" (computers and video cameras) and about the political significance of Spanish, for instance, were limited to statements about working with indigenous intellectuals.

5. Although at the initial stages of the program this was the stated ideal, at least one of the Peruvian students at the institute conducted fieldwork in Bolivia rather than return to his home community in the highland department of Apurimac.

6. Since many indigenous languages are spoken at the PROEIB, out of necessity the lingua franca is Spanish. Classes are taught in Spanish, and all multiethnic meetings are conducted in Spanish. Samuel referred to Quechua brothers and not to Quechua sisters because in 1999 there were no Peruvian Quechua women at the PROEIB. However, of the fifty-two students enrolled at the center at that time, twenty were women.

7. While some of these differences come from long histories of ethnic differentiation (e.g., Aymaras vs. Quechuas), young people are rethinking labels among their own ethnic groups as well.

8. In Peru the selection procedure for the first class was murky. Eleven Peruvian indigenous representatives, from both the highlands and the lowlands, were selected by the UNEBI and by leading intercultural activists. All the Peruvian Quechuas at the PROEIB in 1999 were either community leaders, university-trained teachers, or individuals working in local-level institutions with educational or cultural affiliations and identifying as indígenas. These carefully selected individuals were singled out to become future indigenous leaders in the Andean region. Their ability to speak Quechua, their professional and educational backgrounds, and their claim to indigenous roots became key elements ensuring their selection to the higher education training program mentioned above.

9. See Warren 1992, 1998a; Field 1999, 2000; and Stephen 2002 for discussions about the increasingly frequent collaboration between indigenous leaders and intellectuals and social scientists.

10. In 1982 the Peruvian anthropologist Stefano Varese also used this term to predict the emergence of indigenous peoples in Latin America as a political force.

11. See also Campbell 1994; Rappaport 1994; Jackson 1995a; Warren 1998a, 1998b; and Stephen 2002.

CHAPTER 6. ARTICULATING INDIGENOUS CITIZENSHIP

1. As I write in the summer of 2004, the language of absence becomes even less persuasive as indigenous communities in Peru have begun to mobilize large protests in ways resembling those of their counterparts in Ecuador or Bolivia. "New" protests against coca eradication or the harmful environmental effects of mining are important developments, but they do not diminish the argument I am making here: privileging the large-scale politics of protest can often result in missing other equally important but less visible arenas of contention.

2. Miraflores is one of the more exclusive areas of Lima.

3. For recent discussions of the cultural politics of lynching and communal justice in the Andes, see Goldstein 2003 and 2004. Goldstein argues that these local forms of violence and justice cannot be understood apart from the effects of international neoliberal policies. For this reason, he characterizes recent lynchings as examples of neoliberal violence.

Works Cited

Abu-Lughod, Lila. 1991. "Writing Against Culture." In Richard Fox, ed., *Recapturing Anthropology: Working in the Present*, 137–162. Santa Fe, NM: School of American Research Press.

Agurto, Jorge. 2002. Interview, June 6, 2002, Coordinadora-COPPIP, Lima.

Albó, Xavier. 1994. "And from Kataristas to MNRistas? The Surprising and Bold Alliance between Aymaras and Neoliberals in Bolivia." In Donna Lee Van Cott, ed., *Indigenous Peoples and Democracy in Latin America*, 55–82. New York: St. Martin's Press.

——. 1991. "El retorno del Indio." *Revista Andina* 9(2): 299–345.

——. 1977. *El futuro de los idiomas oprimidos en los Andes*. Lima: Universidad Nacional Mayor de San Marcos, Centro de Investigación de Lingüística Aplicada.

Alvarez, Sonia, Evelina Dagnino, and Arturo Escobar, eds. 1998. *Cultures of Politics, Politics of Cultures: Re-visioning Latin American Social Movements*. Boulder: Westview Press.

Ames, Patricia. 2002. *Para ser iguales, para ser distintos: Educación, escritura y poder en el Perú*. Lima: IEP.

——. 1999. *Mejorando la escuela rural: Tres décadas de experiencias educativas en el Perú*. Lima: Instituto de Estudios Peruanos.

Anderson, Benedict. 1991 [1983]. *Imagined Communities*. New York: Verso.

——. 1990. *Language and Power: Exploring Political Cultures in Indonesia*. Ithaca: Cornell University Press.

Apparudai, Arjun. 1991. "Global Ethnoscapes: Notes and Queries for a Transnational Anthropology." In Richard Fox, ed., *Recapturing Anthropology: Working in the Present*, 191–210. Santa Fe, NM: SAR Press.

Arguedas, José María. 1993 [1968]. "No soy un aculturado." In *Agua: Breve antología didáctica*. Lima: Horizonte.

Arpasi, Paulina. 2001. "Entrevista por Juan Pina." *Perfiles del Siglo XXI*, no. 101, December. Available at www.revistaperfiles.com.

Assies, Willem, et al., eds. 2000. *The Challenge of Diversity: Indigenous Peoples and Reform of the State in Latin America*. Amsterdam: Thela Thesis.

Bakhtin, Mikhail. 1981 [1934]. *The Dialogic Imagination*. Trans. and ed. Caryl Emerson and Michael Holquist. Austin: University of Texas Press.

Basch, Linda G., Nina Glick Schiller, and Cristine Szanton-Blanc. 1994. *Nations Unbound: Transnational Projects, Postcolonial Predicaments, and Deterritorialized Nation-States*. Philadelphia: Gordon & Breach.

Basombrío Iglesias, Carlos. 1998. "Sendero Luminoso and Human Rights: A Perverse Logic That Captured the Country." In Steve Stern, ed., *Shining and Other*

Paths: War and Society in Peru, 1980–1995, 425–446. Durham: Duke University Press.

Bebbington, Anthony. 2000. "Re-encountering Development: Livelihood Transitions and Place Transformations in the Andes." *Annals of the Association of American Geographers* 90(3): 495–520.

Bebbington, Anthony, and Graham Thiele. 1993. *Non-Governmental Organizations and the State in Latin America*. London: Overseas Development Institute.

Becker, Marc. 2002. "Mariátegui y el problema de las razas en América Latina." *Revista Andina* 35: 191–220.

Benavides, Margarita. 2001. "Esta mesa nadie la instala." Interview with Martín Paredes. *Quehacer* 132: 102–106.

Beverly, John. 1998. "Siete aproximaciones al 'problema indígena.'" In Mabel Moraña, ed., *Indigenismo hacia el fin del milenio: Homenaje a Antonio Cornejo-Polar*, 269–284. Pittsburgh: Biblioteca de América.

Blanco, Hugo. 1972. *Land or Death: The Peasant Struggle in Peru*. New York: Pathfinder.

Bonfil Batalla, Guillermo. 1987. *México profundo: Una civilización negada*. Mexico City: Grijalbo.

Bonilla, Heraclio. 1987. "The Indian Peasantry and Peru during the War with Chile." In Steve Stern, ed., *Resistance, Rebellion, and Consciousness in the Andean Peasant World, 18th to 20th Centuries*, 219–231. Madison: University of Wisconsin Press.

Bourque, Susan, and Kay Warren. 1981. *Women of the Andes: Patriarchy and Social Change in Two Peruvian Towns*. Ann Arbor: University of Michigan Press.

Bourricaud, François. 1975. "Indian, Mestizo, and Cholo as Symbols in the Peruvian System of Stratification." In Nathan Glazer and Daniel Moynihan, eds., *Ethnicity: Theory and Experience*, 350–390. Cambridge: Harvard University Press.

Brysk, Alison. 2000a. *From Tribal Village to Global Village: Indian Rights and International Relations in Latin America*. Stanford: Stanford University Press.

———. 2000b. "Globalization: The Double-Edged Sword." *NACLA, Report on the Americas* 34(1): 29–31.

———. 1996. "Turning Weakness into Strength: The Internationalization of Indian Rights." *Latin American Perspectives* 23(2): 38–57.

———. 1994. "Acting Globally: Indian Rights and International Politics in Latin America." In Donna Lee Van Cott, ed., *Indigenous Peoples and Democracy in Latin America*, 29–54. New York: St. Martin's Press.

Burns, Donald. 1971. *Cinco años de educación bilingüe en los Andes del Peru: 1965–1970. Informe final*. Lima: Instituto Lingüístico de Verano.

———. 1968. "Bilingual Education in the Andes of Peru." In Joshua Fishman et al., eds., *Language Problems of Developing Nations*, 403-414. New York: Wiley.

Caballo, Tito, and Stephanie Boyd. 2002. *Choropampa: The Price of Gold*. Video. Lima: Guarango Productions.

Campbell, Howard. 1994. *Zapotec Renaissance: Ethnic Politics and Cultural Revivalism in Southern Mexico*. Albuquerque: University of New Mexico Press.

Cárdenas, Victor Hugo. 2001. "Spaces, International Actors, and Indigenous Development." Presentation delivered at International Conference, "Beyond the Lost

Decade: Indigenous Movements and the Transformation of Development and Democracy in Latin America," Princeton University, March 2–3, 2001.

Castillo, Martín. 1998. "Harawi." Unpublished manuscript.

CENDA. 1988. "Reporte sobre diálogos de conflicto en la comunidad de Raqaypampa." In *Reporte sobre la Educación en Raqaypampa.* Cochabamba.

Centurión, Jerónimo. 2002. "La presencia de Eliane." *AgenciaPeru.com*, June 18. Available at www.agenciaperu.com.

Cerrón-Palomino, Rodolfo. 1989. Language Policy in Peru: A Historical Overview. *International Journal of the Sociology of Language* 77: 11–33.

———. 1988. "Hacia una escritura quechua." *Proceso* 8: 77–98.

———. 1987. *Lingüística quechua.* Cuzco: Centro de Estudios Andinos "Bartolomé de Las Casas."

———. 1985. "El franciscano Ráez y la unificación del Quechua." *Anthropologica* 3: 205–246.

———. 1982. "La cuestión lingüística en el Perú." In Rodolfo Cerrón-Palomino, ed., *Aula Quechua,* 105–123. Lima: Signo Universitario.

Cevallos-Candau, Francisco, et al. 1994. *Coded Encounters: Writing, Gender, and Ethnicity in Colonial Latin America.* Amherst: University of Massachusetts Press.

Cheng Hurtado, Alberto. 1988. "En homenaje a Luis E. Valcárcel." *Perú Indígena* 12(27): 9–11.

Chirif, Alberto. 1991. "Comentario." *Revista Andina* 9(2): 353–357.

Chirinos, Andrés, and Alejo Maque Capira. 1996. *Eros Andino.* Cuzco: Centro de Estudios Andinos "Bartolomé de Las Casas."

CINA. 2002. "Evaluación y perspectivas del movimiento indígena peruano: Conclusiones de una reunión de trabajo." Unpublished document. July 18.

Clifford, James. 2001. "Indigenous Articulations." *Contemporary Pacific* 13(2): 468–490.

———. 2000. "Taking Identity Politics Seriously: 'The Contradictory, Stony Ground . . . '" In Paul Gilroy, Lawrence Grossberg, and Angela McRobbie, eds., *Without Guarantees: In Honor of Stuart Hall.* London: Verso.

———. 1988. *The Predicament of Culture: Twentieth-Century Ethnography, Literature, and Art.* Cambridge: Harvard University Press.

Cojtí Cuxil, Demetrio. 1996. "The Politics of Mayan Revindication." In Edward Fischer and McKenna Brown, eds., *Mayan Cultural Activism in Guatemala,* 19–50. Austin: University of Texas Press.

Comaroff, John. 1996. "Ethnicity, Nationalism, and the Politics of Difference in an Age of Revolution." In Edwin Wilmsen and Patrick McAllister, eds., *The Politics of Difference: Ethnic Premises in a World of Power,* 162–183. Chicago: University of Chicago Press.

CONAPA. 2001. *Reforma constitucional: Bases de una propuesta de los pueblos andinos y amazónicos.* Lima.

Conejo, Alberto. 1998. "La Educación Indígena en el Ecuador: Lineamientos y propuestas." Paper presented at International Conference on Bilingual Education: "Puno vuelve a Puno, 1978–1998: 20 años de implementación de educación bilingüe en Puno." Puno.

———. n.d. "Kwintus." Unpublished manuscript.

Contreras, Carlos. 1996. "Sobre los orígenes de la explosión demográfica en el Perú." Working paper no. 61. Lima: IEP.

Coronel-Molina, Serafín. 2003. "The Intellectualization of Indigenous Languages and Educational Implications." SIT Occasional Papers Series. Brattleboro, VT: School for International Training.

——. 2001. "La intelectualización de lenguas indígenas y su implicación en la educación." Paper presented at the First Hemispheric Conference of Indigenous Education, Guatemala City.

——. 2000. "Piruw Malka Kichwapiq Hatun Qillqa Lulay." *Amerindia* (24): 1–30.

——. 1999a. "Functional Domains of the Quechua Language in Peru: Issues of Status Planning." In Colin Baker, ed., *Indigenous Language Maintenance in Latin America,* special issue of *International Journal of Bilingual Education and Bilingualism* 2(3): 166–180.

——. 1999b. "Crossing Borders and Constructing Indigeneity: A Self-Ethnography of Identity." In James Brown and Patricia Sant, eds., *Indigeneity: Construction and Re/Presentation.* New York: Nova Science Publishers.

——. In progress. "The High Quechua Language Academy in Peru: Language Policy and Planning and Language Ideologies." Ph.D. dissertation, University of Pennsylvania.

Cotler, Julio. 1983. "Democracy and National Integration in Peru." In Cynthia McClintock and Abraham Lowenthal, eds., *The Peruvian Experiment Reconsidered,* 3–38. Princeton: Princeton University Press.

Davis, Shelton. 2001. "Investing in Indigenous Peoples' Development: The Experience of the World Bank in Latin America." Paper presented at the conference "Beyond the Lost Decade: Indigenous Movements and the Transformation of Development and Democracy in Latin America," Princeton University, March 2–3.

Dean, Bartholomew. 2003. "At the Margins of Power: Gender Hierarchy and the Politics of Ethnic Mobilization among the Urarina." In Bartholomew Dean and Jerome M. Levi, eds., *At the Risk of Being Heard: Identity, Indigenous Rights, and Postcolonial States,* 217–254. Ann Arbor: University of Michigan Press.

——. 2002. "State Power and Indigenous Peoples in Peruvian Amazonia: A Lost Decade, 1990–2000." In David Maybury-Lewis, ed., *The Politics of Ethnicity: Indigenous Peoples in Latin American States,* 199–238. Cambridge: David Rockefeller Center Series on Latin American Studies, Harvard University.

Declaración de Lima. 2002. *SERVINDI: Servicio de Información Indígena,* no. 13.

Degregori, Carlos Iván. 1998a. "Harvesting Storms: Peasant Rondas and the Defeat of Sendero Luminoso in Ayacucho." In Steve Stern, ed., *Shining and Other Paths: War and Society in Peru, 1980–1995,* 128–157. Durham: Duke University Press.

——. 1998b. "Ethnicity and Democratic Governability in Latin America: Reflections from Two Central Andean Countries." In Felipe Aguero and Jeffrey Stark, eds., *Faultlines of Democracy in Post-Transition Latin America,* 203–234. Miami: North-South Center Press.

——. 1993. "Identidad étnica: Movimientos sociales y participación política en el Perú." In Alberto Adrianzén et al., *Democracia, etnicidad, y violencia política en los países andinos,* 113–136. Lima: IEP/IFEA.

————. 1990. *Ayacucho, 1969–1979: El surgimiento de Sendero Luminoso.* Lima: Instituto de Estudios Peruanos.

Degregori, Carlos Iván, et al. 1996. *Las rondas campesinas y la derrota de Sendero Luminoso.* Lima: Instituto de Estudios Peruanos.

de la Cadena, Marisol. 2001. "Reconstructing Race: Racism, Culture, and Mestizaje in Latin America." *NACLA, Report on the Americas* 34(6): 16–23.

————. 2000. *Indigenous Mestizos: The Politics of Race and Culture in Cuzco, Peru, 1919–1991.* Durham: Duke University Press.

————. 1996. "The Political Tensions of Representations and Misrepresentations: Intellectuals and *Mestizas* in Cuzco (1919–1990)." *Journal of Latin American Anthropology* 2(1), Fall: 112–147.

————. 1995. " 'Women Are More Indian': Ethnicity and Gender in a Community near Cuzco." In Brooke Larson and Olivia Harris, eds., *Ethnicity, Markets, and Migration in the Andes: At the Crossroads of History and Anthropology,* 329–348. Durham: Duke University Press.

Delgado, Guillermo. 2002. "Solidarity in Cyberspace: Indigenous Peoples Online." *NACLA, Report on the Americas* 35(5): 49–51.

del Pino, Ponciano. 1998. "Family, Culture, and 'Revolution': Everyday Life with Sendero Luminoso." In Steve Stern, ed., *Shining and Other Paths: War and Society in Peru, 1980–1995,* 158–192. Durham: Duke University Press.

Deustua, José, and José Luis Rénique. 1984. *Intelectuales, indigenismo y descentralismo en el Perú, 1897–1931.* Cuzco: Centro de Estudios Andinos "Bartolomé de Las Casas."

Díaz Polanco, Héctor. 1997. *Indigenous Peoples in Latin America: The Quest for Self-Determination.* Trans. Lucía Rayas. Boulder: Westview Press.

Diskin, Martin. 1991. "Ethnic Discourse and the Challenge to Anthropology: The Nicaraguan Case." In Greg Urban and Joel Sherzer, eds., *Nation-States and Indians in Latin America,* 156–180. Austin: University of Texas Press.

DuBois, Marc. 1991. "The Governance of the Third World: A Foucauldian Perspective of Power Relations in Development." *Alternatives* 16(1): 1–30.

Eckstein, Susan. 1983. "Revolution and Redistribution in Latin America." In Cynthia McClintock and Abraham Lowenthal, eds., *The Peruvian Experiment Reconsidered,* 347–386. Princeton: Princeton University Press.

Edelman, Marc. 2002. "Social Movements: Changing Paradigms and Forms of Politics." *Annual Review of Anthropology* 30: 285–317.

————. 1999. *Peasants Against Globalization: Rural Social Movements in Costa Rica.* Stanford: Stanford University Press.

Escalante, Carmen, and Ricardo Valderrama. 1992. *Ñuqanchik Runakuna: Testimonios de los quechua del siglo XX.* Cuzco: Centro de Estudios Andinos "Bartolomé de Las Casas."

Escobar, Alberto. 1984. *Arguedas, o La utopía de la lengua.* Lima: IEP.

Escobar, Alberto, José Matos Mar, and Giorgio Alberti. 1975. *Perú país bilingüe?* Lima: Instituto de Estudios Peruanos.

Escobar, Arturo. 1995. *Encountering Development: The Making and Unmaking of the Third World.* Princeton: Princeton University Press.

————. 1991. "Anthropology and the Development Encounter: The Making and Marketing of Development Anthropology." *American Ethnologist* 18: 16–40.

Fabian, Johannes. 2001. *Anthropology with an Attitude: Critical Essays.* Stanford: Stanford University Press.

Fanon, Frantz. 1963. *The Wretched of the Earth.* New York: Grove Press.

Ferguson, James. 1994. *The Anti-Politics Machine: "Development," Depoliticization, and Bureaucratic Power in Lesotho.* Minneapolis: University of Minnesota Press.

Field, Les. 2000. "The Academic and 'Real World' Analyses of Mestizaje: A Ramble about Privilege, Positioning, and Politics." Paper presented at the annual meetings of the Latin American Studies Association, Miami.

————. 1999. "Complicities and Collaborations: Anthropologists and the 'Unacknowledged Tribes' of California." *Current Anthropology* 40(2), April: 193–209.

————. 1996a. "State, Anti-State, and Indigenous Entities." *Journal of Latin American Anthropology* 1(2), Spring: 98–119.

————. 1996b. "Mired Positionings: Moving beyond Metropolitan Authority and Indigenous Authenticity." *Identities* 3(1–2): 137–154.

————. 1994a. "Harvesting the Bitter Juice: Contradictions of Páez Resistance in the Changing Colombian Nation-State." *Identities* 1: 89–108.

————. 1994b. "Who Are the Indians? Reconceptualizing Indigenous Identity, Resistance, and the Role of Social Science in Latin America." *Latin American Research Review* 29(3): 237–248.

Fisher, William. 1997. "Doing Good? The Politics and Anti-Politics of NGO Practices." *Annual Review of Anthropology* 26: 439–464.

Flores Galindo, Alberto. 1992. *Dos ensayos sobre José María Arguedas.* Lima: SUR Casa de Estudios del Socialismo.

————. 1987. *Buscando un Inca: Identidad y utopía en los Andes.* Lima: Horizonte.

Foster, Robert. 1991. "Making National Cultures in the Global Ecumene." *Annual Review of Anthropology* 20: 235–260.

Fox, Jonathan, and David Brown, eds. 1998. *The Struggle for Accountability.* Cambridge: MIT Press.

Fox, Richard. 1991. "Introduction: Working in the Present." In Richard Fox, ed., *Recapturing Anthropology: Working in the Present,* 1–16. Santa Fe, NM: SAR Press.

Francke Ballve, Marfil. 1979. "El movimiento indigenista en el Cuzco." In Carlos Ivan Degregori et al., eds., *Indigenismo, clases sociales, y problema nacional.* Lima: CELATS.

Fuss, Diana. 1989. *Essentially Speaking.* New York: Routledge.

García, María Elena. 2003. "The Politics of Community: Education, Indigenous Rights, and Ethnic Mobilization in Peru." *Latin American Perspectives* 30(1), issue 128: 70–95.

————. 2000. "Ethnographic Responsibility and the Anthropological Endeavor: Beyond Identity Discourse." *Anthropological Quarterly* 73(2): 89–101.

García, María Elena, and José Antonio Lucero. 2004. " 'Un País sin Indígenas?': Rethinking Indigenous Politics in Peru." In Nancy Postero and Leon Zamosc, eds., *The Struggle for Indigenous Rights in Latin America.* Brighton, UK: Sussex Academic Press.

García Canclini, Néstor. 1995. *Hybrid Cultures: Strategies for Entering and Leaving Modernity*. Trans. Christopher Chiappari and Silvia L. López. Minneapolis: University of Minnesota Press.

Gelles, Paul. 2002. "Andean Culture, Indigenous Identity, and the State in Peru." In David Maybury-Lewis, ed., *The Politics of Ethnicity: Indigenous Peoples and Latin American States,* 239–266. Cambridge: David Rockefeller Center Series on Latin American Studies, Harvard University.

———. 2000. *Water and Power in Highland Peru: The Cultural Politics of Irrigation and Development.* New Brunswick: Rutgers University Press.

Gill, Lesley. 1997. "Power Lines: The Political Context of Non-governmental Organization (NGO) Activity in El Alto, Bolivia." *Journal of Latin American Anthropology* 2(2): 144–169.

Ginsburg, Faye. 1991. "Indigenous Media: Faustian Contract or Global Village?" *Cultural Anthropology* 6(1): 92–112.

Gleich, Utta von. 1994. "Language Spread Policy: The Case of Quechua in the Andean Republics of Bolivia, Ecuador, and Peru." *International Journal of the Sociology of Language* 107: 77–113.

Glick Schiller, Nina, and Georges Fouron. 2001. *Georges Woke Up Laughing: Long-Distance Nationalism and the Search for Home.* Durham: Duke University Press.

Godenzzi, Juan Carlos. 2001. "Política de lenguas y culturas en la educación: El caso del Peru." Paper presented at the 23rd meeting of the Latin American Studies Association. Washington, DC.

———. 1997. "Literacy and Modernization among the Quechua-Speaking Population of Peru." In Nancy Hornberger, ed., *Indigenous Literacies in the Americas: Language Planning from the Bottom Up,* 237–250. New York: Mouton de Gruyter.

———. 1996. "Introducción/Construyendo la convivencia y el entendimiento: Educación e interculturalidad en América Latina." In Juan Carlos Godenzzi, ed., *Educación e interculturalidad en los Andes y la Amazonia,* 23–82. Cuzco: Centro de Estudios Andinos "Bartolomé de Las Casas."

———, ed. 1992. *El Quechua en debate: Ideología, normalización y enseñanza.* Cuzco: Centro de Estudios Andinos "Bartolomé de Las Casas."

———, ed. 1996. *Educación e interculturalidad en los Andes y la Amazonía.* Cuzco: Centro de Estudios Andinos "Bartolomé de Las Casas."

Godenzzi, Juan Carlos, and Janett Vengoa Zúñiga. 1994. *Runasimimanta Yuyaychakusun: Manual de lingüística quechua para bilingües.* Cuzco: Centro de Estudios Andinos "Bartolomé de Las Casas."

Goffman, Erving. 1963. *Stigma: Notes on the Management of Spoiled Identity.* Englewood Cliffs, NJ: Prentice Hall.

Goldstein, Daniel M. 2004. "Human Rights and Private Justice in Cochabamba, Bolivia." Paper delivered at the meetings of the American Anthropological Association, Chicago, November 2003.

———. 2003. "'In Our Own Hands': Lynching, Justice, and the Law in Bolivia." *American Ethnologist* 30(1): 22–43.

Gorriti Ellenbogen, Gustavo. 1999. *The Shining Path: A History of the Millenarian War in Peru.* Trans. Robin Kirk. Chapel Hill: University of North Carolina Press.

————. 1990. *Sendero: Historia de la guerra milenaria en el Perú.* Lima: Apoyo.

Gould, Jeffrey. 1998. *To Die in This Way: Nicaraguan Indians and the Myth of Mestizaje, 1880–1965.* Durham: Duke University Press.

Gramsci, Antonio. 1971. *Selections from the Prison Notebooks.* Ed. and trans. Quintin Hoare and Geoffrey Nowell Smith. New York: International Publishers.

Granda Oré, Juan. 1990. *Los pequeños zorros: Relatos orales de niños ayacuchanos.* Lima: Rädda Barnen.

Gupta, Akhil. 1995. "Blurred Boundaries: The Discourse of Corruption, the Culture of Politics, and the Imagined State." *American Ethnologist* 22(2): 375–402.

Gustafson, Bret. 2002. "Paradoxes of Liberal Indigenism: Indigenous Movements, State Processes, and Intercultural Reform in Bolivia." In David Maybury-Lewis, ed., *The Politics of Ethnicity: Indigenous Peoples in Latin American States,* 267–308. Cambridge: David Rockefeller Center on Latin American Studies, Harvard University.

Guzmán, Abimael. 1988. "Entrevista del siglo. Presidente Gonzalo rompe el silencio." *El Diario,* Lima, July 24.

Hale, Charles. 2002. "Does Multiculturalism Menace? Governance, Cultural Rights and the Politics of Identity in Guatemala." *Journal of Latin American Studies* 34: 485–524.

————. 1997. "The Cultural Politics of Identity in Latin America." *Annual Review of Anthropology* 26: 567–590.

————. 1994a. *Resistance and Contradiction: Miskitu Indians and the Nicaraguan State, 1894–1987.* Stanford: Stanford University Press.

————. 1994b. "Between Che Guevara and the Pachamama: Mestizos, Indians and Identity Politics in the Anti-Quincentenary Campaign." *Critique of Anthropology* 14(1): 9–39.

Hall, Stuart. 1996 [1986]. "On Post-Modernism and Articulation: An Interview with Stuart Hall." Reprinted in David Morely and Kuan-Hsing Chen, eds., *Critical Dialogues in Cultural Studies.* New York: Routledge.

Harvey, Penelope. 1994. *Sex and Violence: Issues in Representation and Experience.* London: Routledge.

————. 1989. *Género, autoridad y competencia lingüística: Participación política de la mujer en pueblos andinos.* Lima: IEP.

Healy, Kevin. 2001. *Llamas, Weavings, and Organic Chocolate: Multicultural Grassroots Development in the Andes and Amazon of Bolivia.* Notre Dame: University of Notre Dame Press.

Hidalgo, María Elena. 2002. "Sendero todavía mantiene cautivas a 200 familias en la Selva Central." *La República* (Lima), December 28.

Hinojosa, Iván. 1998. "On Poor Relations and the Nouveau Riche: Shining Path and the Radical Peruvian Left." In Steve Stern, ed., *Shining and Other Paths: War and Society in Peru, 1980–1995,* 60–83. Durham: Duke University Press.

Hornberger, Nancy H. 1988. *Bilingual Education and Language Maintenance: A Southern Peruvian Quechua Case.* Dordrecht: Foris.

————. 1987. "Bilingual Education Success, Policy Failure." *Language in Society* 16: 205–226.

————, ed. 1997. *Indigenous Literacies in the Americas: Language Planning from the Bottom Up*. New York: Mouton de Gruyter.

Howard-Malverde, Rosaleen, and Andrew Canessa. 1995. "The School in the Quechua and Aymara Communities of Highland Bolivia." *International Journal of Educational Development* 15(3): 231–243.

Isbell, Billie Jean. 1992. "Shining Path and Peasant Responses in Rural Ayacucho." In David Scott Palmer, ed., *Shining Path of Peru*, 59–82. New York: St. Martin's Press.

Itier, César. 1992a. "Lenguas, ideología y poder en el Cuzco: 1885–1930." In Juan Carlos Godenzzi, ed., *El Quechua en debate: Ideología, normalización y enseñanza*, 25–50. Cuzco: Centro de Estudios Andinos "Bartolomé de Las Casas."

————. 1992b. " 'Cuzqueñistas' y 'foráneos': Las resistencias a la normalización de la escritura del Quechua." In Juan Carlos Godenzzi, ed., *El Quechua en debate: Ideología, normalización y enseñanza*, 85–96. Cuzco: Centro de Estudios Andinos "Bartolomé de Las Casas."

Jackson, Jean. 1995a. "Culture, Genuine and Spurious: The Politics of Indianness in the Vaupés, Colombia." *American Ethnologist* 22(1): 3–27.

————. 1995b. "Preserving Indian Culture: Shaman Schools and Ethno-Education in the Vaupés, Colombia." *Cultural Anthropology* 10(3): 302–329.

————. 1991. "Being and Becoming an Indian in the Vaupés." In Greg Urban and Joel Sherzer, eds., *Nation States and Indians in Latin America*, 131–155. Austin: University of Texas Press.

Jelin, Elizabeth. 1998. "Toward a Culture of Participation and Citizenship: Challenges for a More Equitable World." In Sonia Alvarez, Evelina Dagnino, and Arturo Escobar, eds., *Cultures of Politics, Politics of Cultures: Re-visioning Latin American Social Movements*, 405–414. Boulder: Westview Press.

Kapsoli, Wilfredo. 1984. *Ayllus del sol: Anarquismo y utopia andina*. Lima: Tarea.

————. 1980. *El pensamiento de la Asociación Pro-Indígena*. Cuzco: Centro de Estudios Andinos "Bartolomé de Las Casas."

Kapsoli, Wilfredo, and Wilson Reátegui. 1972. *Situación económica-social del campesinado peruano, 1919–1930*. Lima: Universidad Nacional Mayor de San Marcos.

Kearney, Michael. 1996. "Introduction: Ethnicity and Class in Latin America." *Latin American Perspectives* 23(2), issue 89: 5–16.

————. 1995a. "The Local and the Global: The Anthropology of Globalization and Transnationalism." *Annual Review of Anthropology* 24: 547–565.

————. 1995b. "The Effects of Transnational Culture and Migration on Mixtec Identity in Oaxacalifornia." In Michael Peter Smith and Joe R. Feagin, eds., *The Bubbling Cauldron: Race, Ethnicity, and the Urban Crisis*. Minneapolis: University of Minnesota Press.

Keck, Margaret, and Kathryn Sikkink. 1998. *Activists Beyond Borders*. Ithaca: Cornell University Press.

Kleymeyer, Charles. 1994. *Cultural Expression and Grassroots Development: Cases from Latin America and the Caribbean*. Boulder: Lynne Reinner.

Kristal, Efraín. 1991. *Una visión urbana de los Andes: Génesis y desarrollo del indigenismo en el Perú, 1848–1930*. Lima: Instituto de Apoyo Agrario.

Kuptana, Rosemarie. 1988. "Inuit Broadcasting Corporation." *Commission on Visual Anthropology Newsletter*, May, 39–41.

Kymlicka, Will, and Wayne Norman, eds. 2000. *Citizenship in Diverse Societies*. Oxford: Oxford University Press.

Larson, Brooke. 1995. "Andean Communities, Political Cultures, and Markets: The Changing Contours of a Field." In Brooke Larson and Olivia Harris, eds., *Ethnicity, Markets, and Migration in the Andes: At the Crossroads of History and Anthropology*, 5–54. Durham: Duke University Press.

Li, Tanya Murray. 2000. "Articulating Indigenous Identity in Indonesia: Resources, Politics, and the Tribal Slot." *Comparative Studies in Society and History* 42(1): 149–179.

Lockhart, James. 1968. *Spanish Peru, 1532–1560: A Colonial Society*. Madison: University of Wisconsin Press.

López, Luis Enrique. 1998. "La EBI en América Latina: Desafíos y Posibilidades de la Educación Indígena." Paper presented at International Conference on Bilingual Education: "Puno vuelve a Puno, 1978–1998: 20 años de implementación de educación bilingüe en Puno." Puno.

———. 1996. "No más danzas de ratones grises: Sobre interculturalidad, democracia y educación." In Juan Carlos Godenzzi, ed., *Educación e interculturalidad en los Andes y la Amazonia*, 23–82. Cuzco: Centro de Estudios Andinos "Bartolomé de Las Casas."

———. 1995. "Intercultural Bilingual Education and the Training of Human Resources: Lessons for Bolivia from the Latin American Experience." In Raúl Gagliardi, ed., *Teacher Training and Multiculturalism: National Studies*, 25–56. Paris: International Bureau of Education, UNESCO.

Lowenthal, Abraham. 1983. "The Peruvian Experiment Reconsidered." In Cynthia McClintock and Abraham Lowenthal, eds., *The Peruvian Experiment Reconsidered*, 415–430. Princeton: Princeton University Press.

Lucero, José Antonio. 2003. "Locating the 'Indian Problem': Community, Nationality, and Contradiction in Ecuadorian Indigenous Politics." *Latin American Perspectives* 30(1), issue 128: 23–48.

———. 2002. "Arts of Unification: Indigenous Movements and Political Representation in Bolivia and Ecuador." Ph.D. dissertation, Princeton University.

———. 2000. "On Feuds, Tumults, and Turns: Politics and Culture in Social Movement Theory." *Comparative Politics* 32(2): 231–249.

Luykx, Aurolyn. 1999. *The Citizen Factory: Schooling and Cultural Production in Bolivia*. Albany: State University of New York Press.

Lynch, John. 1973. *The Spanish American Revolutions, 1808–1826*. New York: Norton.

Mallon, Florencia. 1998. "Chronicle of a Path Foretold? Velasco's Revolution, Vanguardia Revolucionaria, and 'Shining Omens' in the Indigenous Communities of Andahuaylas." In Steve Stern, ed., *Shining and Other Paths: War and Society in Peru, 1980–1995*, 84–117. Durham: Duke University Press.

———. 1995. *Peasant and Nation: The Making of Postcolonial Mexico and Peru.* Berkeley: University of California Press.

Mannheim, Bruce. 1992. "El renacimiento quechua del siglo XVIII." In Juan Carlos Godenzzi, ed., *El Quechua en debate: Ideología, normalización y enseñanza,* 15–24. Cuzco: Centro de Estudios Andinos "Bartolomé de Las Casas."

———. 1991. *The Language of the Inka since the European Invasion.* Austin: University of Texas Press.

———. 1990. "La cronología relativa de la lengua y literatura quechua cusqueña." *Revista Andina* 8(1): 139–177.

———. 1984. "Una Nación Acorralada: Southern Peruvian Quechua Language Planning and Politics in Historical Perspective." *Language in Society* 13: 291–309.

Manrique, Nelson. 2002. *El tiempo del miedo: La violencia política en el Perú, 1980–1996.* Lima: Fondo Editorial del Congreso del Perú.

———. 1998. "The War for the Central Sierra." In Steve Stern, ed., *Shining and Other Paths: War and Society in Peru, 1980–1995,* 193–223. Durham: Duke University Press.

Marcus, George. 1995. "Ethnography in/of the World System: The Emergence of Multi-Sited Ethnography." *Annual Review of Anthropology* 24: 95–117.

Mariátegui, José Carlos. 1994 [1928]. *Siete ensayos de interpretación de la realidad peruana.* Lima: Biblioteca Amauta.

———. 1972 [1928]. "Prólogo." In Luis Valcárcel, *Tempestad en los Andes.* Lima: Universo.

Marr, Timothy. 1999. "Neither the State nor the Grass Roots: Language Maintenance and the Discourse of the Academia Mayor de la Lengua Quechua." *International Journal of Bilingual Education and Bilingualism* 2(3): 181–197.

Marzal, Manuel. 1995. "Perception of the State Among Peruvian Indians." In Lourdes Giordani and Marjorie Snipes, eds., *Indigenous Perceptions of the Nation-State in Latin America.* Studies in Third World Societies 56. Williamsburg: College of William and Mary.

———. 1981. *Historia de la antropología indigenista: México y Perú.* Lima: Fondo Editorial, Pontificia Universidad Católica del Perú.

Matos Mar, José, ed. 1970. *El indio y el poder en el Perú.* Lima: IEP.

Matto de Turner, Clorinda. 1995 [1889]. *Aves sin nido.* Lima: Mantaro.

Maybury-Lewis, David, ed. 2002. *The Politics of Ethnicity: Indigenous Peoples in Latin American States.* Cambridge: Harvard University Press.

Mayer, Enrique. 1992. "Peru in Deep Trouble: Mario Vargas Llosa's 'Inquest in the Andes' Reexamined." In George E. Marcus, ed., *Rereading Cultural Anthropology,* 181–219. Durham: Duke University Press.

McClintock, Cynthia, and Abraham Lowenthal. 1983. *The Peruvian Experiment Reconsidered.* Princeton: Princeton University Press.

Michaels, Eric. 1991. "Aboriginal Content: Who's Got It, Who Needs It?" *Visual Anthropology* 4(3–4): 277–300.

———. 1986. *Aboriginal Invention of Television: Central Australia, 1982–86.* Canberra: Australian Institute for Aboriginal Studies.

————. 1984. "The Social Organization of an Aboriginal Video Workplace." *Australian Aboriginal Studies* 1: 26–34.

Millones, Luis. 2000. "Hay un país sin indígenas entre Ecuador y Boliva." In Marta Bulnes, ed., *Conversaciones para la convivencia*. Lima: GTZ.

Molina, Guillermo, Rodrigo Montoya, and Rafael Roncagliolo. 1972. *Detrás del mito de la educación peruana*. Lima: IEP.

Montoya, Rodrigo. 1998. *Multiculturalidad y política: Derechos indígenas, ciudadanos y humanos*. Lima: Sur Casa de Estudios del Socialismo.

————. 1993. "Libertad, democracia, y problema étnico en el Perú." In Alberto Adrianzén et al., *Democracia, etnicidad, y violencia política en los países andinos*, 103–112. Lima: IEP/IFEA.

————. 1990. *Por una educación bilingüe en el Perú: Reflexiones sobre cultura y socialismo*. Lima: Mosca Azul.

————. 1986. "Identidad étnica y luchas agrarias en los Andes peruanos." In *Identidades andinas y lógicas del campesinado*, 247–278. Lima: Mosca Azul.

Murin, Deborah Lee. 1988. *Northern Native Broadcasting*. Vancouver: Runge Press.

Nagengast, Carole, and Michael Kearney. 1990. "Mixtec Ethnicity: Social Identity, Political Consciousness, and Political Activism." *Latin American Research Review* 25(2): 61–91.

Narayan, Kirin. 1993. "How Native Is a 'Native' Anthropologist?" *American Anthropologist* 95: 671–686.

Naveda, Igidio. 2002. Interview, June 6, 2002, Oxfam America, Lima.

Niño-Murcia, M. 1997. "Linguistic Purism in Cuzco, Peru: A Historical Perspective." *Language Problems and Language Planning* 21: 134–161.

Obando, Enrique. 1998. "Civil-Military Relations in Peru, 1980–1996: How to Control and Coopt the Military (and the Consequences of Doing So)." In Steve Stern, ed., *Shining and Other Paths: War and Society in Peru, 1980–1995*, 385–410. Durham: Duke University Press.

Oliart, Patricia. 2000. "Cuestionando certidumbres: Antropología y estudios de género en el Perú." In Carlos Iván Degregori, ed., *No hay país más diverso: Compendio de antropología peruana*, 330–355. Lima: Red para el Desarrollo de las Ciencias Sociales en el Perú.

————. 1998. "Alberto Fujimori: 'The Man Peru Needed'?" In Steve Stern, ed., *Shining and Other Paths: War and Society in Peru, 1980–1995*, 411–424. Durham: Duke University Press.

Ong, Aihwa. 1999a. "Cultural Citizenship as Subject Making." In Rodolfo D. Torres et al., *Race, Identity, and Citizenship*, 262–294. Oxford: Blackwell.

————. 1999b. *Flexible Citizenship: The Cultural Logics of Transnationality*. Durham: Duke University Press.

O'Phelan Godoy, Scarlett. 1988. *Un siglo de rebeliones anticoloniales: Perú y Bolivia, 1700–1783*. Cuzco: Centro de Estudios Andinos "Bartolomé de Las Casas."

Ortiz, Alejandro. 1970. "Lenguas aborígenes y educación nacional." *Educación, la revista del maestro peruano* 1(2), October: 12–21.

Palacín, Miguel. 2002. Interview, June 4, 2002, CONACAMI, Lima.

———. 2001. "El problema de la tierra, otra vez: Una entrevista con Miguel Palacín." *Quehacer* 130 (May–June): 110–114.

Paley, Julia. 2001. *Marketing Democracy: Power and Social Movements in Post-Dictatorship Chile.* Berkeley: University of California Press.

Palmer, David Scott. 1992. *Shining Path of Peru.* New York: St. Martin's Press.

Pérez, Wrays. 2002. Interview, AIDESEP, Lima.

Pévez, Juan Hipólito. 1983. *Memorias de un viejo luchador campesino.* Lima: Tarea.

Poole, Deborah, and Gerardo Rénique. 1992. *Peru: Time of Fear.* London: Latin American Bureau.

Portocarrero, Gonzalo, and Patricia Oliart. 1989. *El Perú desde la escuela.* Lima: Instituto de Apoyo Agrario.

Pozzi-Escot, Inés. 1992. "Principios de una política nacional de lenguas y culturas en la educación." In Juan Carlos Godenzzi, ed., *El Quechua en debate: ideología, normalización y enseñanza,* 295–300. Cuzco: Centro de Estudios Andinos "Bartolomé de Las Casas."

———. 1990. "Balance y perspectivas de la educación para poblaciones indígenas en el Perú: 1990." *Allpanchis* 22(35/36): 393–434.

———. 1981. "La educación bilingüe en el marco legal de la reforma educativa peruana." In *Acerca de la historia y el universo aymara,* 113–123. Lima: CIED.

Psacharopoulos, George, and Harry Anthony Patrinos. 1994. *Indigenous People and Poverty in Latin America: An Empirical Analysis.* Washington, DC: World Bank.

Ramos, Alcida. 2002. "Cutting through State and Class: Sources and Strategies of Self-Representation in Latin America." In Kay B. Warren and Jean E. Jackson, eds., *Indigenous Movements, Self-Representation, and the State in Latin America,* 251–279. Austin: University of Texas Press.

———. 1998. *Indigenism: Ethnic Politics in Brazil.* Madison: University of Wisconsin Press.

Rappaport, Joanne. 1994. *Cumbe Reborn: An Andean Ethnography of History.* Chicago: University of Chicago Press.

Remy, María Isabel. 1994. "The Indigenous Population and the Construction of Democracy in Peru." In Donna Lee Van Cott, ed., *Indigenous Peoples and Democracy in Latin America,* 107–130. New York: St. Martin's Press.

Rénique, José Luis. 1991. *Los sueños de la sierra: Cuzco en el siglo XX.* Lima: Cepes.

Rojas, Ibico. 1982. "En torno a la oficialización de las lenguas quechua y aymara." In Rodolfo Cerrón-Palomino, ed., *Aula Quechua,* 82–105. Lima: Signo Universitario.

Rojas, Isaías. 2003. *The Push for Zero Coca: Democratic Transition and Counternarcotics Policy in Peru.* Washington, DC: WOLA.

Roncalla, Fredy. 1998. *Escritos mitimaes: Hacia una poética andina postmoderna.* New York: Barrio Editorial Press.

Roosens, Eugene. 1989. *Creating Ethnicity: The Process of Ethnogenesis.* London: Sage.

Rosaldo, Renato. 1999. "Cultural Citizenship, Inequality, and Multiculturalism." In Rodolfo D. Torres et al., *Race, Identity, and Citizenship,* 253–261. Oxford: Blackwell.

Roseberry, William. 1996. "Hegemony, Power, and Languages of Contention." In

Edwin Wilmsen and Patrick McAllister, eds., *The Politics of Difference: Ethnic Premises in a World of Power,* 71–84. Chicago: University of Chicago Press.

Rowe, John. 1954. "El movimiento nacional inca del siglo XVIII." *Revista Universitaria* (Cuzco) 107: 17–47.

Rubin, Jeffrey. 1997. *Decentering the Regime: Ethnicity, Radicalism, and Democracy in Juchitán, Mexico.* Durham: Duke University Press.

Salomon, Frank, and George Urioste. 1991. *The Huarochirí Manuscript: A Testament of Ancient and Colonial Andean Religion.* Austin: University of Texas Press.

Scott, D. 1991. "That Event, This Memory: Notes on the Anthropology of African Diasporas in the New World." *Diaspora* 1(3): 261–282.

Scott, James. 1990. *Domination and the Arts of Resistance: Hidden Transcripts.* New Haven: Yale University Press.

———. 1985. *Weapons of the Weak: Everyday Forms of Peasant Resistance.* New Haven: Yale University Press.

SERVINDI. 2003. "Declaración pública de los pueblos indígenas del Perú ante la crisis institucional de la CONAPA." No. 30, September.

———. 2002a. "Docientas familias asháninkas sufren terror de Sendero Luminoso." No. 18, December.

———. 2002b. "Evaluación y perspectivas del movimiento indígena peruano: Conclusiones de una reunión de trabajo." Newsletter, July.

———. 2002c. "La CONAPA, un fallido intento de Eliane." No. 18, December.

Sichra, Inge, and Luis Enrique López. 2003. "Las organizaciones indígenas y su papel en un programa de educación superior en los Andes." Paper delivered at International Conference "Movimientos indígenas y estado en América Latina," May 22–24, 2003.

Sieder, Rachel, ed. 2002. *Multiculturalism in Latin America: Indigenous Rights, Diversity, and Democracy.* New York: Palgrave Macmillan.

Smith, Richard Chase. 2002a. Interview, Oct. 6, 2002, Instituto del Bien Común, Lima.

———. 2002b. "Tejido forjado por las vicisitudes de la historia, el lugar y la vida cotidiana: Un marco para visualizar los desafíos para los pueblos indígenas de América Latina en el nuevo milenio: Territorio, economía, gobernabilidad e identidad." Unpublished manuscript/CD-ROM.

———. 2001. "Pueblos indígenas y el estado plurinacional en el Perú." *Quehacer* 129: 82–86.

———. 1996. "Política de la diversidad: COICA y las federaciones étnicas de la Amazonía." In Stefano Varese, ed., *Pueblos indios, soberanía, y globalismo,* 81–126. Quito: Abya Yala.

———. 1983. "Search for Unity within Diversity: Peasant Unions, Ethnic Federations, and Indianist Movements in the Andean Republics." Paper presented at Cultural Survival Symposium, "Iniciativas Indias y Autodenominación Económica." Cambridge, Mass.

Spalding, Karen. 1974. *De indio a campesino: Cambios en la estructura social del Perú colonial.* Lima: IEP.

Starn, Orin. 1999. *Nightwatch: The Politics of Protest in the Andes*. Durham: Duke University Press.

———. 1998. "Villagers at Arms: War and Counterrevolution in the Central-South Andes." In Steve Stern, ed., *Shining and Other Paths: War and Society in Peru, 1980–1995*, 224–257. Durham: Duke University Press.

———. 1994. "Rethinking the Politics of Anthropology: The Case of the Andes." *Current Anthropology* 35(1): 13–38.

———. 1992. " 'I Dreamed of Foxes and Hawks': Reflections on Peasant Protest, New Social Movements and the Rondas Campesinas of Northern Peru." In Arturo Escobar and Sonia E. Alvarez, eds., *The Making of Social Movements in Latin America: Identity, Strategy, and Democracy*, 89–111. Boulder: Westview Press.

———. 1991. "Missing the Revolution: Anthropologists and the War in Peru." *Cultural Anthropology* 6(1): 63–91.

Stavenhagen, Rodolfo. 2002. "Indigenous Peoples and the State in Latin America: An Ongoing Debate." In Rachel Sieder, ed., *Multiculturalism in Latin America: Indigenous Rights, Diversity, and Democracy*, 24–44. New York: Palgrave Macmillan.

———. 1992. "Challenging the Nation-State in Latin America." *Journal of International Affairs* 45(2): 421–440.

Stepan, Nancy Leys. 1991. *The Hour of Eugenics: Race, Gender, and Nation in Latin America*. Ithaca: Cornell University Press.

Stephen, Lynn. 2002. *Zapata Lives!: Histories and Cultural Politics in Southern Mexico*. Berkeley: University of California Press.

———. 1996. "The Creation and Re-creation of Ethnicity: Lessons from the Zapotec and Mixtec of Oaxaca." *Latin American Perspectives* 23(2): 17–37.

Stern, Steve. 1987. "The Age of Andean Insurrection, 1742–1782: A Reappraisal." In Steve Stern, ed., *Resistance, Rebellion, and Consciousness in the Andean Peasant World, 18th to 20th Centuries*, 34–93. Madison: University of Wisconsin Press.

———. 1982. *Peru's Indian Peoples and the Challenge of Spanish Conquest, Huamanga to 1640*. Madison: University of Wisconsin Press.

———, ed. 1998. *Shining and Other Paths: War and Society in Peru, 1980–1995*. Durham: Duke University Press.

———, ed. 1987. *Resistance, Rebellion, and Consciousness in the Andean Peasant World, 18th to 20th Centuries*. Madison: University of Wisconsin Press.

Tamayo Herrera, José. 1980. *Historia del indigenismo cuzqueño*. Lima: Instituto Nacional de Cultura.

Tarrow, Sidney. 1994. *Power and Movement: Social Movements, Collective Action, and Politics*. Cambridge: Cambridge University Press.

Thurner, Mark. 1997. *From Two Republics to One Divided: Contradictions of Postcolonial Nationmaking in Andean Peru*. Durham: Duke University Press.

Tilly, Charles. 1993–94. "Social Movements as Historically Specific Clusters of Political Performance." *Berkeley Journal of Sociology* 38: 1–29.

Torres, Carlos Alberto, and Adriana Puiggrós, eds. 1997. *Latin American Education: Comparative Perspectives*. Boulder: Westview Press.

Turino, Thomas. 1991. "The State and Andean Musical Production in Peru." In Greg Urban and Joel Sherzer, eds., *Nation-States and Indians in Latin America,* 259–285. Austin: University of Texas Press.

Turner, Terence. 2002. "Representation, Polyphony, and the Construction of Power in a Kayapó Video." In Kay Warren and Jean Jackson, eds., *Indigenous Movements, Self-Representation, and the State in Latin America,* 229–250. Austin: University of Texas Press.

———. 1998. *Indigenous Peoples and Cultures in the Contemporary World System.* Videocassette. Lewisburg, PA: Bucknell University.

———. 1995. "An Indigenous People's Struggle for Socially Equitable and Ecologically Sustainable Production." *Journal of Latin American Anthropology* 1(1), Fall: 98–121.

———. 1992. "Defiant Images: The Kayapó Appropriation of Video." *Anthropology Today* 8(6): 5–16.

UNEBI. 1998. *Boletín Informativo* 3. Lima.

Urrutia, Jaime. 2001. "Indios o ciudadanos." Interview by Luis Olivera y Martín Paredes. *Quehacer* 128: 69–78.

Urton, Gary. 1999. *The Legendary Past: Inca Myths.* Austin: University of Texas Press.

Valcárcel, Luis E. 1981. *Memorias.* Lima: IEP.

———. 1972 [1927]. *Tempestad en los Andes.* Lima: Universo.

Van Cott, Donna Lee. 2000. *The Friendly Liquidation of the Past.* Pittsburgh: University of Pittsburgh Press.

———. N.d. "From Movements to Parties: The Evolution of Ethnic Parties in Latin America." Unpublished manuscript.

———, ed. 1994. *Indigenous Peoples and Democracy in Latin America.* New York: St. Martin's Press.

van den Berghe, Pierre. 1978. "Education, Class, and Ethnicity in Southern Peru: Revolutionary Colonialism." In Philip Altbach and Gail Kelly, eds., *Education and Colonialism,* 270–298. New York: Longman.

———. 1975. "Ethnicity and Class in Highland Peru." In L. Despres, ed., *Ethnicity and Resource Competition in Plural Societies.* Chicago: Mouton.

———. 1974a. "Introduction." *International Journal of Comparative Sociology* 15(3–4): 121–131.

———. 1974b. "The Use of Ethnic Terms in the Peruvian Social Science Literature." *International Journal of Comparative Sociology* 15(3–4): 132–142.

van den Berghe, Pierre, and George Primov. 1977. *Inequality in the Peruvian Andes: Class and Ethnicity in Cuzco.* Columbia: University of Missouri Press.

Varese, Stefano. 1996. "The Ethnopolitics of Indian Resistance in Latin America." *Latin American Perspectives* 23(2): 58–71.

———. 1991. "Think Locally, Act Globally." *NACLA* 25(3): 13–17.

———. 1988. "Multiethnicity and Hegemonic Construction: Indian Plans and the Future." In P. Guidieri and S. Tambiah, eds., *Ethnicities and Nations: Processes of Interethnic Relations in Latin America, Southeast Asia, and the Pacific,* 57–77. Houston: Rotheo Chapel.

———. 1982. "Restoring Multiplicity: Indianities and the Civilizing Project in Latin America." *Latin American Perspectives* 9(2), issue 33 (Spring): 29–41.

————, ed. 1996. *Pueblos indios, soberanía, y globalismo.* Quito: Abya Yala.

Vargas Llosa, Mario. 1990. "Questions of Conquest: What Columbus Wrought and What He Did Not." *Harper's,* December, 45–51.

Vargas Llosa, Mario, Abraham Guzmán Figueroa, and Mario Castro Arenas. 1983. *Informe de la comisión investigadora de los sucesos de Uchuraccay.* Lima: Editora Perú.

Vásquez, Fredy. 2002. Interview, June, AIDESEP, Lima.

Velasco Alvarado, Juan. 1995 [1969]. "The Master Will No Longer Feed off Your Poverty." In Carlos Ivan Degregori, Orin Starn, and Robin Kirk, eds., *The Peru Reader,* 264–269. Durham: Duke University Press.

————. 1972. *La voz de la revolución: Discursos del Presidente de la República, General de División, Juan Velasco Alvarado, 1970–1972.* Vol. 2. Lima: Ediciones Participación.

Wade, Peter. 1997. *Race and Ethnicity in Latin America.* London: Pluto Press.

Warren, Jonathan. 1999. *Racial Revolutions: Anti-Racism and Indian Resistance in Brazil.* Durham: Duke University Press.

Warren, Kay. 1998a. *Indigenous Movements and Their Critics: Pan-Maya Activism in Guatemala.* Princeton: Princeton University Press.

————. 1998b. "Indigenous Movements as a Challenge to the Unified Social Movement Paradigm for Guatemala." In Sonia Alvarez, Evelina Dagnino, and Arturo Escobar, eds., *Cultures of Politics, Politics of Cultures: Re-visioning Latin American Social Movements,* 165–195. Boulder: Westview Press.

————. 1992. "Transforming Memories and Histories: The Meanings of Ethnic Resurgence for Mayan Indians." In Alfred Stepan, ed., *Americas: New Interpretive Essays,* 189–219. Oxford: Oxford University Press.

Warren, Kay, and Jean Jackson. 2002. "Introduction: Studying Indigenous Activism in Latin America." In Kay Warren and Jean Jackson, eds., *Indigenous Movements, Self-Representation, and the State in Latin America,* 1–46. Austin: University of Texas Press.

Wearne, Phillip. 1996. *The Return of the Indian: Conquest and Revival in the Americas.* Philadelphia: Temple University Press.

Weismantel, Mary. 2001. *Cholas y Pishtacos: Stories of Race and Sex in the Andes.* Chicago: University of Chicago Press.

Wright, Robin. 1988. "Anthropological Presuppositions of Indigenous Advocacy." *Annual Review of Anthropology* 17: 365–390.

Yashar, Deborah. Forthcoming. *Contesting Citizenship: Indigenous Movements and the Postliberal Challenge in Latin America.* New York: Cambridge University Press.

————. 1998. "Contesting Citizenship: Indigenous Movements and Democracy in Latin America." *Comparative Politics* 31(1): 23–42.

Youngers, Coletta, and Susan Peacock. 2002. *La Coordinadora Nacional de Derechos Humanos del Perú: Un estudio de caso de construcción de una coalición.* Washington, DC: WOLA.

Yrigoyen Fajardo, Raquel. 2002. "Peru: Pluralist Constitution, Monist Judiciary— A Post-Reform Assessment." In Rachel Sieder, ed., *Multiculturalism in Latin*

America: Indigenous Rights, Diversity, and Democracy, 157–183. New York: Palgrave Macmillan.

Zamosc, León. 1994. "Agrarian Protest and the Indian Movement in the Ecuadorian Highlands." *Latin American Research Review* 29(3): 37–68.

Zevallos Aguilar, U. Juan. 2002. "On Andean Archipelagos." Paper presented at "Los Otros Latinos," conference sponsored by the David Rockefeller Center for Latin American Studies, Harvard University.

Zimmermann Zavala, Augusto. 1974. *El Plan Inca, objetivo: Revolución peruana.* Lima: Empresa Editora del Diario Oficial *El Peruano.*

Zúñiga, Madeleine, et al. 2003. *Construcción de políticas regionales: Lenguas, culturas y educación.* Lima: Instituto de Estudios Regionales "José María Arguedas."

———. 2000. *Demanda y necesidad de educación bilingüe: Lenguas indígenas y castellano en el sur andino.* Lima: Ministerio de Educación/GTZ.